From
Prayer to
Pragmatism

A Biography of
John L. Childs

Lawrence J. Dennis

Southern Illinois University Press
Carbondale and Edwardsville

Copyright © 1992 by the Board of Trustees, Southern Illinois University
All rights reserved
Printed in the United States of America
Designed by Linda Jorgensen-Buhman
Production supervised by New Leaf Studio

95 94 93 92   4 3 2 1

*Frontispiece: portrait photograph of John L. Childs. Courtesy of Special
Collections, Milbank Memorial Library, Teachers College, Columbia
University.*

Library of Congress Cataloging-in-Publication Data

Dennis, Lawrence J.
   From prayer to pragmatism : a biography of John L. Childs /
Lawrence J. Dennis.
      p. cm.
   Includes bibliographical references (p.   ) and index.
      1. Childs, John L. (John Lawrence), b. 1889.   2. Educators—United
States—Biography.   3. College teachers—United States—Biography.
I. Title.
LA2317.C482D46   1992
370'.92—dc20
[B]   91-23926
ISBN 0-8093-1777-X   CIP

The paper used in this publication meets the minimum requirements of
American National Standard for Information Sciences—Permanence of
Paper for Printed Library Materials, ANSI Z39.48-1984. ∞

For Maureen

Contents

Acknowledgments

"The most valuable time for a professor is uninterrupted time," a friend said to me the other day. And it was during the uninterrupted time of a sabbatical that I was able to write this book, which was revised, checked, and reworked with difficulty when my time was once more interrupted. My sabbatical turned out to be a time of creation and recreation. For work I went to New York, Madison, and Rockford; for pleasure I went to Italy, where the wonders of the Veneto were revealed to me for the first time. I don't think there is any moral to be drawn, but my experience with all has been immeasurably enriched.

I want to thank those who helped me with this manuscript. It was all made possible by the good offices of the late Mr. Cliff Childs and Ms. Pamela Fox, John Childs' lawyer. I received helpful family information from David and James Donald Childs, Mildred Smith, and Ethel Hoffman. Several students and colleagues of John Childs took the time to reminisce: Professors Donald Arnstine, John Broyer, Raymond E. Callahan, Arthur E. Lean, Robert E. Mason, Cho-Ye To. Reverend Edwin Hunt and several of the staff at Wesley Willows Retirement Community, Rockford, Illinois, generously provided me with information. My friends Donald L. Beggs and William Edward Eaton, respectively my dean and departmental chair, and John A. Beineke were ever supportive.

I am always amazed at the cooperation I receive from librarians, and among those who have been particularly helpful I should mention David Koch and his associates in the Special Collections, as well as Ruth Bauner, the late Alan Cohn, and Lorene Pixley of the Morris Library, Southern Illinois University, Carbondale. I am also grateful to Dagmar Getz, YMCA Archives, now at the University of Minnesota, St. Paul; Bernard Schermetzler, University of Wisconsin, Madison; and David M. Ment and Bette Weneck, Teachers College, New York City. John Portz, Betty and Cash Baxter, and my sons Jolyon and Justin Dennis provided accommodations in far parts. Rosemary Timke and Anintita Posakrisna helped with gathering materials and proofreading. Becky Molina, as ever, has typed and retyped for me and has done so with unfailing generosity. Finally, I thank my wife, Maureen, for, among other things, undergoing the rigors of half pay for twelve all-too-short months to give me "uninterrupted time."

From Prayer
to Pragmatism

1.
Introduction

On a bright, warm June afternoon in 1968, John Lawrence
Childs was awarded an honorary doctorate during the commencement proceedings at Southern Illinois University, Carbondale. It chanced that I received my doctorate at the same
ceremony. Although Childs still lived in Carbondale, he had
retired by the time I had begun my program three years earlier.
He was still advising his last student, and I met him a few
times at department functions. My own interest was in the fine
arts, music in particular, and I intended to return to Canada.
Thus I had little reason to examine Childs' work and none at
all to seek him out to ask questions. But things rarely work
out entirely as planned, and I was shortly back in Carbondale
teaching philosophy of education to undergraduate students

and working more generally in the field of cultural foundations of education.

In the early 1980s, I found myself chair of the George S. Counts Committee, and one of the first things I did was to see if we might be able to obtain for the university archives any papers that John Childs might still have. We already had a small but valuable holding of Counts' papers and a few of those of George Axtelle. These fit nicely with the major collection in the Center for Dewey Studies. It seemed sensible to try to bring the Childs papers here to be joined with those of some of his closest colleagues. We knew that Childs was still alive, and so I sent a letter of inquiry, trying to sound not too "having." My letter was answered by Cliff Childs, who was by this time acting on behalf of his older brother.[1] Cliff Childs replied that he had discussed my letter with John, who seemed to have understood what was being asked and to have given his assent. Thus, shortly afterwards, I received two scrapbooks consisting largely of newspaper clippings, one dealing with the dispute concerning union activities at Columbia University in New York and the other with the American Federation of Teachers.

Then I heard no more. Cliff Childs himself became ill and died in September 1983 just a few months before his brother, but four boxes of papers were eventually sent to Carbondale. They had been cataloged very painstakingly by Cliff Childs.[2] Without these materials, it would have been extremely difficult even to attempt a biography of John Childs, for he was not someone about whom there is a large public record (save in the two instances documented in the scrapbooks). What I did not know at the time was that John Childs' constant occupation during the last years of his life was to sort and resort these papers and probably to relive the times and the people they record. So, in going through the papers, I had this sense that I was looking at Childs' professional life as he himself saw it. Some might assume that it is as he wanted it seen, but that would not be altogether fair in the case of the unusual John Childs. Childs passed even harsher judgments on himself than he did on others, and I have no feeling at all that things had been "edited out"; rather, it seemed that they had been whittled down. What I did not find was very much about Childs the person, but that in itself gave me a clue—I do not think there was much difference between the public and the private man. Even in advanced old age, John Childs would insist on wearing a suit and shirt and tie every day. The workers at Wesley Willows Retirement Community told me that they would have to take the suit away at night, unnoticed, so that it could be cleaned. He had a sense of propriety, of what was proper and what was not. When he came to sell his house in Carbondale, he insisted on telling all prospective buyers that the basement leaked. As almost all basements leak in Carbondale on account of the thick, hard clay, he probably need not have bothered; but, the warning was a matter of principle— a moral necessity. From stories such as these, I sense no dislocation between his public and private faces. In fact, Childs himself stated that "a good life is a life devoted to some form of socially useful work."[3]

My own doctoral dissertation concerned John Dewey, esthetics, and music. Although I had one class with George Counts and several with George Axtelle, my interests were focused on art and education, about which Childs and Counts have almost nothing to say. With Dewey, of course, it is quite a different matter.

The work of John Dewey has dominated thinking about American education during the twentieth century. True, what has taken place in the country's classrooms has not reflected that work to the same extent, but no discussion of the matter can long avoid bringing in the ideas of the great philosopher; for this there are many reasons. Dewey had an exceedingly long career, and education was not peripheral but absolutely central to his thinking. Consequently, educators could find theoretical justification for a variety of innovations in his writings. But Dewey was not always clear or even free of ambiguity. Dewey himself described the difficulties he encountered when he moved from his earlier Hegelian position to his later pragmatic one. Instead of basing his work on a settled reality, he now had to base it on process. The English language is not readily amenable to process. There are too many nouns. R. Buckminster Fuller commented on this fact and suggested we should do more "verbing." Dewey would have been more easily understood if he had been specific. For example, he might have told teachers to arrange their students' chairs in a circle or to have them study certain books. He did not. Rather he attempted to describe the goals to be striven for and the means to reach them. Even as late in his career as 1938, he had to write one more book to set matters straight, but without careful contextual reading, even the luminous *Experience and Education* is not easy for the tyro. Nonetheless, Dewey still dominates educational discourse in America and probably will long continue to do so.

Dewey had taught at the University of Michigan, Ann Arbor, and worked closely with teachers and schools. At the time of his move to Chicago in 1894, he had discarded his earlier philosophic views and had come under the intellectual sway of C. S. Peirce, William James, and, during the Chicago years, George Herbert Mead. He went to Chicago, William Rainey Harper's new and to-be-great-instantly university, as chair of the Department of Philosophy, Psychology, and Pedagogy. He thus became the prime mover behind the experiments that were carried on in the so-called Lab School. He wrote his first, and tremendously popular, books on education—*Child and the Curriculum* and *School and Society*—which sold well and were widely read. These were critical and formative years. In 1905 Dewey went to Columbia University; there, in his early forties, he settled in for a long stay and the glories of a brilliant intellectual career.

At Columbia Dewey wrote his most important work, which included his classic educational treatise (derived from class lectures in philosophy of education) *Democracy and Education*. He produced similarly seminal writings in logic, inquiry, esthetics, metaphysics, and so on. His influence in these areas was great; in education itself it was enormous. Who since Plato had presented a full-blown educational philosophy of such power? Rousseau's *Émile* changed the face of education, a fact that Dewey recognized readily. His ideas were made accessible through Johann Pestalozzi and Friedrich Froebel. Maria Montessori produced a practical guide to education. The work of such people as Francis Wayland Parker, Rudolf

Steiner, Bertrand Russell, A. S. Neill, and Susan Issacs was important. But none of them, influential as each was, approached Dewey's systematic presentation of education in its wider aspects and implications. It is not surprising, therefore, that New York City began to attract people sympathetic to Dewey's point of view. Thus, Teachers College, in the period between the wars and for some time beyond, became a gathering place for students from all around the world. Teachers College was during Dewey's life the most important institution devoted to the study of education in the New World, and among its faculty were many who played large parts in bringing Dewey's work to a wider audience. William Heard Kilpatrick may well have been the most influential of these partly because of his popularity as a teacher and also because he was able to translate aspects of Dewey's thinking into understandable classroom practice. Others came to Teachers College: Harold Rugg, Jesse Newlon, George Geiger, George Counts, and John Childs. Several of these—Kilpatrick, Geiger, and Childs—had actually been students of Dewey, others were sympathetic to his views. Among the most radical were Counts and Childs.

George Counts had received his doctorate at the University of Chicago in 1916, long after Dewey left, under Charles Hubbard Judd. He was the first doctoral student there to major in education and minor in sociology. He had studied philosophy as an undergraduate at Baker University in Baldwin City, Kansas, but his orientation was predominantly, and remained, sociohistorical.

John Childs had taken only three courses in philosophy as an undergraduate at the University of Wisconsin. He showed no evident interest in the study of education. He became a missionary and went to China. His graduate work in the 1920s, done jointly at Union Theological Seminary and Teachers College, was a different matter. His focus was education, with an emphasis on philosophy. His mentor was Kilpatrick, and later, in his doctoral studies, he had three courses with Dewey. As will be seen, Childs was ready for Dewey. He accepted the pragmatic viewpoint with fervor and enthusiasm, an enthusiasm that had earlier been satisfied by the teachings of

Jesus. Now the message changed; the enthusiasms remained. From absolutism to experimentalism is a big jump for anyone. It was for Dewey, and it was for Childs. In Dewey's case it led to a revolution in his thinking; in Childs' case it meant a transfer of allegiance. The transition took more than a decade, and it seemed to have been made relatively smoothly. The missionary of the gospel of the New Testament became the missionary of experimentalism, and his zeal remained undimmed for the next fifty years. Admittedly, Childs' preaching was never quite orthodox, and he was not long in China before he developed his own version of the social gospel. His was no empty mouthing of received truth. It was a rigorous and reasoned analysis, but it was still a gospel, still good news.

Childs, as do many disciples, also went a little beyond Dewey. He joined his colleague Counts in calling for an educational agenda that would not shrink from describing the society to be created out of the disappointments of the early 1930s and later out of the ruins of World War II. They both asked teachers to create a new social order. They became the flag bearers of the left-wing group of Dewey followers, who were given the appellation *social reconstructionists*. But they were not mere utopians. Both believed that their convictions demanded action, not only for others but for themselves also.[4]

John Childs and George Counts were born in 1889. Their lives and careers did not merely run parallel, they also became close colleagues. They were educated in midwestern, rural America, whose values they carried with them for almost one hundred years; both were raised as Methodists; both had intense foreign experience and interests (in Counts' case, his Russian studies continued until the end of his life, whereas Childs' China experience dimmed in his mature years); both taught at Teachers College over the same period; both were engaged in political and union activities and shared similar roles; both returned to the Midwest for their last professional assignments; and both died in Illinois. Those are the obvious similarities. But both, and this may in part have been due to the external similarities, spearheaded the left wing of the Teachers College progressives. In fact, both were accused of having communist tendencies, although each man subsequently played a major part in opposition to communism in the American Federation of Teachers and in the American Labor Party. This is a book about Childs, but from 1930 onward Counts runs in and out of its pages.

As long as Dewey's work still has meaning for education, Childs will be of some importance. His presentations were transparently clear, his arguments persuasive, and his writing stylish. Moreover, Childs represents pragmatism at its most active. Faith without works is dead, said St. James, and Childs had no doubt that the apostle was correct on this point. It is perhaps appropriate now, shortly after his centennial, to examine the life and work of John Childs. Lawrence A. Cremin and William Van Til have suggested that the work of Dewey's disciples is worthy of examination, even as the Center for Dewey Studies reports (January 1990) that as many as seven biographies of Dewey are underway. Although no biography of George Counts has been written (he did write an autobiography), several books examining his work have been published.[5] Childs has received little attention, indeed his death in 1985 passed virtually unnoticed. It is time now to look at Childs' contributions to education, to look at his career, and to show the significance of his work. For Childs, it was not sufficient to write and speak. One's life must also reveal one's deepest beliefs and convictions—a philosophy demonstrated as Childs, a former missionary, became a respected and outspoken professor, who was able to command notice in the pages of the leading newspapers of the country; as he played for a while on the political stage; as he taught the ways of democracy to the Chinese and went on to teach them anew at Teachers College; as he strove to make Dewey's work intelligible and accessible to large numbers; as he moved from belief in the efficacy of prayer to belief in the efficacy of pragmatism.

2.
Early Years

John Lawrence Childs was born in Eau Claire, Wisconsin, on January 11, 1889. He lived more than ninety-six years, and after his death in Rockford, Illinois, on January 31, 1985, he was buried, as he wished, in his hometown. The values he appropriated from growing up in western Wisconsin remained with him throughout his life and profoundly influenced his thought. His father was a logger "in the original pine forests of northwest Wisconsin," whose son spent his first winter at a logging camp.[1] Although the community was dominated by sawmill operators and loggers who had struck it rich, it was essentially a one-class community. The value of hard work was instilled in John Lawrence from his early years. Productive labor was both a social and a moral obligation; "we made a gospel of it," he wrote seventy-five years later.[2] Childs' commitment to work is evident in the self-control that marked him later as one of the severest thinkers and teachers of the "frontiersmen."

Childs was the second son of John Nelson Childs and his wife, Helen Janette (Nettie) Smith, who was ten years his junior. They were married in Augusta, Eau Claire County, in 1884. John Nelson had emigrated from Old Chelsea, Quebec, Canada, and had settled in Eau Claire in 1880 as a young man of twenty-six. He was of English-Irish extraction. John Childs' grandfather James Childs was unable to read or write; his paternal grandmother, Levina Allen, evidently could. They were married in St. James Angelican Church, Hull, Quebec, on January 28, 1858. Nettie Smith was born in Toronto. It may be that John Junior overplayed his rural roots, for John Senior was more than a logger; he handled the teams of horses. Lois Barland says that he was a superintendent of logging camps.[3] In any event, he retired at a fairly early age and went into the ice and fuel business, operating on one side of Half Mile Lake. He was sufficiently well-to-do to buy a large house at 539 Lake Street, on the corner of 6th Street. In later years he could afford to shut up the house from October to April and travel by train to winter in Long Beach, California. John Nelson died at the age of eighty-five in 1939, after falling off the steps of the back porch of his summer cottage at Prairie Lake, Wisconsin.

The local belief in the efficacy of work was accompanied by faith in education. Education was regarded "not as a means of escape from the responsibilities of life and labor, but rather as an agency which would equip the young for greater competence."[4] In fact, Childs came to deplore the shift in the schools from an orientation toward work and responsibility to an orientation toward preparation for worthy use of leisure time. "I consider," he wrote, "that the conception of man as a producer and a creator is grounded in a sounder human psychology, than the alternative conception which regards him as a consumer, a hobby faddist, or as the passive enjoyer of the arts of others."[5] He was raised a Methodist, a branch of Protestantism that has traditionally valued good works. The puritan in Childs is clear, although it was, intellectually at any rate, a broad-minded form of puritanism that was fostered in Eau Claire. The community was mixed both ethnically and religiously. Later Childs became an outspoken critic of parochial education, or at least of public support for parochial education; he was proud that the local parochial school was attended only by a segment of the Catholic children of Eau Claire. Others attended the local public elementary school. His fellow students in high school included those from German, Norwegian, Swedish, and French backgrounds; there were some black students as well. Speaking of his school years, he said:

Through our classroom studies we learned of the history, the principles, and the institutions of democracy, but we learned the spirit of democracy through our daily associations with one another. From these common school experiences of work and play we gained the appreciations, the understandings, and the live and help live attitudes which are the foundation of a democratic way of life. Nor does the evidence show that enrollment in the common school, committed to the scientific method of thought and to the democratic way of life, made us indifferent to the claims of religion. Participation in the community school and participation in the activities of the family church went hand in hand.[6]

The high school principal was Michael S. Frawley, himself a Catholic but of an ecumenical bent. He was an 1873 graduate of the University of Wisconsin and served as the school principal from 1880 until 1913. After his retirement, he bought a cheese factory, which he ran with his brother, William H. Frawley, who had served as mayor of Eau Claire for five one-year terms. Mike Frawley died in 1925.[7] It is clear that Childs much admired Frawley, who may have played a part in Childs' decision to go to Madison. At any rate, Frawley, or "The Professor" as he was affectionately called, was a respected personality in Eau Claire.

Thinking people of Childs' generation saw clearly that America was moving quickly and inexorably from being an agrarian society to becoming an industrial one. Childs worked on a farm as a teenager, and there he came to know the dignity of hard work, the meaning of honest wages and thrift, but he also learned that labor was hard and exacting. In describing his life on the farm, he stated:

I am also a product of agrarian America. At the age of thirteen, I went, not to a boys camp to spend my summer vacation, but, instead, to a farm fifteen miles from my home town to work as a hired hand for $10.00 per month and keep. My day began at five in the morning as I regularly milked four cows before breakfast; it closed at dusk with the same round of milking plus a half-hour of pumping fresh water into the tank where the milk cans were stored until picked up by the wagon from the cooperative creamery of the district. My first job was to plant beans on a strip of *breaking*—that is, a plot of freshly turned under sod which had never been cultivated. At the end of the summer, I walked back to Eau Claire with two ten dollar gold pieces and two silver dollars wrapped in a handkerchief and sewed under my belt. During the five-hour homeward journey, I felt my belt many times to make sure that the net from my summer earnings was still there.[8]

In 1960 Childs wrote, "Although I am a child of the 19th century, sixty years of my life have been lived in the 20th century. It was inevitable therefore that eventually the principles of life and thought assimilated from my frontier and agrarian childhood would collide with the realities of the emerging industrial and urban civilization of our country. Fortunately for me, this encounter began during the four years I spent as an undergraduate at the University of Wisconsin."[9] Those views first encountered at Madison were modified for almost thirty of those sixty years, but the work there was critical to his development.

After graduating from high school, Childs took a freight-trucking job as a means of earning quick money, which he would need to go to Madison. In September 1907, Childs entered the University of Wisconsin as a student in the College of Letters and Science. He decided to major in journalism, a career he never practiced but a skill he used to advantage. The program at Madison consisted of a broad training in the cognate areas of English, history, political science, economics (or political economics as it was then called), and philosophy, with a total of only five courses offered in journalism. This limited number of journalism courses was arranged "in the belief that the greater part of the time should be devoted to a study of the subjects . . . which are fundamental to journalistic work."[10] Some choices were permitted among the suggested courses, but Childs followed a fairly predictable program of study throughout his four years. The only real surprise was a full-year course in Norse, which was actually a study of the plays of Ibsen conducted in English.

The University of Wisconsin was one of the great loves of Childs' life, a contention supported by his having left the university a sizable portion of his estate upon his death. Childs recorded that the changes brought about in him during his undergraduate years were sufficiently strong for him to conclude that "it is a mistake to assume that all crucial learnings are acquired during childhood."[11] His major advisor was Willard G. Bleyer, actually the only faculty member in journalism at the time. Of Bleyer, Merle Curti and Vernon Carstensen write that his "leadership was vigorous and imaginative. He conceived of educational journalism not merely in terms of the techniques of writing . . . but increasingly in terms of historical, social, and economic forces affecting the newspaper and magazine world."[12] His other teachers included A. L. P. Dennis for British history; Paul Samuel Reinsch and Howard Lee McBain for political science; William B. Cairns for American literature; and Rollo Lyman for public speaking.[13] His philosophy teachers were Frank Chapman Sharp, whose chief interest was in ethics; Evander Bradley McGilvray; and Max Otto, who, at the time, was still a graduate student.

In later life, Childs wrote, "I have always been grateful for what I received from my university teachers during the first decade of this century. These pioneer thinkers helped orient me to the world that was in process of formation, and they gave me a perspective from which to interpret the bleak and challenging events of the great depression of the thirties."[14] He went on to mention particularly the influence of two of the greatest luminaries among the faculty at the time, Richard T. Ely and John R. Commons. Although Ely's text, *Outlines of*

Economics, was used for one of the courses Childs took in political economics, it does not appear that he actually took a class from either Ely or Commons.[15] He seems to have been in close contact with Dennis and Reinsch, both also distinguished members of the Wisconsin faculty, but they were not singled out in 1960 for special mention. Of course, the Madison campus still had well under five thousand students at the time Childs was there, the physical campus was much smaller than it is now, and the ideas of Commons and Ely would have spread well beyond their classroom walls.

Richard Theodore Ely (1854–1943) was born in New York and earned his doctorate at Heidelberg, Germany, in 1879. Two years later he went to teach at Johns Hopkins University. Calls for his dismissal came after the publication of his first book, which detailed the history of the labor movement. In 1892 he moved to Wisconsin. History repeated itself, and he was called before the Board of Regents to answer charges brought by State Superintendent of Public Instruction Oliver E. Wells, who was an ex officio member of the board. Wells alleged that Ely was advancing unsound ideas about economics, property rights, and organized labor. Ely not only won his point but so impressed the board that it drafted a statement on the freedom of teaching, part of which was later cast in bronze and placed at the entrance to the Main Hall of the university, now Bascom Hall.[16] Needless to say, one of Ely's ideals was the freedom of teaching. But his other values also struck a response in Childs. In an interview Ely gave to Joseph Medill Patterson in 1908, he stated, "I believe that such natural resources as forests and mineral wealth should belong to the people; . . . that labor unions should be legally encouraged in their efforts for shorter hours and higher wages; that inheritance and income taxes should be generally extended; and that child education should be substituted for child labor."[17] Childs himself frequently mentioned the influence that Ely had on him and noted particularly "that whereas heretofore the great economic problem of the human race had been one of more adequate production, we were entering a period when much more conscious attention would have to be given to the problems of more equitable distribution."[18] The transition from an agrarian to an industrial age was showing up in economic theory well ahead of John Maynard Keynes.

Ely's views on organized labor were largely shared by another of Childs' Wisconsin mentors—John Rogers Commons (1862–1945). Commons had been attracted to Ely's work while still a student at Oberlin College in Ohio. He began work on his doctorate at Johns Hopkins and became an assistant to Ely, helping him put together the *Outlines of Economics*. However, Commons failed his history examination, which dashed his hopes for a third-year fellowship, and he never completed his doctorate. After a somewhat checkered career both in and out of academe, Commons, largely through Ely's influence, moved to Wisconsin in 1904 with the purpose of writing a history of labor. Commons was an iconoclastic thinker and an unorthodox teacher. He himself wrote, "When a subject became routine I lost initiative."[19] He believed that the problem of education is how to jerk up routine into, to use C. S. Peirce's phrase, the initiation of doubt.

Of Commons, Childs wrote:

> Any report of my undergraduate experience at Wisconsin would be most incomplete if it did not mention the work of Professor John R. Commons. From him, I learned that my father had been misinformed when he condemned organized labor as a regimented system hostile to the freedom of the individual worker. Through my study with Commons, I began to realize that it was only through organization that workers could share in determining the conditions under which they labored, and also have a real part in deciding how that which was produced should be distributed among owners, management, workers, and consumers. Through patient, objective analysis, Professor Commons led us to realize the way in which press reports often distorted what was the actual situation in an industrial dispute. I also learned, from him, that coercion may be a function of impersonal economic practices as well as a function of man-made laws. He helped us to perceive that the right to a job is foundational, and that this right is an empty one in a situation in which there are no jobs to be had. Under his tutelage, the concept of human freedom began to mean something more than the mere abscence [*sic*] of external restraints.[20]

The other great intellectual influence on Childs, and probably on most of his contemporaries at Madison, was University President Charles R. Van Hise. It was under Van Hise that the University of Wisconsin achieved the status, at least in the eyes of Charles Eliot, president of Harvard, as "the leading state university."[21] During his last year at the university, Childs had fairly close contact through his journalistic activities with this great administrator. Journalism majors were encouraged to work on the staff of one of the student publications, although such was by no means limited to them. Childs reported that since his early college days he had been a member of the staff of the *Daily Cardinal*, the university newspaper. In June 1910, he was elected to be its editor-in-chief for the 1910–11 academic year. Election to the position was through merit and competition and was made on the recommendation of the outgoing staff of the *Cardinal* by President Van Hise and three professors, including Willard Bleyer. Childs' salary was forty-five dollars for the year. In his position as editor-in-chief of the *Cardinal*, Childs had many personal conferences with Van Hise. And he wrote that he, a disturbed and confused editor, interviewed Van Hise "to gain perspective on complex current issues."[22]

It seems that universities will constantly be subject to outside pressures to curb free inquiry. In the light of the regents' response to the charges against Ely in the 1890s one might suppose that, at the University of Wisconsin at any rate, no such thing would occur again. But it did, and during Childs' years there, Max Otto, who had just joined the faculty of the Philosophy Department replacing his teacher, Boyd H. Bode, was charged with holding distinctly heretical views on religion. President Van Hise mounted a strong defense of Otto, which was highly lauded by Childs, even though Otto's views at the time conflicted with his own. However, Childs came quickly to see that the academic tradition is mortally injured if "the process of inquiry, of education, and of proposal is curbed or suppressed."[23] In fact, this experience so impressed him that he stated that he never lost the capacity for indignation at the abuse of public responsibility or his conviction that public service can be a means to advance the general good.

But a university is more than its teachers, important as they may be. Childs noted three characteristics of life at Madison that struck him powerfully. The first was the commitment of the university to the entire population of the state. This was a two-way street, with the university broadening its curriculum and outreach in response to the needs of the citizens, and with members of the university playing a lively part in the affairs of the people. Second, the university not only functioned as an expression and an interpreter of its culture but, because of the commitment to free inquiry, played its part in actually shaping the culture. Third, the relationship between education and politics became clearer. Picking up on the ideas of John Dewey and George Herbert Mead, Childs noted that "a primary test of the American political and educational system is its ability to institutionalize the process of revolutionary reconstruction."[24] And one of the main strands of this reconstruction was for Childs that "the *interdependence* of rapidly forming industrial-urban society was rendering obsolete the historic system of laissez-faire."[25] He became convinced that there was no beneficent invisible guiding hand governing the economy, yet he believed sincerely that such a guiding hand governed most other things.

But that was an older Childs speaking, and while what he said then should not be discounted, during his Wisconsin years, and for some time after, he held much more orthodox views, and these found their way into his job as editor. If one compares the issues of the *Daily Cardinal* during Childs' tenure with those of the previous year, there is considerably more extensive reporting of national and international news, with a corresponding decline in the reporting of local news and general advertising. There was much less coverage of sports events and entertainment and more about the activities of the faculty, particularly of those who had taught Childs— Dennis and Reinsch, for example. Perhaps even more notab ly, for anyone looking, the activities of the Young Men's Christian Association (YMCA), and to a lesser extent those of the women's YWCA, became front-page items.

The YMCA at Madison was formed in 1870; it was officially founded the following year with its object "to promote moral and religious influences among the students."[26] Within ten years, division occurred between those with an evangelical bent and those with a liberal one, but they were reconciled in time.

For the period 1902–8, James T. Honnold lists three program developments. The first was increased emphasis on Bible study; the second, the establishment of a health committee in 1904, as there was no hospital or infirmary on campus; and the third, an increase in giving to the support of missionaries overseas. "[O]rganized campaigns were sponsored to raise money for students to support Y. M. C. A. men in the field who had been previously connected with the University."[27] However, membership was dropping, and the association had been somewhat compromised by agreeing to lease part of its building to the university as a social center for its students. In the fall of 1908, Arthur Jorgensen arrived on campus to become general secretary of the YMCA in Madison. He decided to try to enlist the services of John W. (Jack) Wilce, a prominent member of the student body, captain of the football team, and stroke on the rowing crew, to accept the presidency. Wilce agreed, and Jorgensen reported that his decision "marked the beginning of a new era in the history of the University Y. M. C. A. of that period."[28] Jorgensen continued to get student leaders interested in the work of the association. Honnold reports: "One of those whose positive Christian leadership had a powerful effect on the Association for several years was John L. Childs."[29]

There can be little doubt that Childs used his position as editor-in-chief of the *Daily Cardinal* (1910–11) to publicize and promote the work of the association. Hardly an issue passed without reference to the YMCA and what activities were going on; many of these were front-page items. For example, the October 3, 1910, issue contained a description of a YMCA mixer attended by between three and four hundred students. The student president of the association, David S. Hanchett, urged his peers "to live clean lives, to get the best out of their college course, and to get that through the association with Christian work."[30] Childs himself "impressed the students with the smallness of themselves." Characteristically,

he also "urged the freshmen to get out for one of the publications."[31] On October 25, it was announced that "J. T. Childs"
[*sic*] would act as toastmaster at a "booster banquet."[32] On
November 17, readers were informed that C. T. Wang, secretary of the Chinese Students' association of North America,
would address members of the association about "the influence
of Christianity in the awakening of China."[33] On December
16, there was a report of a meeting held the previous day when
"Jack" Childs, president of the YMCA, chaired a meeting
at which several talks were delivered, including one by the
International Student Secretary of the YMCA A. J. Elliott,
whose office was located in Chicago and who would later
become a relative by marriage to Childs. In January 1911, the
thirty-sixth annual state convention of the YMCA was held in
Madison. The *Daily Cardinal* of January 13 notified its readers
that a dinner would be held that evening; those expected to
speak included Senator John M. Whitehead, Justice John B.
Winslow, and John L. Childs, who was listed as vice president
of the Madison YMCA. In fact, Childs and Hanchett shared
the presidency during the 1910–11 year.

Clearly Childs was deeply involved in the work of the
YMCA and became even more so after graduation. However,
during his final year he was also involved in other activities,
as he had been throughout his four-year stay in Madison. He
was a member of several fraternities, including Sigma Delta
Chi for journalism and Delta Sigma Rho for debators. He was
variously literary editor, managing editor, editor, and associate
editor of the *Western Intercollegiate Magazine*, which ran for
less than two years, from October 1909 until April 1911. He
was a member of the YMCA Senior Honor Society and a senior
orator on the Intercollegiate Debate Team. In December, he
spoke to the university regents "to make a request for a yearly
appropriation for intercollegiate debating."[34] He was also
working on his graduation thesis.

Undergraduate degree candidates in journalism were required to write a thesis, which had to "represent some phase
of the student's work in the major study and shall be of a
scholarly character."[35] Childs registered for three thesis hours
in each of his final two semesters. His major professor re-

mained Willard G. Bleyer. Childs' thesis is titled *A Study of the Editorials of the New York Evening Journal* and runs sixty-nine pages without the appendix, which consists of all the *Journal*'s editorials from January 16 until March 18, 1911. Childs analyzed these for both content and style.

The work is solid but unexceptional. Childs began by assigning the eighty-five editorials to five groups: political (38), social (27), moral (11), religious (3), miscellaneous (6). It is ironic that, in view of Childs opposition to William Randolph Hearst and his activities in the 1930s, the study is generally favorable to the work of the *Journal*, which was a Hearst paper. At that time, Hearst followed a populist policy, and there was considerable muckraking in the *Journal*. Childs summed up his view of its editorial policy by stating, "The *Journal* fights hard and is willing to go to any scheme in favoring those things it believes to be right, and in most cases it is safe to assume it has right on its side."[36]

The tone of Childs' thesis is definite, opinionated, and inclined to self-righteousness. For example, in commenting on the work of the editor, he wrote, "He sees a poor woman in rags on the street and without stopping to consider whether or not the woman's poverty may be due to her own lack of initiative, he generalizes about the injustice of the present economic system."[37] Again, "The Journal may be intended to be a poor man's paper, and yet it is barely awake to the shortcomings of this class. Nor does it fail to upbraid the members of this class for their indifference to their responsibilities."[38]

Childs' interest in editorial policy and writing was obviously occasioned not only by his major focus of study but also by his responsibilities at the *Daily Cardinal*. Its editorials were, of course, unsigned, so it is not possible to state definitely those that were written by Childs. But the topic, as well as the somewhat sanctimonious tone of this editorial, echoing his thesis writing, suggests it is an example of Childs work:

Religion for Men
The Young Men's Christian association in scheduling a series of Sunday afternoon talks on religious subjects is attempting to ade-

quately meet a real need of our community. A need that has long been apparent. One that is felt in every higher educational institution where legal restrictions are placed upon sympathetic instruction in the greatest of all religions, Christianity.

In the past, too many men have come to Wisconsin with firm religious beliefs, and after having spent four years in assimilating her training, have passed out of her jurisdiction with a well-developed mind and body, but with a spiritual nature both flabby and unresponsive. A large number of our graduates are equipped with an intellectual and physical training of the highest university grade, but with a religious experience that was originally conceived in "prep" school days, and one that has lost most of its primary vitality through disuse. Instead of developing spiritual leaders, we are producing men who consciously, or unconsciously, are becoming established in the belief that religion is for women and children, and, perhaps, a few sentimental men.

This year an opportunity will be extended to each man to learn of religion under the teachings of the foremost authorities of the country. Speakers of national and international names—men who are eminent Christian leaders in the social, political, and religious fields have seen the possibilities in such instruction for university men, and have willingly consented to speak here. The association has assumed an expensive and arduous task in bringing such men to Wisconsin. It believes, however, that it is doing a work worth while; one that will be productive of results. We hope the men of the university will appreciate the significance of these meetings sufficiently to attend them.[39]

Childs' zeal for the work of the YMCA was rewarded following Arthur Jorgensen's resignation as secretary in early 1911 to become general secretary of the YMCA in Tokyo, Japan. Frank H. West from Grand Rapids, Michigan, was named his successor, and it was announced at the same time that John L. Childs was appointed to fill the new position of assistant secretary. "Childs will devote his entire time to the work and receive $1,000 a year."[40] Thus, Childs entered the next stage of his life and career, upon his graduation from the University of Wisconsin in June 1911 with a bachelor of arts degree.

Particularly in view of Childs' later pragmatic position, it is surprising to discover his early commitment to the work of the YMCA and to an evident, wholehearted religious conviction. Whatever the early influences from his home, they were reinforced by the experiences at Madison. He was a highly involved and fervent supporter of the work of the YMCA at the University of Wisconsin. Had any doubts developed, although there appear to have been none, they must have been completely dispelled by the time John R. Mott visited the university.

In March 1910, John R. Mott (1865–1955) came to Madison and was to play an important role in Childs' life. Mott had been involved in work with young people for many years. In 1888 he became chair of the Student Volunteer Movement; he was both founder and leader for thirty-three years of the World Student Christian Federation. His association with the YMCA went back to the mid 1890s, and he became general secretary to both the National Council and the International Committee of the YMCA. Later, in 1946, he was cowinner of the Nobel Peace Prize.

Mott was a powerful personality, "a man blessed with a genius for organization, unlimited energy, massive good looks, and a staggering capacity for raising money."[41] Under his leadership, twenty-two missionary school student associations were formed in China in the fall of 1896 alone. No wonder this impressive man impressed the impressionable twenty-one-year-old John Childs.

"Mott week" received comprehensive coverage in the *Daily Cardinal*. During the convention, Mott gave several addresses ("Moral and Mental Atrophy," "My Experience with Students in Russian Universities," "The Battle Ground of Students in All Countries," "The Greatest Handicap to Success in Student Life," "Why an Increasing Number of Students throughout the World Believe in Jesus Christ"), and he held a special meeting with some of the Chinese students on campus. At the end of the week, it was reported that "it is confidently expected that over 1,000 men will be enrolled in the work next week."[42] Childs was mentioned as a member of the committee backing the recruitment drive.

Many years later Childs wrote to Mott, "You . . . spoke with tremendous power to our student body, not as the official head of a great organization with vast material resources in wealth, buildings, and workers, but as a pioneer in a spiritual crusade. The lives of many of us were fundamentally altered at that time because of the vision you were able to give us of Christ and the adventure of life in following Him."[43] Childs was obviously speaking for himself.

Childs stayed at the Madison post for only ten months. At the Board of Directors' meeting on April 28, 1912, he was formally released. He seems to have made an impact during his short tenure. Alfred P. Haake, the YMCA student president for 1914–15, noted years later that Childs was a tower "of strength in the student body and stood for all that the 'Y' represents."[44] He further stated that Childs "represented that which was most genuinely religious in the student body." James Honnold wrote that Childs' "positive Christian leadership had a powerful effect on the Association for several years."[45]

Childs' involvement in full-time work for the Madison YMCA coincided with the departure of the well-liked and respected general secretary, Arthur Jorgensen. Jorgensen had passed on to his successor, Frank H. West, "an untried idea . . . which was destined to become an important part of the future of the Y. M. C. A. program."[46] This idea was to work with "foreigners and boys" to ensure that their living conditions were suitable. However, the concern was not simply moralistic but included good health. It was, in short, social in intent as much as it was religious. Honnold notes that West brought to his assignment "an unbounded enthusiasm for the work coupled with a keen sense and ability for organization and administration that had been unequalled by any of his predecessors."[47] West revamped the organizational structure. "The old Advisory Committee was abolished and its powers were incorporated into the Board of Directors. A Board of Trustees was organized the function of which was limited to responsibility for the mortgaging or sale of the real property of the organization. General administrative powers were given to the Board which relieved the division of function that had formerly existed between the Advisory Committee and the

Board."[48] Childs' position was retitled, and he acted as secretary to the board for a short while before he left Madison.

Childs' new position, which he held for the next three years, involved fieldwork in the Middle West for the Student Department of the International Committee of the YMCA. He was based at the Y's western office in Kankakee, Illinois. His working area comprised Wisconsin, Minnesota, and the two Dakotas; it did not include Illinois. The job was a large one, handicapped by rapid changeover in staff, lack of financial support, and inexperienced colleagues. "One of my primary efforts has been to cultivate the presidents of the Christian colleges. With a number I have gained considerable entrez [sic] and I am just getting them into a hearty spirit of cooperation. For instance, at Dakota Wesleyan, the president, at the suggestion of the students and of myself, is favorably considering a considerable appropriation from their budget for the securing of a local secretary."[49] However, the head office was trying to get Childs to work overseas (Cairo, Egypt, in addition to China, being mentioned as possible postings), but he was reluctant. "Personally the state university problem appeals to me strongly, inasmuch as I . . . have such a tremendous conviction about the place which the Young Men's Christian Association should have in the religious life of these schools that I cannot but feel deeply this attitude which is expressed by certain church leaders, which is undercutting the energies of some of our secretaries in state institutions." He expressed the focus of his concern: "The question I am facing is, whether or not I cam [am] called upon to make the sacrifice of my foreign work. . . . I am hoping and praying that the will of God in the matter may be made clear."[50] Whether or not this was the cause, in 1915 Childs became secretary to the Special Evangelistic Mission to Colleges of the United States and Canada, working with Raymond Robins, but still, apparently, based in the Kankakee office.

During this period, Childs met Grace Fowler on the way to a conference in Colorado. She was teaching English and commercial subjects at Kankakee High School. Grace Mary Fowler was two years older than Childs and a graduate in

English from Northwestern University, Evanston, Illinois. She was born in Danforth, Illinois, on January 2, 1887; but at the time of her meeting with Childs, her parents, John Fowler and Hannah Crawford Fowler, lived at 240 North Harrison Street, Kankakee.[51] John Childs and Grace Fowler were married on July 22, 1915. The wedding was held in the bride's home and was conducted by Arthur J. Elliott, who was a cousin of Grace's. One of the two flower girls at the ceremony, which was an elaborate affair, was Elliott's daughter, Eleanor; the other was Grace's double niece, Mildred Fowler. Gertrude Fowler was the matron of honor. The honeymoon was spent on Lake Chetek, Wisconsin, which was a favored summer resort for the entire Childs family. It was to be a long and happy marriage; they had no children. Grace Childs was, like her husband, a Methodist. Her parents were quite well-to-do and owned a farm just west of Gilman, in Iroquois County, Illinois. Grace was an only child and eventually inherited the farm, which was leased to long-term tenants by the name of Monk. In fact, it was only after Childs' eventual retirement and the couple's move to their last residence in Rockford that they actually sold the farm to the Monk family.

Grace Childs must have been relieved that her husband was enthusiastically considering "a unanimous call from the Board of Directors of the Association at the University of Illinois to accept, at the conclusion of this school year, the position of general secretaryship of their Association."[52] Childs believed that, although there were serious problems with the association's relations at many state universities, "Illinois is possibly the most hopeful situation . . . in our entire student section." The alternative to the position at Illinois seems to have been foreign work in China. "I am wanting to make my decision between these two opportunities just as quickly as possible."[53] Mrs. Childs' relief was short-lived, for China won, and on September 7, 1916, John and Grace Childs sailed from Vancouver, British Columbia. They arrived in Shanghai on September 24, where they stayed a few days, and reached Peking in early October. Arrangements had been made for them to live in the U.S. Compound, and they boarded with the Mills family.[54]

The YMCA had first established a foothold in China in 1895 at Tientsiu, and it was, for those colonial-missionary days, extremely ecumenical in orientation. D. Willard Lyon, who spearheaded the Chinese connection, pledged "to start not a movement that would be an alien growth, but one that would become truly indigenous."[55] A wide latitude was permitted the secretaries, who frequently tended to a liberal Christian position, which disavowed orthodoxy. The spirit of the Chinese wing, right from the start, "was one of service, not conversion."[56] The secretaries tried to give their work local flavor and to develop local leadership. They succeeded, and in brief time the YMCA gained the trust of the Chinese, so that, after the 1900 Boxer Rebellion, "the Association . . . found itself playing a far larger role in China's modernization than it had expected."[57]

By 1910 the orientation of the YMCA's Peking branch had shifted from Bible study to efforts to meet the practical social needs of the Chinese people. Under the secretary of the time, John Stewart Burgess, it turned "to studying social, political, and economic questions on a systematic basis."[58] Shirley S. Garrett writes, "Despite the rapid discrediting of liberal institutions, the period between 1911 and 1925 represented a high point for moderate Sino-American organizations. During that time there was reasonable agreement between China's self-diagnosis and Western prescription."[59]

Childs went to China as secretary of the Foreign Department of the International Committee of the YMCA in Peking. His work was partly supported by donations from the Wisconsin in China project and privately by a generous gift from Mrs. S. M. Clement of Buffalo, New York, whose own son was in China with the Yale in China project. Within a few weeks of his arrival, Childs wrote, "I am one of the most profoundly grateful men in the whole world that events have so shaped themselves that in all probability the best working years of my life will be spent in China under the direction of the Young Men's Christian Association."[60]

The Wisconsin in China project of the University of Wisconsin, further reinforced Childs' Wisconsin connections. It generated considerable enthusiasm on the campus when it was initiated, but it fizzled out fairly quickly as events and personnel changed. It was described by the distinguished sociology professor Edward A. Ross, who was vice-chair of the committee.

"Wisconsin of China" is a representative committee of over a hundred students and professors, formed in 1915 for the purpose of keeping a University of Wisconsin man working among the students of Chinese colleges. The movement sprang from a feeling that it would be a brotherly and inspiring thing for us to acquaint the intellectual young men of the Orient, lately for the first time gathered in student bodies, with the best ideals which have been wrought out in the experience of American students—the ideal of self-mastery, of being hard with one's self, of all-around development, physical, social and religious as well as intellectual. In this we line up with other institutions like Yale, Princeton, Pennsylvania, Illinois, Michigan and Oberlin, which for a number of years have maintained such a work in China.

Last spring the committee secured from the Faculty and students $1350 and hopes to raise annually $2000, which is necessary to maintain a man in the field. . . . It is hoped that the undertaking will appeal to the Alumni and parents of Wisconsin students as a noble extension of the University's influence.[61]

The project was endorsed by several people, including Amos P. Wilder, a former U.S. consul general in China: "It is good news that the University of Wisconsin is to join the procession of American Universities taking a part in the development of the New China . . . The effort to put one-fourth of the human race, and such a capable people as the Chinese, on the high way of better living and thinking is a glad thing. . . . When a University enters on a work of this sort, it becomes great and the onlooker catches a glimpse of the majesty of the passion for truth in action."[62] The committee that sponsored Childs included F. O. Leiser, secretary of the YMCA who was himself a Madison graduate and a missionary to China from 1905 until 1914. Childs' former English teacher, Frederick W. Roe, was on the Faculty Committee; and Childs' brother Marshall, who attended the University of Wisconsin for a while, served in the United States Army in World War I, and died in the

1920s, was a member of one of the fifteen Student Campaign teams. From an examination of the accounts of the Madison YMCA, it does not appear that much was actually paid to Childs' work in China, and Professor Ross probably exaggerated the receipts to date. In 1916 the amount paid out was $603.65, dropping to $30.84 in 1917. In a response to the New York headquarters, E. G. Hersman noted "we have received pledges and cash amounting to $1378.65 for Wisconsin Fund for Jack Childs for 1917. Of this amount, you have already received $600.00. I would call your attention to the fact that this figure does not allow for any shrinkage in subscriptions. I am somewhat astonished at the large shrinkage in all the subscriptions made here this year. . . . In my opinion, you will not be justified in depending upon Wisconsin for more than a total of $1,000.00."[63] Hersman was far too sanguine, for in subsequent years the amount was zero; although, largely through Ross' efforts, a small amount was raised in the 1920s when efforts were made to revitalize the project. And thus the high hopes of the project failed to materialize, but Childs' work in China continued until 1927.

Childs quickly came to love and respect the Chinese. "China is indeed a land of wonderful people, and it cannot but mean personal growth to be associated with them."[64] He was encouraged by the progressive movement in China but quickly realized that most Chinese who had studied in the United States did not retain American values. "Some of those same men I found apparently so enthusiastic for service while in America, have lost the motive now that they are actually at home in the land that needs them so tremendously."[65]

The boot was on the other foot for Childs himself, and he immersed himself in Chinese life, beginning with language study, which he found laborious and extremely difficult. However, the story of Childs' China years centers on his gradual shift from a more or less Christian orthodoxy to a pragmatic reconstructionism. The tendency is there from the beginning as he writes in January 1917: "I am also developing a tremendous interest in seeing what can be done toward relating the student and official classes to the social problems of a typical Chinese community. Now that we have gained such a wonderful contact with the influential classes it seems to me that a double responsibility is ours to see that they tie up the task of social re-construction which China so badly needs. The opportunity ... to win these men into the Christian life and then to tie them up to initial tasks of community work grows upon me the more I contemplate it."[66] Yet in this same letter, he was able to write, "I can only say that I believe both of us are now confident that God was in the decision that led us out here."

As Peking secretary, Childs wrote regular reports, which make fascinating reading and present a very personal picture of the so-called Chinese renaissance. They also reveal the changes in Childs' own thinking. In his first report for 1917, he wrote,

Only last week a delegation . . . from the Peking government university, came to my house asking that the Association provide a leader for the Bible class they had organized entirely on their own initiative. What a challenge to capture these institutions in the days of their youth for the program of Christ! In the plastic years when the traditions and the character of these institutions are being formed, to build into the warp and the woof of their life those traditions which will be friendly to the program of Christianity. Surely our Association is called of God to move forward to the occupation of this field.[67]

Over the next few months domestic political problems increased. China, along with America, entered the European war. Then came the great floods in the north of the country, which occasioned appalling suffering, surely to be followed by severe famine and plague. The tone of the final report of this same year is different. Childs' journalistic background is clearly evident in the piece, but it is sufficiently vivid to justify reproduction in full.

Old and Young China

He was returning from a committee meeting. The meeting had not gone well. In spite of all the efforts of foreign members the attempt to get honest and efficient administration of the public flood-relief funds seemed about to fail. It was a December evening and as he walked along the crowded street of Peking, the sweep of the cold

North wind caused him to pull his long heavy coat more closely about him. He thought of the letters from the rural districts which he had been reading in the afternoon. He knew that that night over a million people in his province were going to bed hungry and cold, some of them lying down, perhaps to sleep the sleep from which there is no waking. He thought of men wading into icy streams to get a little fuel for their homes. He pictured others trying to live on chaff, leaves and roots; of those who were reported to be tearing up the tender sprouts of winter wheat to get that nourishment that might keep alive a little longer the vital spark of life. He knew that these men were not idlers, but men who wanted to sell their labor and there was no market. He remembered how some of them had jumped with joy when they had been chosen to leave home, to walk many miles to the place where they were to work for $6.00 Mexican [sic] a month on the road that was being constructed out of flood-relief funds. He knew that many others had cried bitter tears when they were told that no more could be accepted from their district.

He also knew that in Manchuria the government had grain that could have given much relief but thus far the Department of Communications had refused to give it transportation. He knew that out in those flooded districts were the well filled granneries of many wealthy land-owners, who were letting the people round about them go hungry while they were hoarding the grain. Out in those same districts the starving people could not get food, and yet the distilleries had their grain.

As he walked along the street he saw rickshaw men shivering in their rags, calling to him to let them haul him to his destination. At the side of the streets were little children and mothers blue with the cold; crying to him: "Kind Sir, pity us; give us a copper." He saw the dirty shops, he thought of the many cold cheerless homes that were to be found in that capital city. He thought of all this, and more, and then his brain grew numb. It refused to carry the picture further. He said to himself: "After all is there any hope? Is there any power able to build out of circumstances such as these a civilization with at least tolerable living conditions? Was he right in believing that there was that which was sacred in all this human life? That in every one of these suffering perishing people there were God-like possibilities? If so where were the men with the faith and the courage to lead in the gigantic task of re-construction?"

What is this jostling and jam of pedestrians, rickshaws, carriages, and automobiles such as only a street in Peking affords? He looked to see what building it was whose entrance all were striving to reach.

To his surprise he discovered that it was only the pressing of the crowd which had prevented him from walking past his destination, for the building was the Y. M. C. A. and he was intending to look in on a reception of returned students.

Once inside the well-lighted lobby, surrounded by alert well dressed young men, both Chinese and foreign, it seemed that he was in another world. In truth he was. Outside was Old China; inside was Young China. On all sides he was greeted by friends. In the reception hall which ordinarily served as the gymnasium, there were no less than 150 young Chinese who had been educated in either England or America. Many fellow foreigners were there also. Many of the returned students wore the coveted scholastic keys of Phi Beta Kappa and other honorary scholarship socities [sic]. Not a few had successfully completed graduate work leading to a Phd. [sic] degree in their respective fields of study. Here were twenty from the faculty of Tsing Hua College; over there was a group of professors from Peking Government University; the Higher Normal college was represented by an able number; standing at one side of the room engaged in conversation with a foreigner about forestry was the dean of the Agricultural College, and here fresh from study was a clean-cut young fellow who was just taking up his work as professor in the new Union Theological Seminary of Peking. Among the younger and more capable men in the official life of China who were there in good numbers were representatives from The Department of Foreign Affairs; The Ministry of Commerce and Agriculture; The Board of Finance; The Department of Communications; The Board of Navy; The Ministry of Justice; The Ministry of the Interior; and the Board of Education. The editors of some of the leading papers in North China were included in the crowd. This unassuming young man serves in his spare hours as the superintendent of a Sunday-school numbering over a 1000, and he was also efficiently leading a teachers Bible training class. Men were there who were giving their lives to the cause of Western medicine in China; others who were attempting to solve some of the complex engineering problems of the land; and still others who were having large share in the developing industrial life of the nation. All of these were there and others. And what, as the British Minister later declared, was more wonderful they were not there alone but were accompanied by their wives and sisters. One saw in the presence of these educated, refined ladies, the proofs positive that the emancipation of women in China was soon to be an accomplished fact.

A little later the chairman of the evening, a graduate of Yale, and the director of the Peking-Hankow Railroad, called the gathering together and a short program of speeches was given. With what emotion our friend listened to those speeches. The first without apology to anyone proclaimed the gospel of exercise; this in China where all physical exertion has long been considered an evil to be avoided. The next speaker dwelt on the flood situation and the responsibility that was resting upon them to do all in their power to relieve the distress of the many poor. That he was thinking in terms of real sacrifice was indicated by the fact that he finished with an appeal for each man to either give or raise $200 for a relief fund. The next man dwelt upon the importance of these men using and not abusing the leisure time that was theirs. The final speaker spoke of the work that was awaiting them in building the new China, and ended with the statement that all of their building would be in vain were it not based on the bed-rock principles of Jesus Christ.

Following the talks by the returned students, the British and the American Ministers spoke briefly. How fortunate it is that in this period of critical transition China should have the service of two such men as Sir John Jordan and Dr. Paul S. Reinsch. Their desire to see the best in the life of China prevail is relied upon by everyone. It is evident that they do not conceive their offices as limited to the protection of their nation's interests, but rather as mediums through which they can bring the resources of their countries to the assistance of China. That the purpose of diplomacy may be service and not exploitation is clearly demonstrated by their examples. In the best sense both ministers deserve to be classed as friends of China. Perhaps the deepest office of their friendship is their unwavering faith that the righteous is going to triumph in the nation's life, and that within China is to be found the leadership capable of redeeming her.

With the conclusion of the formal program, our friend not tarrying for refreshments, was shortly once more upon the street. This time he yielded to the importunities of a rickshaw man and was sonn [soon] gliding homeward. What were his thoughts as he thus came to the end of a long, crowded day? Surely the need and the suffering of the great common life of China were no less real to him. A man of his wide experience in China could not fail to know that even in that group he had just left were many whose thought was of self rather than their nation's good. But other thoughts also were his. In that group were others whose spirit of moral earnestness had borne the mark of reality. Some-day they would not be the underlings in the affairs of China. True they were not many, but then he remembered that Jesus had only twelve men with which to change the whole world. If these few, and others of their type scattered over China were moved by the spirit of the Master, might they not as truly do for China what the twelve had done for the world?[68]

It is interesting to compare Childs' account of the occasion with that written by Paul S. Reinsch, who, it will be remembered, was one of Childs' Madison professors. It seems not unlikely that Childs was in fact the young man "just come out from Wisconsin" referred to by Reinsch. If he was, it gives a brief insight into Childs' mode of working with people.

The intimate feeling of cooperation between the British and American communities expressed itself in many meetings, in some of which the Chinese, too, participated. Thus, on December 8, 1917, there was held a reception of the English-speaking returned students. The Minister for Foreign Affairs; a number of his counsellors; the British minister, Sir John Jordan, and his staff; the American Legation; the missionaries; all who had received their education in the United States or Great Britain, were here present. It was a large company that gathered in the hall of the Y. M. C. A., including a great many Chinese women.

The hum of the preliminary conversation was suddenly interrupted by a loud voice issuing from a young man who had hoisted himself on a chair in the centre of the room. He proceeded to give directions for the systematic promotion of sociability and conversation. The Chinese guests were to join hands and form a circle around the room, facing inward; within that circle the British and American guests were to join hands, forming a circle facing outward. At the given word the outer circle was to revolve to the right, the inner circle to the left. At the word "halt," everyone was to engage his or her vis-à-vis in conversation. To eliminate every risk of stalemate, the topics for conversation were given out, one for each stop of the revolving line, the last being: "My Greatest Secret."

The young man who proposed this thoroughly American system of breaking the ice had just come out from Wisconsin, and it was his business to secure the proper mixing in miscellaneous gatherings. The British seemed at first somewhat aghast at the prospect of this rotary and perambulatory conversation; yet they quite readily fell in with the idea, and when the first word of halt was given, I noticed Sir John duly making conversation with a simpering little Chinese girl opposite him.[69]

During his entire time in Peking, Childs focused his concerns in one way or another on education. One of his major preoccupations was with the extraordinary waste of talented people, who had been trained in the West or in Japan, but who were denied real opportunities to contribute to Chinese affairs and help in the country's reconstruction. For example, he played a leading role in a conference which was held in Peking in March 1918 of 137 delegates from North and Central China. Speakers included not only officials of the YMCA but also the American attaché in Peking and the British minister. Four committees were appointed as a result of the conference as follows: "(1) To launch a movement to organize the Western educated men in China that they may more effectively serve one another and their country; (2) To start a publication that will give opportunity for their voice to be heard on national issues of vital moment [this goal came to fruition with the publication of *The Life*];[70] (3) To assist in a movement to establish a modern library in Peking; (4) To make arrangements for a similar conference to be held again within a year."[71]

It is clear that Childs threw himself wholeheartedly into the work of the YMCA in China. His main bases, where in a sense he continued the work he had been doing in American colleges before he went to China, were Customs College and Tsing Hua College. But in 1918, for example, he spoke to students at "Peking Government University, the Higher Normal College, the Peking University, the Y.M.C.A. Day Schools at Peking and Tientsin, the Government Middle School, the Anglo-Chinese College, and Nankai College at Tientsin."[72] He also attended evangelistic conferences at Shanghai and Tientsin. He organized meetings, met with people in his home, arranged schedules for other speakers whenever possible, and helped conduct surveys because, he wrote, "As social facts are fundamental to any intelligent program of social reconstruction, it is expected that the results of this year's effort will lay the foundation for a real program for constructive social work in Peking. It is our hope that the revealing of the actual living conditions will enable us to challenge many of the students and the returned students to social service work who thus far have remained indifferent to the appeal."[73]

At this time Childs, along with the rest of the world, was looking towards the end of World War I. He felt that missionaries had a responsibility to bring "to the attention of their respective countries the legitimate claim that China has upon their support."[74] He thought there would be little doubt that China would become increasingly Westernized, but he expressed the hope that

the Western civilization which wins the day in China is built upon spiritual foundations; that the principles of Christ are made the working principles of the New Order in China; that a Christian conscience will sit in moral judgment upon all of its activities; that it will be based upon the conception of the sacredness of life which Christ gave to the world; that it will have a soul able to use its new found powers for the advancement of human liberty and freedom in China and the world; that it will be possessed of such a faith that will enable it to carry all of this weight of material civilization and at the same time triumph in the things of the spirit.[75]

Childs was not upholding a denominational view as he enjoined unity, but he was clearly embracing a social gospel: "The Christianity which is to prevail out here must be loyal to the social implications of its Gospel."[76] Childs put his beliefs into action when he assumed the job of executive secretary of the United War Work Campaign, which raised within China 1.4 million dollars in gold.

Childs continued to immerse himself in the life and language of China, to sensitize himself to the ways of thinking of the Chinese people, and increasingly to assume their point of view. He came to see that although the West sent its missionaries it also sent its traders and its gunboats. He became aware that something other than altruism motivated the Western powers in their dealings with China, and he was shocked when he heard that the Treaty of Versailles resulted not in a world made safe for democracy but in a gift of the Shantung Province with its millions of people to Japan. "Seldom has a more cruel blow been struck at the idealism of youth. Even many of the

Christian Chinese found it a shock to their faith from which they have never wholly recovered, believing that hereafter faith must be reposed in industrial and military force rather than in the ideal of international justice held by Western nations."[77]

The annual report ending September 30, 1920, strikes a new tone. After listing the activities for the year, he refers to the fund-raising effort for North China famine relief. And, for the first time, Childs mentions John Dewey: "'One cannot be in China long without arriving at the conclusion that her greatest need is for men of personal character,' declared Dr. John Dewey in a recent conversation. Dr. Dewey who has been in China for over a year as special lecturer for the National University and The Government Teachers' College, is known as a warm friend of China, as well as a keen observer of contemporary conditions."[78]

3.
Transition

During the 1918–19 academic year, John Dewey took a sabbatical leave from Columbia. After a few months of lecturing in California, Dewey and his wife, Alice, decided to spend some time in Japan, where he was asked to lecture at the Imperial University in Tokyo. George Dykhuizen takes up the story: "The Deweys' stay in the Far East was unexpectedly extended when Dewey . . . received an invitation to lecture at the National University in Peking during the academic year 1919–20, his duties to begin in June 1919 and end in March 1920. The invitation was the result of the efforts of some former Chinese students of Dewey who believed that he could make a significant contribution to the liberal movements then taking root in China."[1] Dewey did not spend all his time in Peking or in teaching only at the National University. As

Dykhuizen reports, "Dewey visited thirteen of the twenty-two provinces of China, speaking in the capitals of most of these."[2] However, he found time to deliver a total of sixty-four lectures at the National University, including sixteen on philosophy of education and fifteen on ethics. "The lectures were delivered in English, interpreted in Chinese as they were being given, and written down by recorders for use by the daily press and learned periodicals."[3]

Almost certainly Childs attended at least some of Dewey's lectures. In the preface to *Education and the Philosophy of Experimentalism*, he wrote, "For two years through lectures, writing, and teaching he [Dewey] gave, in person, a powerful reinforcement to the work of the Chinese Renaissance leaders. Living as I was in Peking at the time, my first introduction to Experimentalism came as I watched it grapple with the complex and difficult problem of present-day China."[4] Moreover, the Deweys "lived temporarily in the home of John L. Childs" in July—just after the Treaty of Versailles was signed on June 28.[5] July marked the rainy season. Dewey wrote home, "It was impressed upon us yesterday afternoon, when the side street upon which we live was a flowing river a foot and a half deep. The main street on which the Y. M. C. A. building is situated was a solid lake from housewall to housewall, though not more than six inches or so. But the street is considerably wider than Broadway, so it was something of a sight."[6]

In a more revealing passage, for our purposes here, a passage that certainly makes indirect reference to Childs, Dewey wrote:

I asked the principal [of a private high school] what the effect of the missionary teaching was on the Chinese passivity and non-resistance. He said it differed very much as between Americans and English and among Americans between the older and the younger lot. The latter, *especially the Y. M. C. A.*, have given up the noninterventionalist point of view and take the ground that Christianity ought to change social conditions. The Y. M. C. A. is, he says, a group of social workers rather than of missionaries in the old-fashioned sense—all of which is quite encouraging. Perhaps the Chinese will be the ones to rejuvenate Christianity by dropping its rot, wet and dry, and changing it into a social religion [italics added].[7]

Edward W. (Will) Lockwood, writing from Shanghai to the
New York YMCA headquarters, gave his opinion on the sig-
nificance of the visits to China by Dewey and Bertrand Russell.
He had a low opinion of Russell but grudging admiration for
Dewey.

This American educator has lectured in many provincial capitals. In
one place there were a thousand middle school students who did not
have tickets to hear a lecture. They marched in a body to the hall,
broke past the armed policemen at the door and jammed in against
the walls of an already filled hall of listening students. . . . When
questioned about religion he only says that religion and education
are not related. In justice to him it should be said that his general
influence upon Chinese students is good. He advocates reform in
education and does it mighty well for an intellecualist. The Chinese
like him and he likes the Chinese.

Lockwood added rather ruefully that "it is from our viewpoint
a tragedy that this educationalist does not bring a Christian
faith into his messages to Chinese students."[8]
   With or even without Dewey, Childs was being changed
by his China experience. He was certainly of the opinion that
faith without works was empty; it was an opinion shared by
the Chinese. He had the opportunity to put his convictions to
the test when, in 1920, he played a major part in providing
help following the devastating flood. Elaboration comes from
Dewey: "Missionaries and Y. M. C. A. workers took a large
part of the burden of recent flood-relief work. The Chinese in
the devastated region who had remained calmly impervious to
prior preaching, were so impressed with the exhibition of
kindness that was gratuitous that they flocked into the
churches."[9] In Childs' own words, "I was serving as the executive secretary of the National Famine Relief Drive. In all we
raised in China close to $2,500,000. and I think results which
came from the effort more than justified my giving up for the
period my regular student responsibilities."[10] It was reported,
"This money was so wisely used that 500,000 lives were saved.
. . . As this was the first nation-wide popular appeal ever made
in China for philanthropic purposes it created wide comment.

For this service Childs was honored by the Chinese government and given the Fourth Class decoration of the Abundant Harvest—a decoration given only to civilians."[11] John Dewey was one of the members of Childs' relief committee, which also included "three former premiers, six cabinet members, all the foreign ministers, . . . and a number of bank presidents."[12]

Childs clearly recognized that the Chinese would not now accept a religion that held itself aloof from the social arena. In his annual report for 1921, he "made pointed reference to the Association's hesitation and confusion over labor problems, a timidity that was damaging its reputation as an innovator in the community."[13] Criticisms of the association's work occur frequently in the report, and are perhaps best summarized by Childs, who wrote, "I am afraid that more and more we are coming in China, as well as in the West, to be an institution which exists for itself rather than for service to the community as a whole."[14] His own convictions were surfacing and were further reinforced by events the following spring.

In May 1922 the World Student Christian Federation sponsored a National Christian Conference in Peking. A few months before the conference, Childs published some principles that he believed should guide the delegates. In sum, these called for unity but not at the expense of compromise. The piece is revealing because it demonstrates the transitional stage in Childs' own thinking. On the one hand, he makes a strong plea for orthodoxy: "With no thought of presenting a formal statement of belief, could not the Christian forces utilize this conference to place before China the Person of Christ and the way of salvation through Him?"[15] On the other, the influence of Dewey is apparent.

[W]e could clearly state our conviction about the vital importance of the spread of modern education, and our realization that the method of science should be applied fearlessly and thoroughly to the whole life of China including the field of religion. The impression now lingering in the minds of some that Christianity is opposed to, and afraid of, modern science and education should be vigorously dispelled. In the spirit of Jesus who is quoted as saying: "Ye shall know the truth, and the truth shall make you free," in this conference

composed of His followers, we might proclaim our warm interest
in those who are honestly searching for the truth. The relation of
Christianity to the democratic movement in the world, and the social
ideals of Jesus could be stated with much meaning for contemporary
life in China.[16]

It is hardly surprising that, in the aftermath of the Great
War, the topic that received the most attention at the conference was the question of Jesus' attitude toward war. In their
opinions the delegates were divided, with one camp holding
that Jesus' command that ye love one another precluded kill-
ing. The other camp held that there are occasions when war
is justifiable, and indeed occasions when it would be one's
Christian duty to fight for one's country. Later, Childs used
this as an argument against there being a single Christian point
of view. The conference was virulently attacked by the growing
body of young Chinese Marxists as being one more manifestation of capitalist exploitation. Foreign delegates to the conference were impressed with the success of the conference; Childs,
who was by this time sensitively tuned in to the nuances of life
in China, was not. He thought that the conference was not
only disappointing but that it exposed the weaknesses of the
movement.

By the time the conference opened, Childs had left China
temporarily. Prior to the event, he wrote to Edward A. Ross
at Madison, "I am working hard to see that we adopt a clean
cut courageous program on social, industrial, and international issues. Increasingly these questions seem to me to be
world issues."[17] In the 1921 report, Childs mentioned a forthcoming furlough and his hope that he would have sufficient
time to take up some form of study. On April 22, 1922, he
and Grace Childs left Peking and arrived in Vancouver on
May 8. In New York a few weeks later, he met with Willard
Lyon and Edward Jenkins, to whom he expressed doubts
about continuing to work for the YMCA. However, they persuaded him to remain with the association. He was also given
a free hand to promote the policy changes that he believed to
be essential. He expressed similar doubts to John R. Mott and
his wife during a personal visit, concluding that it was unwise

for someone holding his views, religious as well as political, to remain with the association. He was moved to write a passionate letter to Mott.

In this letter he discussed at some length his views on the relation between Christianity and the modern world—or, more accurately, the role that America should and should not play in the Far East. He differentiated between religion and theology and deplored the efforts of the reactionaries in America to maintain old dogmas and superstitions, including their belief in the literal truth of the Bible. Rather, he held to the ideal that science and religion must work hand in hand to save the world. Childs noted that the spiritual results of the work of the YMCA in Peking were disappointing, not due to a lack of piety and zeal on the part of its workers but because the association had not grappled with the living issues of the day. The program had been devoted to shielding boys and young men from temptations of the flesh rather than in arousing in them a desire to support social and labor issues. He urged that the association seize the opportunity "to unite the youth of the world in a crusade against militarism and war as the recognized legal method of settling international disputes." And so we hear one of Childs' most persistent refrains of his mature years—the need to build a world society. In his letter to Mott, Childs mentioned that he would have failed in his duty to his employer had he not given the reasons he believed the Peking conference had failed. He correctly saw that Chinese youth were "impatient for advance and yearn to see these new visions of truth translated into practical deeds."[18] Mott wrote a kind but noncommittal reply. Clearly, Childs was embracing a social gospel, and he continued to do so for the rest of his life.

In October Childs was called back to Madison to intervene in a dispute that had developed there. Honnold takes up the story:

The Regional and National Committees had proposed a statement of purpose for all student Associations that included two stipulations: (1) that one of the primary functions of the student Y. M. C. A. was to lead students "into membership and service in the Christian

Church,["] and (2) "that all elective officers of the student association shall be members of good standing of the churches recognized by the general association movement." [Frederick E.] Wolf and the student leaders representing the Association in the intercollegiate movement made a vigorous protest and proposed a statement of purpose excluding any mention of the churches. Some of the students went so far as to threaten that the University Y. M. C. A. would withdraw from the Y. M. C. A. Movement if it were made mandatory that all Associations adopt the recommended statement of purpose.[19]

Among those who supported the views expressed in the statement of purpose was Grace Childs' cousin, Arthur Elliott. Honnold continues, "Two prominent alumni, Lester Rogers and John L. Childs, came to the campus to investigate the charges against the University Y. M. C. A. and after three days of 'investigation and conferences' recommended that it was necessary for the organization to maintain its 'liberal policy' of operation."[20] In spite of these recommendations, the Board of Directors "adopted a resolution substantially accepting the statement of purpose."[21] Nancy D. Sachse reports that, through the efforts of Rogers and Childs, a break "with the National Committee was prevented, and the Wisconsin Association permitted to maintain its liberal policy."[22] Wolf had, however, lost the confidence of the members of the Regional Committee, and in December 1923 he resigned, to the disappointment of the local board.

On his way to Madison, Childs had stopped off at Chicago to attend a YMCA conference at the University of Chicago. "Its purpose was to further the welfare work of . . . institutions in China and India."[23] Professor Edward A. Ross spoke at the meeting, and Childs was described as "another prominent figure at the convention."[24] Ross tried to revitalize the Wisconsin in China project at Madison. A leaflet put out at the time outlined Childs' work in China and sang his praises. Childs himself was a little troubled by the hyperbolic terms in which his efforts were described "by well meaning but over-enthusiastic friends" to the Madison community.[25] His opinion reflected a natural modesty, but he thought that the general tendency "to over-emphasize the dark side of Chinese civilization and to exaggerate greatly what we of the Y. M. C. A. are doing to ameliorate the situation" would be provocative to the Chinese students at the university.[26] Edward A. Birge, who succeeded Charles Van Hise as president at Madison, wrote, "The work of Childs in China is the one enterprise for moral betterment in a foreign land which is supported by the university as a whole. Childs is working with those Chinese who have a foreign education and is successfully trying to promote and maintain among them not only the general spirit of Christian civilization but also those specific aims and ideals which are represented here in Wisconsin. He is in every high sense of the word our representative in China. We must sustain his and our work there in full vigor."[27] Ross himself wrote, "I think of Childs as an ambassador from the fortunate students of this university to the educated young men in Peking. How fitting it is that the sons of the oldest republic should greet fraternally the sons of the youngest republic and that we should send them the most precious and famous thing we have."[28] A student committee was set up to support the campaign and a faculty committee was also formed. Ross even raised a small amount of money. But either simply because Childs remained in America until 1924 or because interest died this time as it had in 1917, the effort again fizzled out. In any case, Childs, ensconced in New York, had other fish to fry.

In February 1923, Childs began graduate study in religious education. He enrolled at Union Theological Seminary. His major professors were George A. Coe and Harrison Sacket (Sunny) Elliott. Coe had taught at Union since 1909 but had moved to Teachers College a few months before Childs' arrival; he retired at the beginning of 1927. He was interested in religion, morals, and education. Elliott actually lived in China from 1905 to 1908 and then began a long association with the YMCA; from 1910 to 1927 he was secretary of the International Committee. He taught at Union and was an associate professor at the time of Childs' arrival. He had just received his master's degree from Teachers College the previous year. Elliott later became a founding member of Kilpatrick's famed Discussion Group.

Once Childs got down to serious study he realized that it

would be necessary to increase the length of his furlough if he was to obtain a graduate degree. He convinced Charles A. Herschleb, of the New York headquarters of the YMCA, who made his case to Will Lockwood in Shanghai. A few weeks later, even without hearing from China, Herschleb gave Childs permission to complete his degree.

Since February 1st, or the opening of the second semester of work at Union Theological Seminary, Jack has been giving his time to study. Gradually he has come to realize how far behind he was when he came and how much he is still in need of further training in order to cope with the situation as he will find it on his return to China. The reason for this primarily is that during his course at the University of Wisconsin, he received no training whatever in religious thought, except that which was received in a voluntary way in connection with the Student Y. M. C. A. He, therefore, has felt handicapped as he dealt with religious and philosophical problems in Peking, both with the students and faculty members.

Childs has given himself willingly to the financial task and because of the pressure that has been upon us in the securing of our funds, it will be possible for him to secure but three and one half months of work at the Seminary. In view of the present student situation in China, we sympathize with his feeling of need for more thorough training if he is to bring the maximum contribution to the work on his return; and to this end, it is proposed that he remain for another academic year for work both at Columbia and Union, where he will study primarily such subjects as History of Christian Thought, a critical study of the Bible, Philosophy of Religion, and something of the social problems under Dr. Ward.[29]

The association recognized his abilitites and put some pressure on him to return to China as soon as his degree was completed. In a presumably confidential report, it was noted that "Mr. Childs has a strong and winning personality. Few men in our movement are his equal as a speaker. He was so effective in his work with his Chinese associates that they unanimously and urgently requested his return to China as early as possible."[30]

At the beginning of the 1922–23 academic year, a new arrangement had been worked out between Union Theological

Seminary and Teachers College, just across Broadway, by which the departments of religious education in the two institutions could be treated as one. There was a joint program of studies "from which the students of either institution may elect courses, and use the same for credit in either institution under the general regulations of the institution concerned."[31] The expressed purpose of the program in religious education and psychology was "to meet the needs of, first, prospective pastors and missionaries who wish to utilize the results of educational thought and experience, and second, persons who intend to make religious education their life work."[32] This arrangement was tailor-made for Childs, who with his wife moved into an apartment one street over on 121st Street.

In fact, Childs took most of his courses at Union, including Bible with Harry Emerson Fosdick; History of Christian Thought with Arthur Cushman McGiffert, then president of Union; three courses in philosophy of religion with Eugene William Lyman; two in Christian ethics with the left-wing Harry Frederick Ward; and two in religious education with Elliott. All this did not leave much room for work at Teachers College, although he took two courses in which George Coe and Harrison Elliott team taught along with others, and two courses in educational psychology with Arthur I. Gates. Finally, Childs took two courses, which as events turned out were probably the most important of all, in philosophy of education with one of the stars of Teachers College: William Heard Kilpatrick.

Kilpatrick at that time was listed as "Lecturer in Religion" at Union, but his primary affiliation was, of course, with Teachers College. His two courses that Childs enrolled in were Education 441 and 442, which were advanced versions of the earlier 241 and 242. The catalog description in part reads, "[E]ducation will be studied as a social agency in relation especially to other factors at work in a democratic society. . . . [T]he effort will be made to construct a satisfactory working theory of democratic education, considering principally such topics as the nature of education, the principles of the curriculum, and the bases of method."[33]

Kilpatrick must have quickly come to find Childs, then

aged thirty-four, congenial and in October included him in one of his Sunday socials for students, which represented, as was Kilpatrick's wont, a mixed bag of domestic and foreign students. The following spring, Childs discussed with Kilpatrick some of the difficulties of the cooperative program between the two institutions. In April 1924, Kilpatrick took part in a discussion with Union students "as to the nature of God as demanded by the democratic criterion."[34] He commented, "So far as I could judge Elliott . . . and Childs all agreed with me."[35]

On completion of his degree, Childs had a conference in New York with Charles Herschleb and E. C. Jenkins, when it was tentatively arranged that, on his return to China, Childs would be transferred from his old post to an industrial position with the National Committee of the YMCA. He laid down some terms to the head office and admitted a certain dogmatism. The new master's degree candidate had already been changed by his experience in graduate school. "My whole thought with regard to our industrial program is that we should approach it in a *frankly experimental manner*. . . . I do feel that experience has shown that if we are to play a worthy part in bringing in a Christian industrial order that the Association must maintain its independence and have the freedom to stand for a program that is much more comprehensive than simply that which is often put on in a paternalistic way under the direct support of the employers [italics added]."[36]

The Childs spent the early summer weeks at their beloved Lake Chetek, together with other members of the family. Just before sailing for China, Childs wrote to Professor Ross at Madison, thanking him for his support over the years. He expressed the hope that the Wisconsin in China movement would not stop now that he personally had been reassigned. Grace and John Childs sailed from San Francisco on July 22 aboard the *President Wilson* and reached Peking on August 12, 1924. Things were to be different from now on. The first stage of his transition to pragmatism had been completed.

The main purpose of the YMCA's Industrial Department was to find a place for the association in the development of

a comprehensive program which would hold the most promise
of success in dealing with the complex problems it faced with
regard to the industrial institutions of China. But Childs' New
York studies had further hardened his ideas. Writing at the
beginning of 1925 to C. V. Hibbard, general secretary of the
Madison branch of the YMCA, he said, "My own view is that
the time is at hand when radical changes will have to be
made in mission methods on the field . . . if the total effect of
missionary work is to continue to make for international good-
will and understanding. . . . Traditional and, in my opinion,
false views of white race superiority, of the superior nature of
Western Christian civilization will have to be replaced by
attitudes of mutual appreciation and mutual exchange."[37]

On May 30, 1925, a group of students staged a demonstration in Shanghai, and thirteen of them were killed or
wounded by British-officered police; the incident then ex-
ploded into a large national strike. Three weeks later Childs
took on Bishop Frank Norris and the Church of England
Mission in the pages of the press. Although the bishop had
not excused the activists for their precipitate and fatal action,
Childs saw the students' action as justifiable in the face of
discrimination. "Unless I entirely mistake the spirit of Jesus I
doubt if he would find it at all necessary to hesitate to say
where the major share of the responsibility lies. Who can
imagine Jesus for one moment looking upon the racial discriminations practised in China, the arrogant and unfounded assumption of superiority by the white man, his contemptous
[contemptuous] disregard of the Chinese people, without believing that there is implicit in such a situation that which
would profoundly stir his moral indignation."[38] Childs was
clearly becoming more political than theological in this respect; his anger was shared by other YMCA workers. Later in
the year he took the courageous if unwise step of publishing
an intellectual autobiography in which he noted the changes
in his thinking from the time of his arrival in China to the
present. Childs rarely wrote about himself, and one must assume that this self-revelatory article was intended to bring
about some change in direction in the work of the association
in China. It sounded "a high moral tone," as did a talk he had

given the previous year to the ladies of the YMCA in New York. However, the effects of his work at Union are evident for they formed the basis of his "altered view of the nature of religion and appropriate methods of religious education."[39]

In his article in *The Life*, which appeared simultaneously in English and Chinese versions, Childs presented a strong indictment not only of the missionaries themselves but also of the nature of the Christianity they practiced. He criticized the exclusive character of the Christian religion and related a conversation he had with one of the national leaders of the Chinese Christian movement, who stated, "Christianity would be much more useful in China if it were to put off this view of its exclusive nature, which, as he saw it, was the child of the twin forces of the Western aggressive desire to dominate, and the ancient Hebrew idea that salvation was for the elect few."[40] But Childs went further when, in the light of modern scholarship, he criticized the traditionalist view of Jesus himself. He pointed out that "Jesus was by no means infallible, and that in some of our ethical and religious thought that we have gone beyond him."[41] One way that we have gone beyond him is by making the world, through modern communication and transportation, smaller than formerly. This has necessitated a universal religion which "gathers into itself the best the whole race has ever thought and experienced," a necessity that cannot be met by the "with me or against me" nature of Jesus' religion.[42]

But there was more. Childs quoted his teacher George Coe, who denied mysticism and religious intuition. Childs confessed that what he once thought to be divine revelation had a naturalistic explanation; it was simply the outcome of building on experience. In fact, so strong was his new conviction that he held completely invalid the insights derived from prayer. A critical, even a pivotal, point in his career had been reached. He had come to view the self as inherently social, thus, as he stated, "the social environment in which I have lived is the very warp and woof of my conscience, my ideals, and my ultimate standards of right and wrong. . . . Prayer has its unique power to refine and purify desire, and to help me choose the better from the worse, but it would seem generally only to have that power when a conflict, conscious or unconscious, of alternatives in conduct is before me."[43]

Having taken shots at the nature of Jesus and the limitations of prayer, Childs then asserted that even the Bible does not provide an adequate basis for social action. Social action takes place in a specific cultural context, and the general principles of, for example, justice, love, brotherhood are poor guides to action. Childs asked "what justice to the criminal offender shall include, or what justice to all of the various races would mean for our imigration [sic] policy, or what justice would mean for labor and capital under present industrial conditions, or, to take a simple, individual problem, what would justice mean for the sick beggar boy who stands outside my gate in Peking?"[44]

From doctrinal issues, Childs moved to the motives and activities of the missionaries themselves. He deplored their ethnocentricism and concluded that Christianity does not have exclusive ownership of virtue. He asked if conversion is really necessary before the moral nature of non-Christians, particularly the Chinese, can be trusted? "Are . . . Christian missionaries so superior in moral and spiritual insight that we have the right to . . . ask others to accept the authority of the Christian God, the Christian Bible, the Christian Church?"[45] If, at the end of this piece, Childs did offer warrant for the missionary enterprise, the damage was nevertheless done, and the article evoked instant and strong response. A letter from a Shanghai resident appeared in the *China Press*, in which the word *impudent* was used several times. The writer's views on Childs were summed up when he stated, "My own opinion is that he has fallen into the snare of the devil. Such illusions have accompanied Satanic working, though they are more often connected with the delusions of Popery than of Modernism."[46]

Childs sent copies of his own article to a number of friends and associates, among them Willard Lyon, who happened to be in Shanghai. Lyon expressed the fear that it might cause some confusion among English-speaking Chinese. (He was apparently unaware that the article had also been published in the Chinese edition of the journal.) He believed that it was not fair for the nationals "that they should be plunged into water much over their heads. . . . In using this figure, I want to make it plain that I believe an effective way to teach a person who cannot swim to keep afloat, is to put him in water over his head; but that method can hardly be called a safe one, unless the instructor is in a position to rescue the one who is learning, from actual drowning."[47] This paternalistic view of the Chinese is precisely the major complaint raised by Childs in both his article and his correspondence. His position is echoed in a letter from T. C. Ch'ao to Y. C. Shu, the editor of *The Life:* "I have often said that the great responsibility before us now is to fuse Western and Chinese culture. We need to catch the essential spirit of each in order that we may be equipped to achieve the creation of a new world culture."[48]

There can be little doubt that the heretical article in *The Life* marks the climax of Childs' move from prayer to pragmatism. This shift was recognized by his friend C. G. Dittmer, a faculty member in the Department of Economics at Madison, who wrote,

> The evolution of your religious belief is, I think, one of the most remarkable things I have ever met. You have succeeded in arriving at a religious faith for which you can have intellectual respect and intellectual integrity. I had to go through the same process and it was only through Union that I was able to get my feet on the ground at all but I have never attempted to carry the analysis as far as you have. I can not help wondering what will be the result of the publication of your article in China. What will the missionaries think and do? I can see heavy seas ahead for you.[49]

Among other recipients in the United States of the article was George Coe, who called it "a very important contribution because it clearly tells the truth upon certain fundamental issues."[50] C. V. Hibbard, his Wisconsin contact, thought that Childs' sympathetic approach to Chinese life more than justified his selection for the job in Peking. Daniel Johnson Fleming, of Union Theological Seminary, told Childs that, in his opinion, it was the frankest, bravest statement he had seen in print by any regularly appointed missionary. However, even his friends, while admiring his courage, wondered whether Childs had been wise in taking such a strong public stand, particularly as he had focused so strongly on the negative aspects of missionary work.

But Childs was unrepentant, and on Sunday, February 21, 1926, he spoke at a morning service. Although he did not take potshots at missionaries this time, he did expound the modernist view of religious topics. "[O]ne of the reasons for much of the ineffectiveness of Christian people is that we have been so much occupied in preaching and restating in one form or other . . . generalized ideals that we have neglected to make the social study and experiments which are necessary to give intelligent expression to these principles." On theological topics Childs moved farther from orthodoxy: "In the whole series of spiritual leaders of the human race, we may, indeed, be justified in giving Jesus the supreme place, but a scientific handling of the evidence no longer permits us to say that all truth is in Him, and that all others move in a moral and spiritual realm entirely different from that of Jesus." He was now questioning the divinity of Christ: "We recognize that Jesus died for the welfare of the human-race. But so does the scientist who dies while he voluntarily exposes his body to bacteria in order that an adequate test may be made of a long sought-for anti-toxin. Jesus died because of the sin of the world. Yes, but so did my College room-mate who was called back from educational work in Japan to give his life along with ten million other young men in the madness of a War which he did not will, and which was fought against a people for whom he held no hatred."[51]

As with the *Life* article, Childs sent copies of this sermon to friends, whose responses were much as the previous ones were. C. V. Hibbard responded with his customary forbearance. Childs was becoming strident, and what was happening was clear. He was evidently preparing himself, psychologically at least, to withdraw from the work in China. He was distancing himself from the missionary work of the association, and his almost reckless disregard for the consequences of his words, in terms of the association anyway, is a clear indication of his state of mind. Then, sure enough, in early August he stated his decision openly to Dr. David Yui, by training a journalist and educator and by that time general secretary of the National Committee of the YMCA stationed in Shanghai. Yui had given a series of impassioned speeches following the Shanghai incident of the previous year to make it clear that the YMCA had taken a pro-Chinese stand throughout the business. He appreciated Childs' position. To Yui, Childs wrote,

> For sometime I have not been getting genuine satisfaction out of my work in the Association. . . . As nearly as I can analyse my own situation I believe that my difficulty arises from a lack of interest in the administrative, promotional, and executive aspects of my work. I find that I am increasingly drawn to the opportunity which the teaching profession affords. For the past two years I have been doing a certain amount of regular teaching work and the experience has been so satisfying that I am coming to the conclusion that for me my best contribution can probably be made in that relationship rather than that of an executive officer of the Association Movement.[52]

Childs stated that he expected, after more graduate work, to return to China. He also mentioned that his interest now lay in social and educational subjects. Within two weeks he had made up his mind to leave Peking, even though he did not receive a reply from Yui until November. Once again, C. V. Hibbard was most sympathetic and even ventured the opinion that there might be a place for him on the faculty of his alma mater in Madison. However, Childs stuck to his intention to return again to graduate school.

Although Childs' own dissatisfaction with his work was largely personal, he was doubtless also aware that, even as he had long urged, control of the association was passing into Chinese hands. As Garrett said of 1926, "The golden years of the West in China had come to an end."[53] There was, however, another private reason for his desire to leave China. Grace Fowler Childs was an only child, and her parents were in their seventies and in bad health. It behooved both John and Grace Childs to be closer to their families.

Already, late in 1926, Childs had applied for admission to the doctoral program at the University of Chicago, where he was offered a tuition scholarship and a missionary apartment. The financial picture brightened when he learned in mid-April that his application for a fellowship from the National Council on Religion and Higher Education had been successful. His twelve-month stipend was to be sixteen hundred dollars. He asked several of his associates to write letters of recommendation for him, including his teachers George Coe and Harrison Elliott, and his YMCA supervisors Stephen Brockman and G. Sherwood Eddy. Eddy wrote that Childs "is one of the best minds and most fearless spirits that we have in our entire force of picked Y. M. C. A. men in all Asia. He will probably be the strongest man who applies to you this year for a fellowship. He needs it. He will use it in the best way and will prove, I predict, one of your most useful students in the future."[54]

Plans to go to Chicago changed abruptly on account of a two-week visit to Peking at the beginning of May 1927 by one of his professors from Teachers College, William Heard Kilpatrick. It was from Kilpatrick, during the time of study for his master's degree, that Childs had got a better notion of his new approach to philosophy and education, which over the years would "grow in meaning and in significance."[55] Kilpatrick was on an extended round-the-world trip, which took him to Egypt, India, Ceylon, Japan, England, Germany, and the Soviet Union. His Chinese visit was sponsored by the National Association for the Advancement of Education in China. Childs saw a great deal of Kilpatrick while he was in China and even had the opportunity to discuss not only his future plans but also a possible dissertation topic. Kilpatrick urged Childs to get his doctorate, combining, as he had for his master's degree, work at Union Theological Seminary with work at Teachers College.

With the die cast and Grace Childs already in Korea, Childs left Peking in early June to join his wife. He wrote to David Yui, "I shall be ever thankful for the years I have had in the work here."[56] And so closed the Chinese chapter, after his years in Eau Claire and those in Madison, the third great "crucial learning" of his life. Before their departure from the Orient, John and Grace Childs went to Japan, where they again met Kilpatrick who promised to see them in New York in September. They sailed from Kobe, Japan, on June 28, 1927, on the *Empress of Russia*. John Childs never returned to the East, neither did he make frequent reference to it—the book was almost closed. But, in 1944 he did briefly open its pages when he spoke eloquently and poetically of his China experience.

Many years have passed since Mrs. Childs and I said good-bye to our home in Peking in order to return to our work here in America. We had spent more than ten years in China—happy years which have left us many valued memories of the country and its people. As former Ambassador, Paul S. Reinsch, used to remark, the Peking of those days was one of the most impressive and charming capital-cities of the whole world. Its temples, its spacious parks and courtyards, its palaces, its pagodas, its bright colored street arches, its schools and universities, its friendly and artistically furnished homes, its market-places, its theatres, and its shops were admired and recognized as the seasoned products of a mature, integrated and humane way of life. I was particularly fascinated by the massive wall which encloses the major part of the city of Peking. Often at evening, I would go south on Hatamen to the City-Gate, and after ascending the wall walk there for an hour or so. I never tired of watching the sun sink in a purple haze into the Western hills which seemed at dusk to blend with the graceful and beautiful tiled roofs of the old Imperial City.[57]

Eleven years is a long time in anyone's life, but the ages from twenty-seven to thirty-eight are critical, and John Childs spent them in China. He had undergone a profound spiritual-intellectual transformation. Ahead of him lay the work for the doctorate at Teachers College and then instant prominence with the publication of his dissertation, *Education and the Philosophy of Experimentalism,* and collaboration with Dewey on two chapters in Kilpatrick's *Educational Frontier.* The pragmatic "moralist" would then be ready to take his place alongside others of the Dewey contingent. It could be argued that "the best working years" of his life were to be spent not as a Christian missionary but as the moralist of the left wing of the progressive educators.

On their return to New York, Grace and John Childs

moved into the Missionary Apartment House, which was run by Union Theological Seminary. These apartments were located at 99 Claremont Avenue and were "available to missionaries on furlough who intend to return to the mission field."[58] They later moved to 509 West 121st Street. Union and Teachers College were now offering a joint doctorate in philosophy of education. The program was described in the 1928–29 Union catalog.

[T]he Seminary faculty shares directly with the faculty of Teachers College in the student's work for the doctor's degree. Seminary students majoring in religious education or related fields, are recognized as specializing in the teaching of religion, and may, therefore, include in their work for the degree, as "approved equivalents" to courses in education in Teachers College, such courses in the Seminary as are recommended by the major professor as inherently necessary to the proper preparation of the dissertation or to success in the field in which the candidate is to specialize. These courses must be approved by the committee on higher degrees. No definite requirement is made as to the proportion of courses to be taken in the Seminary or Teachers College, this depending upon the dissertation and the field of specialization. The subject of major interest and the major professor may be either from the Seminary or Teachers College, and members of the faculty of the Seminary will share with members of the faculty of the department of educational research of Teachers College in a joint advisory system for the approval of students' programs for the doctor's degree, in matriculation examinations, in the committee for the guidance of the dissertation, and in the oral examination, and the final approval of the dissertation as appointed and approved by the dean of the faculty of philosophy.[59]

Thus it was that Childs' major professor continued to be, as it had been for his master's degree, Harrison Elliott, for his degree was to be officially in the field of religious education. This time, however, he took more courses from Teachers College and Columbia University, where his professors included not only Kilpatrick but also Goodwin Watson, Edward H. Reisner, George S. Counts, Herbert Schneider, John Herman Randall, and John Dewey himself.

Childs did not entirely close his eyes to what was going

on in China, and some time in 1928 he gave a talk to associates of the magazine *World Tomorrow*. It was a strongly worded indictment of United States' policies in China and included a denunciation of U.S. Minister to China John Van Antwerp MacMurray, who had been appointed in 1925. In contrast to his predecessors, MacMurray seems to have avoided contact with the Chinese and demonstrated little feeling for the situation in China. Childs described MacMurray as having "an indoor mind."[60] Kilpatrick realized that Childs was taking a chance with such an outspoken statement. Whether it was the reception to the talk, Kilpatrick's warning, or simply the pressure of his doctoral studies, Childs concentrated increasingly on educational philosophy, an area in which he realized his shortcomings. Years later one of his classmates recalled that "you were moaning over doctoral requirements and whether you would ever surmount them."[61] His future references to China were comparatively rare, although he and Grace did resort to speaking Chinese, particularly in front of their nephews and nieces, when they did not want to be understood.

Kilpatrick, while not Childs' official advisor, acted very much as Childs' mentor during the doctoral years, and he was sufficiently enthusiastic about his work to nominate him as a temporary teaching substitute for R. Bruce Raup for the following year. Kilpatrick did not take long to see that Childs was offered the job at a salary of fifteen hundred dollars a year.

May 8, 1928, marked the inauguration of Kilpatrick's famous Discussion Group, whose purpose was "to discuss the more significant matters that interest us in the educational field."[62] The original group included William C. Bagley, Harrison Elliott, Jesse Newlon, Harold Rugg (not present at the first meeting), George Counts, Percival M. Symonds, Goodwin Watson, and Bruce Raup. Isaac Kandel was added that first day. Originally the number was to be limited to twelve people, but that was soon forgotten. John Dewey attended for the first time in December. Even though in his diary Kilpatrick listed Childs as a member on January 1, 1929, the entry is in a different color ink. It seems that Childs first attended on April 20, 1931.

As early as February 1929, Childs discussed his dissertation topic, at least in general terms, with Kilpatrick. The title at that time was "The Implications of Experimentalism for Education." The pair had frequent talks, or "walks," which Kilpatrick was fond of taking with his friends. Kilpatrick expressed the hope that Childs would be kept in the department after Raup's return, although Childs himself had some doubts. But for the 1929–30 academic year, Childs did continue as a half-time instructor "with very definite success."[63] For both semesters that year, Childs was enrolled in Dewey's seminar in philosophy. The course was open to a limited number of students, who were encouraged to pursue their own fields of interest. Individual or joint conferences were arranged with Dewey.

The course work completed, having obtained an almost perfect A average, Childs was free to work on his dissertation. Kilpatrick thought it "distinctly good," and was sufficiently enthusiastic to talk to Dean William F. Russell concerning Childs' fitness for a permanent position at Teachers College as an assistant professor.[64] The dean was not altogether of the same opinion and told Kilpatrick that "Childs did not seem a strong man and that it seemed wiser to bring in a man of different philosophy."[65] Childs sent a copy of his almost-completed dissertation to the dean so that he could judge for himself the quality of the work. But Childs' name did not appear on the list of new appointees issued a few days later. Kilpatrick wrote, "The future has suddenly grown dark"; however, he was not ready to give up, and before he went to see Russell once more he summoned the support of others, including Raup and Counts. "I tell him I don't understand. I don't seem to know where I stand. He is quick to see that I feel pretty low in spirit. He begs me not to feel so, offers in fact to make the appointment if that will cheer me up. I say neither yea nor nay to this."[66]

Kilpatrick continued to press, although Russell was obviously reluctant. "Walk with Dean R. We have a long and earnest but entirely friendly talk about Childs and the situation. In the end the Dean gives in and says he will appoint Childs Assistant Professor at $4500. He seemed particularly interested as to whether Childs has a mind of his own. I feel immensely better and let Raup and Childs know as soon as I can. Childs had about given up hope."[67] In the event, Dean Russell would not formally appoint Childs until after the publication of his dissertation, which came out in June 1931. Kilpatrick commented that he was "highly delighted" with the good-looking volume.

Kilpatrick continued to confide in Childs. One evening in July, he visited Childs in his new home, which he had rented for fifteen months from his Union teacher Harry F. Ward. As was customary, they took a stroll. "After dinner we sit and talk about various matters. In a way I am initiating him into the secret history of the College and our department, etc. I like Childs very much." He saw the anomaly in the situation and wrote, "A former student and former missionary in China."[68] Childs never forgot his gratitude to Kilpatrick and remained on cordial terms with his mentor until the latter's death at the age of ninety-two in 1965. With such support, Childs was well placed to move quickly into prominence. Now the student days were at last over, Childs, at the comparatively late age of forty-two, was about to have a certain greatness thrust upon him. The transition from faith in prayer to faith in pragmatism was complete.

4.
Philosopher of Reconstructionism

Largely through William Heard Kilpatrick's advocacy, Childs became a full-time member of the faculty of Teachers College, where he was to remain until his retirement in 1954; it was to be a distinguished career. As stated, Dean William F. Russell would not approve Childs' appointment until his dissertation had been published. In July 1931, Childs' first book, *Education and the Philosophy of Experimentalism*, was published by Century as the first in a series edited by Willis L. Uhl, dean of the School of Education at the University of Washington, Seattle. It was dedicated to Grace Childs. Kilpatrick had written an enthusiastic recommendation to Scribner's: "It is one of the very best pieces of thinking yet done in the field of the exploitation and criticism of Professor Dewey's ideas."[1] Macmillan was also offered the manuscript, but the company wanted Childs himself to pay for the plates. Century not only made the first offer but moved promptly to meet a July publication date. As the title indicates, the book deals primarily with the implications of experimentalism for education, or more precisely, as Herman H. Horne pointed out, with the educational work of John Dewey. It must be readily admitted that the book is by no means a practical manual.

Childs held that experimentalism, a term he preferred to both *pragmatism* and *instrumentalism*, is a genuine American philosophy, it, like America itself, is firmly grounded in the European, particularly the English, tradition. This basis is demonstrated by what it owes to modern science, the experimental method, and the theory of evolution. The four distinct aspects of American life that conditioned the thought of the experimentalists are

1. the absence of a rigidly fixed system of ancient traditions, customs, and institutions that tend to orient the life of a people towards the past rather than the future;
2. the primitive quality of life on the frontier that made it evident that there was little that was fixed in either the natural or the social environment;
3. the reality given to the ideas of social democracy and human progress in a new world where natural resources were abundant and people relatively scarce;
4. the extensive development and unparalleled use made of the machine in serving human ends.

In spite of these factors, which have fostered the experimentalist disposition, there is an opposing strain in American life that has not been as hospitable. It is the mentality that encourages superstition, that is reactionary, fundamentalist, bigoted, formalist, and dualistic. Most particularly, the tradition of "rugged individualism" is inhospitable to the experimentalist temper. A philosophy of excessive individualism, fertilized in a frontier-agrarian society, is inappropriate in an inextricably interdependent technological society. This side-by-side existence of the two mentalities makes education an area of special interest to the experimentalist, for it underlines the importance of thinking critically even about those things that have become assumed truths, such as religious dogmas or allegiance to the flag.

Childs looked at the underlying principles of experimentalism and answered some of its critics. He responded first to the charge that experimentalism has no metaphysical base. This is a debate he was to take up again in the early 1950s with Boyd H. Bode. While previous philosophies had been dualistic, the experimentalists' belief in the primacy of experience, in which things are simply as they are experienced, is fundamental to the entire philosophy. Therefore, its metaphysics can be deduced from it methodology. The experimentalist can be said to reject any transempirical reality, to deny all sorts of supernaturalism, to refuse to look for support to anything beyond experience, and to assert that no spiritual experience can contribute knowledge about this world. While the older philosophies sought certainty, the experimentalist accepts the reality of ambiguity, uncertainty, indeterminateness, and incompleteness. We live in a world that is a mixture of the regular and the changing, of the uncertain and the fixed, of the stubborn and the precarious. Thus, absolute dogmas give way to hypotheses.

Hypothesis testing focuses on the scientific method, which is at the heart of experimentalism. Thinking is inquiring not mere musing, and it starts with the problematic situation, which Childs called a *situation of ambiguity*. He made the interesting comment that knowledge is that which has a significant opposite. Experience in itself is neither true nor false; it is simply what it happens to be. Knowledge is not gained by our immediate consciousness. It is our judgment about that experience and our interpretations of it that are true or false and that therefore yield knowledge. It is the use of intelligence, *creative intelligence* is a term Childs liked, that occasions this knowledge. Intelligence is insight into the behavior of persons and things; it is the mental ability to guide present activity in the light of foreseen consequences. Intelligence guides choice, which always goes beyond the tried-and-true (if it did not it would be either mere habit or the result of simple conditioning), and therefore involves an element of risk. Hence *creative* intelligence. Søren Kierkegaard said, "Life can only be understood backwards; but it must be lived forwards."[2] Childs would agree wholeheartedly, although he might phrase it somewhat differently: knowledge comes after the experience.

One of the central themes in all Childs' work is that choice making is necessarily a moral undertaking. No choice, no morals. "[W]henever a significant choice has to be made between a better and a worse in experience, we face a genuine moral situation. . . . The moral factor in any choice-situation is proportional to the significance of the various sets of value consequences which follow from the alternative courses of action. To discriminate and anticipate such consequences is an intellectual act of the highest quality."[3]

Childs then moved to a discussion of values—the values of freedom and democracy in particular. Both, however, are not ends in themselves. Goods are individual and particular; a democratic society makes these goods more readily available than do other societal forms because it can more readily accommodate variations. "[M]oral autonomy implies freedom from the imposed control of others, and equally freedom from habits that inhibit the capacity to change and grow. The individual who is controlled by fixed ideas and habits is no more free to grow than is the individual whose behavior is dictated by others."[4] Now we get to the importance of education. "For the experimentalist the only justification for the existence of a school is that it can through intentional effort produce an environment in which the experiences of youth will be more truly educative than they otherwise would be."[5] Childs continued, the basic educational aim "is to develop individuals who can intelligently manage their own affairs, at times 'alone,' more usually in shared or joint enterprise."[6] Childs, reflecting his experimentalist views of the self as found in and through interaction with others, held that education is the sharing of experience. Formal education must "develop individuals who through critical experimental procedures come to possess the resources needed to carry on this responsible work of social reconstruction."[7] He placed emphasis on both the individual *and* society. While he expressed faith in the fullest development of the individual, he rejected roundly the philosophy of individualism. Interdependence is a fact of industrial society. And in a phrase that predated that of George Counts, Childs asked, "Dare the schools be adventurous enough to permit children to have meaningful intercourse with the wider community activities?"[8]

Childs had arranged with Century for complimentary copies of the book to be sent, at his own expense, to about fifty friends and colleagues. He received congratulatory letters from many of them, among the most enthusiastic coming from Boyd H. Bode, who responded, "It presents the point of view of experimentalism much more discerningly than anything which I have seen for a long time."[9] Several people commented favorably on the section on psychology and the individual. Herman H. Horne wrote that "experimentalism has here been expounded ably, criticized slightly, and sympathetically defended."[10] Alice V. Keliher called it "an important book."[11] And, Willis L. Uhl, the series editor, told Childs he was "greatly pleased" with the book.[12] In short, the reviews and comments were good but not ecstatic. However, the book drew from Ann Shumaker, a former student and by 1931 the editor of *Progressive Education,* a request for an article based on chapter 6, "Education and Freedom." This was the first of many articles Childs wrote for the journal.

In fact, the article that appeared in *Progressive Education* deals succinctly with the notion of freedom in education and is not merely a restatement of the book chapter.[13] In it Childs laid down five conditions for freedom, which require

1. mastery over appropriate techniques or skills;
2. intelligent understanding of what one is about and the ability to share in shaping the ends that govern our activities, or, as Dewey was to write later, the power to frame purposes;
3. harmonious ordering of life to give maximum expression to varied desires;
4. healthy emotional adjustment;
5. a discriminating mind that can see a variety of possibilities.

Childs pointed out that freedom is not given but is something achieved; it is a function of habits, attitudes, and basic intellectual and emotional dispositions that are acquired. Hence the importance of an appropriate education. Freedom is won in experience; it is desirable because it enables us to control more effectively our life situation. This is a nice little article, and its brevity shows Childs at his best.

Kilpatrick continued to keep Childs under his wing. On October 6, 1931, after a meeting of the famed Discussion Group, Kilpatrick wrote, "Bagley asks what I think of inviting Childs to membership, that he wishes it. I say I wish it, but had hesitated. B. then moves that C. be invited, and puts the motion which is carried."[14] One week later, Kilpatrick celebrated Childs' new appointment and held a dinner at the Faculty Club. "In honor of Childs's promotion to the Assistant Professorship we have a departmental table: Dr. and Mrs. Raup, Professor and Mrs. Childs, Miss Ostrander, and Margaret and I. It was a pleasant occasion."[15]

As was mentioned in chapter 3, Childs had taken Kilpatrick's philosophy of education course (Education 441–42) for his master's degree. For this course Kilpatrick had prepared a seventy-five-page syllabus and used it in conjunction with his 1923 *Source Book in the Philosophy of Education*.[16] Kilpatrick was a master teacher, and his method has been well detailed by Samuel Tenenbaum in *William Heard Kilpatrick: Trail Blazer in Education*.[17] Like many successful teachers, Kilpatrick himself expressed doubts about his own abilities. The classes were run as large discussion groups based on questions contained in the syllabus and answers derived from a suggested list of readings. Kilpatrick rarely supplied answers or conclusions himself. Rather, he posed a problematic situation, such as, "Are the unborn to be included in society?" and "In the light of the foregoing how do you define a society?" During the course of his doctoral program, Childs had already been helping his teacher with revisions to both the syllabus and the *Source Book*. Kilpatrick noted on September 4, 1931, that he found Childs of great help. "We block out the general scheme and in greater detail the first two chapters."[18] Childs retained his copy of the syllabus, which is liberally covered with notes and inserted pages. When the revised *Source Book* was printed in 1934, Childs had provided material for the first four chapters, in point of fact, considerably more than Kilpatrick wanted.[19] Childs' original forty pages for chapter 2 were cut to thirty, and Kilpatrick wanted a further reduction. For chapter 3, Childs provided sixty-seven pages, for chapter 4, seventy-two! For his efforts, Kilpatrick offered Childs 10 percent of the royalties, which by the third year of publication amounted to a little over a thousand dollars. Childs declined the offer. The *Source Book* is a collection of excerpts from educational writers, and it is hardly surprising that over half of the excerpts that Childs selected for his four chapters are from C. S. Peirce, William James, John Dewey, and Kilpatrick himself, with Dewey, inevitably at this stage of Childs' career, being far and away the favored author.

Shortly after publication of the revised edition of the *Source Book,* Kilpatrick published a new edition of the *Syllabus* and included Childs' 1931 book frequently in the lists of suggested readings.[20] At the same time, he enlisted Childs' assistance in writing *The Educational Frontier,* a book written jointly by both of them and five other like-minded writers, including John Dewey and Boyd H. Bode. Although the writing was shared, it was preceded by several long discussion meetings.

At an initial meeting in New York in April, it was agreed that the book should be written "from the point of view of the philosophy of education on the social situation," and a tentative table of contents was approved.[21] The authors agreed to meet again early in July. By that time Dewey had visited Columbus, Ohio, and differences appeared between the New York group (Kilpatrick, Childs, Raup, and V. T. Thayer) and the Ohio group (Bode, H. Gordon Hullfish, as well as Dewey). At the end of three days of meetings between July 2 and 4, the topics had been reassigned, and "Dewey and Childs were to make the social analysis and write the chapter on the philosophy of education."[22] Kilpatrick still hoped that they would produce a good book, but he was concerned that Dewey was not altogether in accord with his colleagues; he also was a little worried that Childs was being somewhat recalcitrant. Shortly after the July meetings had concluded, Kilpatrick noted, "Childs troubles me a little. I fear that he takes at times a merely contrary attitude."[23] The irritation did not last, although it recurred occasionally over the years.

The entire group met again in late September at Briarcliff, Pennsylvania. The chapters that by then had been written were read and discussed. Kilpatrick, at any rate, was pleased with the results, but he was critical of Bode's tendency to "see education almost exclusively in terms of school."[24]

The group met for the last time in mid-November, when the revised chapters were further discussed. Kilpatrick felt that the Dewey-Childs chapter on the socioeconomic situation took "strong clear ground," largely thanks to Childs.[25] A few days later Kilpatrick went through the final version of this second chapter and called it "very fine of content, but rather badly written in spots."[26] Their other chapter, meanwhile, had hit a snag. On December 7, Kilpatrick, Dewey, Counts, and Sidney Hook dined at the Childs' home. Charles A. Beard, who was then working closely with Counts on the American Historical Association's (AHA) Commission on the Social Studies in the Schools, arrived later. In Kilpatrick's words, "Childs arranged this meeting to discuss experimentalism as to whether it is available to get us out of the present trouble. Counts has been saying no. In the end I thought we cleared up the points: [that] E[xperimentalism] . . . is not limited to pacifist means if no others will work and wisdom so points; that the free use of intelligence is our only safe hope, and any substitute is to be feared."[27] The meeting seems to have been productive, for, on Christmas Eve, Kilpatrick pronounced the chapter "an admirable short statement of Dewey's philosophy."[28] It was sent off to the publisher two days later. In reviewing the copy proofs in mid-February, Kilpatrick noted that "Dewey had made the greatest contributions."[29] It is precisely these contributions to *The Educational Frontier* that have caused several commentators to note Dewey's flirtation with social reconstructionism. The influence of Childs here cannot be in doubt, especially when looking closely at their exchanges.

In a memorandum from Childs to Dewey, some of Childs' fundamental concerns about their collaboration were addressed. He noted the necessity for educational reform to be linked with social reform: "educational reconstruction and social reconstruction are correlatives, and, therefore, the two must develop together. For us as educators to try to solve our present problems through exclusive attention to school procedures leaves too much out of account to promise success. Any attempt to work through the school problem—to say nothing of the educational problem as a whole—inevitably leads into a consideration of the prevailing economic and social situation."[30]

Childs hoped that he and Dewey might recommend ways in which students could be actively involved in community affairs. He reiterated the difficulties inherent in moving from the older tradition of individualism to an emerging collective, interdependent mode. Childs asked Dewey, "[H]ow far can and should the school go in educating for a cooperative community life when the actual life of the community is still controlled by the policy of individual initiative and private competition?"[31] On the one hand, we must conserve "the essential values of our democratic social experience," while at the same time, we must adjust to an emerging society. Dewey's reply was somewhat unexpected. He preferred to take a higher view than the one occasioned by the social conditions of the early 1930s and noted that he and Childs should "not be too much concerned with the apparent *immediate* situation. I take it that we would all agree that the most ultimate look ahead would give us a glimpse of a community of resolute men and women intelligently controlling social traditions, institutions and arrangements for the promotion of a significant human life on the part of all concerned. This is the goal we should hold in mind."[32] The two men seemed to have approached the project from different vantage points—Dewey looking at perhaps the bigger picture and wanting to lay down general principles, Childs concerned that the book have immediate "practical" value. However, the work progressed, and Dewey himself prepared the final version of the manuscript for the press.

The first of the two Dewey-Childs coauthored chapters, "The Social-Economic Situation and Education," contains much that is already familiar to readers of the work of Dewey and of Childs. At the heart of the then-current educational debate was that, as has already been mentioned, the traditions of the agrarian-individualistic past were not altogether useful in the industrial-collectivist present of the 1930s. Although ideas for social reconstruction had gained widespread *verbal* acceptance, even in educational circles, they had not been organically connected with educational practice, largely because school subjects had not been taught in a social context. Industrialism had been accompanied by chronic insecurity, by the rationalization that the successful were somehow the more moral, by an exaggerated significance being given to business and money, by excessive competitiveness, by the belief that social planning was somehow harmful to the moral fiber of the nation, and by the conviction that the demands of democracy were achieved, in the face of economic autocracy, so long as its political forms were retained. The authors quickly pointed out that there was nothing inherently wrong with science and technology (a point overlooked by one of the reviewers of the book); rather, the "man-made legal and political system under which technological industry operates is the cause of our troubles rather than machine-industry itself."[33] To address the dislocation we needed new modes of thinking.

What might these new modes be? For Dewey and Childs the answer was almost self-evident, and Dewey, at any rate, had been talking about them for years: science itself is a mode of thinking; it is a method. This method has had a revolutionary impact on daily life, largely in the form of technology; it has been taken for granted in technological fields, while it has hardly had any impact at all in social fields. Yet, they said, in scientific method we have a "potential agency for ridding the present situation of its confusions and conflicts and for making the transition to a society which will be emancipated from many of the undesirable traits" of life.[34] This is why education is so important. It needs to awaken "to a sense of its identity with the cause of a community which employs science and technology for experimental planning and action in the common interest."[35] Consequently, not only do the methods of instruction need to be changed but also subject matter and objectives. The overall educational goal is "to prepare individuals to take part intelligently in the management of conditions under which they will live, to bring them to an understanding of the forces which are moving, to equip them with the intellectual and practical tools by which they can themselves enter into direction of these forces."[36]

Perhaps this chapter sounds more like Counts (and indeed he is referred to here) than either Dewey or even Childs, although Childs did share basic views with Counts. They disagreed with him on the meaning of *indoctrination*—Dewey and, to a lesser degree, Childs believing that what they were advocating was more open-ended than any explicit agenda implied by the use of the offending word. Counts, however, held that his colleagues were in fact calling for a form of indoctrination. The difference was more than semantic, and perhaps Counts here was more honest. Norman Foerster, who wrote a damning review of *The Educational Frontier*, drew attention to this point and, in effect, agreed with Counts: "When it does not please us, we call it propaganda; when it does please us, we call it education."[37] However, Foerster is wrong in noting that the authors called for a planned society, for Dewey and Childs made it clear that they proposed not a planned society but a *planning* society. The distinction is important.

The typescript of the final chapter of *The Educational Frontier* is not available, but Dewey and Childs, while admitting that theirs should not be taken as *the* philosophy of education, clearly shared the perspective of the other "frontiersmen." Education, as they conceived it, "is a process of social interaction carried on in behalf of consequences which are themselves social—that is, it involves interactions between persons and includes shared values."[38] It may be difficult to judge the value of those social consequences but Dewey said it must be done on the basis of "their educative effect, by what they do in the way of liberating, organizing, integrating" human capabilities. Therefore, "[i]t is the function of education to see to it that individuals are so trained as to be capable of entering into the heritage of . . . values which already exist, trained also in sensitiveness to the defects of what already exists and in ability to recreate and improve."[39] After all, no society is free from negative aspects, and to minimize them requires that intelligent choices be made, on the basis of an appreciation of probable consequences.

All this may seem to suggest that Dewey and Childs were focusing too much on means, on methodology, and not sufficiently on ends. Foerster certainly thought so, and there is some basis for his criticism, unless one accepts the experimentalist view that "genuine values and tenable ends and ideals are to be derived from what is found within the movement of experience."[40] But "association," "democracy," "humanizing of the economic system," and "reconstruction of society" are not educational aims that are in themselves too helpful, particularly to practicing educators, but they were about as far as the authors would go. There is little doubt that Childs and Dewey placed emphasis on emerging rather than on a priori ends. They made this plain when they wrote, "Ends cannot be conceived as operative ends, as directors of action, apart from consideration of conditions which obstruct and means which promote them. . . . Ends may begin as the plan and purpose in the rough. This is useful if it leads to search for and discovery of means."[41] Dewey and Childs believed that the dualism between means and ends is inherited from past philosophic thought and reinforced by educational practice; but, they felt that the separation could be overcome if we were to view "knowledge as instrumentality of action."[42]

Dewey and Childs proceeded next to a discussion and explication of the experimental method, already familiar to their readers. They suggested that to the bare bones of the methodology we need to add intelligence, and Dewey stated that the method of intelligence, in which method *and* goals are united, would only be possible when all have the opportunity to "develop rich and diversified experience, while also securing continuous cooperative give and take and intercommunication."[43] The method of intelligence is, therefore, completely compatible with the democratic way of life for it enlarges the area of common understanding, of shared meanings. The authors believed they fulfilled their own rule that "[i]t is the business of a philosophy of education to make clear what is involved in the action which is carried on within the educational field, to transform a preference which is blind, based on custom rather than thought, into an intelligent choice—one made, that is, with consciousness of what is aimed at, the reasons why it is preferred, and the fitness of the means used."[44]

This chapter poses a problem for Dewey scholars, especially taken in tandem with the earlier chapter, for it is a radical extension of his philosophy of education; Childs' influence is patent. The writing also has, as has been mentioned, a Countsian tone in its railing against entrenched and vested interests; in its outspokenness on behalf of common folk, it smacks more of Childs than of Dewey. Sidney Hook recognized this in his review for the *New Republic* when he noted that it is a "radical reformulation of the position of America's leading educators."[45] But, as has been seen, both Counts and Hook had something to say about the work before the final version had been received by Kilpatrick. For his part, Kilpatrick wrote in his diary, "More work has gone into the making of this by much than anything I have yet done"; not a light admission for such an indefatigable worker as Kilpatrick.[46]

The Educational Frontier came out in the early part of 1933 and received generally good reviews, although the one by Norman Foerster, already referred to, is particularly negative. He deplored the work of the Teachers College frontiersmen. John C. Almack was kinder on account of "the good will which the reviewer tends to hold toward the collaborators." He called it "a brave and honest attempt on the part of a little group of men, unequally qualified, in general untrained in science and skeptical of the value of its method, to assert their right to lead. That they have not succeeded is due to several reasons, most notably that they have no new place to go and no means of conveyance."[47] Almack called the final chapter "the weakest of the lot," and "not Dewey at his best."[48] However, as much of the last chapter elucidates the method of science (the method of intelligence) and advocates its use, it is hard to see how Almack could have described the authors as skeptical of the value of its method.

On the other hand, Sidney Hook was, not unexpectedly, most enthusiastic. He called it, "By far the most progressive and significant statement of the new educational philosophy

which is emerging from the depression."[49] Indeed, Hook felt
the book was not quite revolutionary enough because it did
not describe how America is to move from a class to a classless
society. Hook here suggested the Countsian solution—that
teachers take up common cause with other workers, farmers,
and professionals and gain political power. The reviewer in
Progressive Education thought the book would "arouse teachers and educators who are not too lazy to read it."[50] It received
a favorable notice from the *Times (London) Literary Supplement*, where it was described as "an original, courageous and
thought-provoking book, the value of which is not for American readers alone."[51]

Childs was now closely associated with Dewey and over
the years achieved the reputation as being the leading interpreter of Dewey's educational theory. As such, he not only
stepped into that role during the events honoring Dewey on
his eightieth birthday, but subsequently on the ninetieth, and
eventually during the centennial celebrations. Paul Arthur
Schilpp chose Childs to write the essay, "The Educational
Philosophy of John Dewey," in the first of his *Library of Living
Philosophers* series. Dewey himself, commenting in the book
on the discussions by Childs, Kilpatrick, Joseph Ratner, and
George Geiger, all former students, wrote, "I have to express
my appreciation of the way in which these contributers have
seen and reported the direction in which my thoughts have
moved, of their sense of what it is I was doing and what it is
I was after."[52]

Childs' essay is cogent and powerful; he believed that
Dewey's work was a call to action, to active reconstruction,
just as earlier he had believed that Jesus called His followers
to spread the gospel and to feed His sheep. But, whereas the
power of Jesus was derived from supernatural sources, the
power of Dewey, or rather of his ideas, was their appeal to a
thoroughly naturalistic outlook. Childs admitted that method
is primary in Dewey's philosophy and that method "does
not automatically prescribe a complete set of metaphysical
theses," but the method of experience inevitably leads to a
naturalistic outlook, which does *eliminate* certain metaphysical assumptions.[53] Experimental naturalism "calls not only for

a reconstructed view of mind, it also calls for a reconstructed view of the nature of the world in which man lives, moves, and has his being."[54] Childs summarized Dewey's views on nature and mind and proceeded to consideration of things social and to Dewey's commitment to the democratic way of life, not merely as a statement of preference but as the inevitable outcome of the arguments used thus far. Childs concluded his essay by looking at the implications for education that could be derived from the argument:

1. each individual possesses intrinsic worth and dignity;
2. individuals have the status of ends, while institutions have the status of means;
3. individuals must be educated to be competent judges of values;
4. individuals are unique, thus differences between them must be prized, and the opportunities for free association with others must be encouraged;
5. the school must permit the young actual experience in the process of adjustment "by the method of conference and mutual give and take";[55]
6. present conditions in American society constitute a real threat to American democracy.

The last point shows Childs himself pushing perhaps a little farther than Dewey had. He took a strong stand here when he wrote:

Existing economic and legal arrangements have so concentrated wealth in the hands of a small class that equality of opportunity has been destroyed in the economic sphere. This privileged class also seeks to maintain its position by restricting that free expression of thought, and that experimental use of intelligence which are foundational in a democratic society. . . .[B]oth democracy and education demand that the anarchy of the present competitive profit economy be supplanted by a planning society in which production is democratically controlled for the good of all.[56]

To support this position Childs, significantly, quoted Dewey's essay from *The Educational Frontier*, the very essay that, it will be remembered, had been coauthored by Childs: "An identity, an equation, exists between the urgent social need of the present and that of education. Society, in order to solve its own problems and remedy its own ills, needs to employ science and technology for social instead of merely private ends. This need for a society in which experimental inquiry and planning for social ends are organically contained is also the need for a new education." Childs then added, in his own words, "The supreme task of our generation is to bring about this social transformation."[57] As will be seen, this is exactly what Childs himself was engaged in throughout the 1940s.

Childs' chapter in the Schilpp book was reprinted together with Kilpatrick's in a short monograph, for which Kilpatrick wrote the introduction. They discussed their respective contributions together, and each generally reinforced the other's views. Schilpp also sent to them a controversial chapter to review. It consisted of a Marxist attack on Dewey, and Schilpp was urged by Kilpatrick and Childs to reject it. Dewey himself did not like it, and Sidney Hook was "violently opposed" to its inclusion.[58]

A decade after the chapter written for Schilpp, Childs contributed an essay to Sidney Hook's symposium that was published in 1950 and that was "developed in conjunction with the activities of the National Committee to Celebrate the 90th Birthday of John Dewey."[59] After a résumé of Dewey's educational principles, Childs looked, also briefly, at three groups who had departed from them. Although Dewey acknowledged the supreme importance of intelligence, the child-centered devotees had neglected to realize that children's interests may not be what they appear to be and that adults "must be trained to see beneath these surface manifestations to the more significant personal needs that underlie them."[60] He then looked at where Bode differed from Dewey. Bode believed it was the prime obligation of the citizens of a democracy to be intelligent, and it was the teacher's obligation to bring this about; it was not, for Bode, the teacher's job to "predetermine the nature of the future social order" or to develop programs of social improvement.[61] Childs next looked at the social reconstructionists who agreed unreservedly with Dewey and Bode that "the growth of the child is the supreme purpose of democratic education" and that this growth is best provided when children are "engaged in purposeful projects of construction and inquiry."[62] However, the social reconstructionists saw this as only one side of the educational task. They "reject the notion that inquiry is all that is involved in the nurture of the immature members of a democratic society" and hold "that understanding of the cultural heritage along with the characteristics and trends of contemporary society is also basic."[63] Childs concluded this essay by stating that Dewey himself saw value in all three of these educational conceptions, which were supplementary rather than antagonistic to his own. Childs himself took a definite tilt in favor of the social reconstructionists as he again quoted from his and Dewey's essay in *The Educational Frontier*. It was probably in response to this essay that Dewey wrote to Childs in flattering terms, "Thanks for sending me the copy of your paper and still more for writing it. Your knowledge of my position is so thorough that you don't need my assurance that you have understood it and reported it correctly, and that the correct understanding and report are all the more valuable since they are expressly set over against popular misconceptions."[64]

Dewey died in 1952, and in the ensuing years Childs continued to be a leading interpreter of his work. The centennial celebrations provided Childs with several opportunities to speak about his former teacher. He was a member of the Columbia University Centennial Committee and gave an address in the Horace Mann Auditorium on October 20, 1959, Dewey's one hundredth birthday, entitled "John Dewey and American Education," which was subsequently published in the *Teachers College Record*. He was invited to write an article for the *Progressive* ("John Dewey and American Thought"). On November 14 he gave an address at New York University at a meeting of the Middle Atlantic States Philosophy of Education Society ("Inquiring and Acquiring in Dewey's Educational Theory"). He turned down invitations to speak at the University of Tennessee, Knoxville, and at Columbia's Philosophy Department.

In October he did return to the University of Michigan and gave an address entitled "Enduring Elements in the Educational Thought of John Dewey." Childs gracefully began by noting Dewey's ten years at Ann Arbor, and he recalled that while there one of his tasks was to visit and evaluate the work of the public schools. Thus Dewey learned first hand "much about the life of pupils and the problems and opportunities of education."[65] Childs then looked at two common educational approaches that were not in accord with Dewey: the child-centered movement and the great books approach. Both ignored Dewey's "civilizational theory," which covered not merely the past but also the new and emerging world order. Childs stated that Dewey believed that a "civilizational interpretation is inherent in all educational construction, and that the manifestation of an educational preference is necessarily a manifestation of a civilizational preference."[66] Democracy is both a moral and a political conception.

Childs admitted that Dewey's theory was not free of ambiguity, and he focused next on inquiry. There are two aspects to inquiry, or research, according to Childs: "one, in which we inquire into that which is already known in order to master a developed system of meanings; the other, in which we inquire in order to attain the answer to a problem which as yet no one has achieved."[67] The latter is obvious to anyone reading Dewey. The former is not so obvious, although Childs believed that Dewey did include it in his notion of inquiry. "[P]uposeful inquiry into that which is known and fruitfully organized into systems of meaning and practice" was as important to Dewey as original problem solving.[68] As will be discussed later, for Childs himself this even came to include the administration of true-false tests. There is such a thing as organized subject matter, and Childs said that Dewey himself deplored that the "newer schools" ignored its existence. However, Childs admitted that Dewey did not show how his earlier formulations of inquiry should be qualified.

It should be seen, even in this later work, that Childs tended to interpret Dewey's work, or at least to take it to its logical conclusion, from the perspective of his own social reconstructionism. He summed up his Michigan lecture by stating, "Above all, Dewey has taught us that education is a civilizational undertaking."[69] Dewey was sufficiently friendly to Childs' point of view, held even more strongly by George Counts, to join them both, along with Kilpatrick, Harrison Elliott, Hook, and others, as members of the board of directors of a new educational journal.

The driving force of the journal was Kilpatrick, who was himself much troubled by the effects of the depression. Early in 1933, he, closely aided by Childs, Counts, and William C. Bagley, had drawn up a manifesto, which was subsequently presented to President Franklin D. Roosevelt, calling for the new president to organize a "National Coordinating Council empowered to devise policies and to recommend appropriate institutional machinery" to take care of current social needs.[70] Although the statement, which was signed by 220 educators representing all levels of schooling, was printed in several newspapers, it was delivered to Roosevelt at an inopportune time and apparently fell on deaf ears. The appeal is reconstructionist in tone, but Bagley, for example, thought the situation sufficiently grave to add his "well-known conservatism" to the general chorus.[71]

By 1934, attendance at the Discussion Group had been dwindling. In reflecting on the reasons, Kilpatrick wrote, "Possibly there are too many committee meetings, possibly we have come to know each other too well. Partly, it is that the social situation absorbs some to the exclusion of almost every interest, and this is not an 'action' group."[72] In fact, by the following October, when the group reconvened after a break of several months, only six people were in attendance, one of whom was Childs. On that occasion, it was decided to recess for a year. As part of Kilpatrick's retirement festivities in 1938, the same six men (Kilpatrick, Childs, Newlon, Raup, Edmund deS. Brunner, and Percival M. Symonds) met again and were joined by other old members (Counts, Bagley, Rugg, F. Ernest Johnson, Edward H. Reisner) and by younger colleagues (R. Freeman Butts, Kenneth Benne, George Hartmann, and James McKeen Catell). In a meditative mood, Kilpatrick recalled, "After dinner, we drew around in a circle. They asked me what they should discuss (recalling the old Discussion Group), I asked them to raise questions regards my lectures just closed. And we had a rigorous discussion for about two hours."[73]

Kilpatrick's intellectual leadership of the new journal was acknowledged when he was appointed chair of the organization, but he accepted with the proviso that Jesse Newlon would chair the executive committee and do the work. In February 1934, Counts was invited to become editor-in-chief, with Norman Woelfel and Mordecai Grossman, who soon made something of a nuisance of himself, as assistant editors. Counts accepted in mid-April, and by the end of July, three months before the first issue was out, nine hundred subscriptions had already been received. By the end of the year, this number had grown to well over three thousand.

The *Social Frontier*, a "Journal of Educational Criticism and Reconstruction," first appeared in October 1934. Counts stated that the *Social Frontier* was launched "to arouse teachers and others to the magnitude and gravity of the crisis facing American democracy and education."[74] In an interview with a reporter from the *New York Times*, Counts is quoted as saying, "It will advocate the raising of American life from the level of the profit system, individualism and vested class interests to the plane of social motivation, collectivism and classlessness. . . . Particularly since The Social Frontier is interested in public education, it will place human rights above property rights."[75] Childs was fully in accord with the prevailing views of the editors of the *Frontier* and had a review article published in the second issue. He continued to be a regular contributor during the following decade.

In 1937 Childs became a member of the Board of Editors of the *Social Frontier,* contributing many editorial items over the next five years. He resigned from that board during the academic year 1942–43, on account of his work in the Commission on Education and the Problems of the War and the Peace, but rejoined the editorial board a year later, along with Counts, Kilpatrick, and others, for the final three issues. After his retirement, Childs had intended to write a history of the journal, but he seems to have done no more than keep a complete run of the *Social Frontier,* and then, apparently, destroyed it at some point. This is a pity, as he was a close colleague of many of the principals as well as being a regular contributor.

In late fall of 1943, the Board of Directors of the Progressive Education Association voted overwhelmingly to discontinue the publication of *Frontiers of Democracy,* as the *Social Frontier* had by then been renamed. By that time Harold Rugg was chief editor, and he wrote a bitter attack on the directors of the Progressive Education Association for refusing further support. Although money was the immediate cause, the political fervor of Rugg and his associates was probably the efficient cause. In the editorial of the October 1943 issue, Rugg called the thirteen months between then and the November 1944 election "the Year of Great Decision." He proposed a social agenda that the journal would vigorously pursue (actually reiterating Henry A. Wallace's three-point program):

First, responsibility for the enlightenment of all the people.
Second, responsibility for mobilizing peace-time production for
      full employment.
Third, responsibility for planning world cooperation.

Rugg asserted that "the *Frontiers* will not be neutral. On every issue it will take sides."[76]

Rugg suggested that the board lacked commitment, and he expressed contempt for the directors' proposal "that progressive education shall popularize accepted truths rather than develop new ones. . . . [T]heir program avoids the controversial issues of community life."[77] He concluded his comments with the most damning phrase he could find, "it is safe." Rugg, speaking almost certainly on behalf of the others, felt more than betrayed, particularly as he saw nothing in recent developments to contradict the continuing philosophic orientation of the journal since its beginning in 1934. As Kilpatrick had written in the very first issue, "Its founding is definitely related to the new spirit of creative social inquiry which has been apparent among American educators and teachers during the past three or four years. If the hopes of its founders are to be realized, this new journal must become the expressive medium of those members of the teaching profession who believe that education has an important even strategic role in the reconstruction of American society."[78]

The financial basis of the journal had not been good for

some time, so that a projected loss of two thousand dollars for 1943–44 was expected. For five years, Rugg, along with Counts, Kilpatrick, Elliott, F. Ernest Johnson, *and* Childs had personally helped finance it.[79] They actually considered the possibility of taking over the journal themselves but reluctantly concluded that the financial burden on them would be too great. Thus, the radical journal, the organ of the reconstructionist wing of the experimentalists, came to an end. It had lasted barely a decade.

This, however, all lay in the future at the time Childs published his first article in the *Social Frontier* in November 1934. It was an extensive review of *Conclusions and Recommendations,* the report of the AHA's Commission on the Social Studies in the Schools. This summary volume of the commission, of which Counts was director of research, was authored by Counts, Charles A. Beard, and August C. Krey, although Krey's illness prevented his doing much in its later stages.[80]

Conclusions echoed much of what Childs stood for, and that could be seen already in his book on experimentalism and the two chapters in *The Educational Frontier.* He described the controversial volume as "one of the most penetrating and forthright statements of position which American scholars have as yet produced."[81] The report, Childs suggested, stood as a challenge to the three prevailing emphases in American education: that education can be an exact science, that the interests of the child can be an adequate basis for educational programs, and that education is a technical affair controlled by efficiency experts. The fundamental fallacy in all three is that they assume that education is an autonomous process separated from a social philosophy or outlook. In contrast, the signers of the *Conclusions* took the view that education is not "socially neutral, and, by its inherent nature, never can be."[82] This is a theme that Childs himself was to hammer home constantly. He saw the report directed mainly at those teachers "who have the capacity, the freedom, and the courage to initiate and to think for themselves," who must be "liberally trained individuals who are intelligent about the world in which they now live, and who, organized effectually in their own professional movement, will cooperate with other work-

ers' groups to achieve essential economic and moral security."[83] It was Kilpatrick who immediately saw the main limita-
tion of the book and attacked it in private "as having an
inadequate conception of method."[84] Indeed, the book had
little to say to practicing teachers, thus many reviewers thought
it was a disappointing wrap-up from a commission that had
held out high hopes of real educational reform.

In other writings Childs frequently made reference to the
Conclusions, always in laudatory terms. He was one of the
contributors to the 1935 yearbook of the National Education
Association (NEA), *Social Change and Education.* His chapter
was titled "Preface to a New American Philosophy of Education." The "new" philosophy had to be based on a "social
philosophy whose central doctrines are formulated in terms of
the characteristics of the power age."[85] Childs expressed the
hope that the *Conclusions* would "encourage other educational groups to carry their thinking into the realm of policy
construction."[86]

As early as May 1933, Childs had been appointed to
the Commission on Education for New Social and Economic
Relationships. The objective of the group was to produce
the 1935 yearbook on the overall topic of social change and
education. The commission was chaired by John W. Studebaker, U.S. commissioner of education and formerly superintendent of schools, Des Moines, Iowa. The other ten members
included, in addition to Childs, three members of the AHA's
Commission on the Social Studies in the Schools: Frank W.
Ballou, superintendent of schools, Washington, D.C., who had
refused, for political reasons, to sign the *Conclusions;* Fred J.
Kelly, chief, Division of Higher Education, U.S. Department
of Education; and Jesse Newlon, principal of Lincoln School
and a Teachers College colleague. There was little unanimity
among the members of the new commission, and it was early
agreed that each should sign the chapter he authored.

Childs was also one of a five-person subcommittee,
chaired by Studebaker, that prepared the opening chapter of
the book, "Meaning of Social Change." The subcommittee
decided, rather than attempt to resolve or iron out their differences, to provide three responses to the four contrasting inter-

pretations of American life and the ten social trends listed in the chapter. The responses themselves covered three positions—radical, liberal, and conservative. The radical interpretations carry Childs' mark.

Childs' own chapter is as radical an expression of his reconstructionist posture as can be found. He noted that American society was undergoing a profound change as a result of scientific and technological developments. In contrast, the nation, and accordingly also the schools, continued to cling to a traditional system of ideas. He listed the four most important of these ideas and the conflicts they presented to industrial society. "1. Our traditional economy has been based on the assumption that the supreme human problem was to find ways to produce enough to feed, clothe, and shelter the population."[87] The contemporary problem, on the other hand, had not been one of production but of distribution. The former economy of scarcity had been replaced by one of abundance, yet the profit system, with the full acquiescence of business, militated against the more equitable distribution of goods. "2. Our social life has been organized on the principle that all who wanted work could find it in the private business activities which care for the production of material goods and services."[88] The problem of unemployment lay in the industrial conditions, which left to themselves would not be ameliorated. The intervention of the state was required in order to devise fairer methods of distribution of income. But before that could happen, we needed a new conception of the activities of government. "3. [O]ur society is based on principles of competition and of conflict."[89] Conditions in the mid 1930s mandated genuine democratic participation, which would require collective ownership and greater centralized control. The laissez-faire doctrine, which actually encouraged the competitive principle, permitted the free play of excessive individualism with the consequent exploitation of the workers. "4. In any society those who have the property also have a disproportionate share of the power."[90] Modern industrialism had divided the society along economic lines, and there was no point in glossing over the fact with fine-sounding platitudes.

Childs held strongly to the view that in that present crisis it was more necessary than ever to develop a social philosophy; for educators it was a professional obligation. Educators could "play it safe," but that is not neutrality at all; it is allying oneself with the forces of conservatism. Educators could also side with the forces of reconstruction. Either way educators *act* because "public education is not a self-enclosed movement, but is inherently linked with the culture of a people." For Childs the choice was clear: this "period of fundamental social reconstruction will also prove to be a period of educational reconstruction."[91]

The yearbook provided the basis of a prolonged discussion at the meeting of the NEA's Department of Superintendence held in Atlantic City during the last week of February 1935. All the members of the commission were present. In his opening remarks, Chairman Studebaker acknowledged the fundamental conflicts in the points of view represented, conflicts that arose "chiefly from varying assumptions as to the nature, the needs, and the purposes of society."[92] Newlon and Childs represented the radical wing of the group, with Newlon being the more outspoken. Childs tried to clarify his perception of the emerging social order by mentioning three items: that "we are living in a collective, interdependent world";[93] that we are living in an economy of potential abundance, but we are not able to marshal our resources on behalf of the masses of the people; and that society requires some sort of conscious planning and control. Of the social agenda he had in mind he said little, but it emerges clearly in the chapter he wrote for the yearbook.

It was at this point in his career that Childs, as befits a former missionary, became an overt activist and moved into the political arena. At first he confined himself to an injustice he saw at Teachers College. It says something for the tolerance of the dean that Childs had, effective July 1, 1935, been promoted to the rank of associate professor at an annual salary of five thousand dollars. Exactly three years later, he attained a professorship with his salary raised another five hundred dollars. His pay was supplemented by teaching during the summer school, which he did almost every year of his employ at Teachers College.

5.
Political Activities

Both his personal history and his state of mind made it virtually inevitable that John Childs would move into the political arena. His activism, apparent while still at the University of Wisconsin, had intensified during his years in China. His doctoral studies had necessitated some withdrawal, as he thought through his newly adopted pragmatism. His rather abrupt thrust into the ranks of the leading experimentalists demanded articulation of his ideas, and Childs was as forceful as any in promulgating them. But these ideas also required action of their adherents. Thus it is not surprising that in 1935 he joined some of his colleagues in membership in the Columbia University Chapter of Local 5 of the American Federation of Teachers (AFT), although this was just about the time that John Dewey resigned. By the summer of 1935 Childs was publicly urging teachers to join the labor movement and to take sides on social and economic questions. The next year he represented the chapter in the delegate assembly for Local 5.

Since 1931 Childs had been a member of Kilpatrick's Discussion Group, which beginning in the winter of 1928 met more or less bimonthly for ten years. As Lawrence A. Cremin wrote, "in the course of these many talks certain agreements and ideas emerged."[1] Agreements were not total, and Childs and Counts were to the left of most of the others. Intellectually, Childs was, and continued to be, closely allied with his colleague and friend George S. Counts, and his demands were no less uncompromising. Childs took the view that teachers "must ally themselves with the workers, not only with professional groups, but with the workers of factory and farm. Unless we are going to be sentimental or Utopian, we must face the recognition of special interests. Teachers with their special function to perform for society, are linked with labor."[2] A month later, the *New York Post* reported Childs' advocacy of the AFT: "We shall do all in our power to support the American Federation of Teachers. . . . Should any move be made in the American Federation of Labor [AFL] to revoke the charter of the teachers' federation, we will vigorously oppose it."[3]

In late October 1935, Dean William F. Russell, an outspoken opponent of unionization himself, responded to a group of Teachers College faculty, including Counts, Kilpatrick, R. Bruce Raup, and Goodwin Watson, to form a committee to investigate charges following the firing of four workers in the college dining halls. The trouble had been simmering for some time. Most educational institutions had been having financial problems as a result of the continuing depression. Teachers College faculty had already taken a salary cut of 15 percent.[4] During this period, however, it was reported that the already-low wages of many of the full-time workers had been reduced 40 percent.[5] The dismissal of four men, all members of the union—one of whom, Manuel Romero, was the father of five children, while the others possessed distinctly non-Anglo names (Yuranovich, Astreas, and Kolokithias)—appeared to many to be unjustified, even in the context of a difficult financial situation. Beyond this immediate issue was a much deeper question: should Teachers College be run on democratic lines?[6] Russell asked Childs to chair a special committee of three faculty members and two students "to investigate the circumstances surrounding the failure to re-employ certain employees in the dining halls of Teachers College."[7] Childs himself called the request "The Bolt out of the Blue" and initially refused the assignment on the basis that the college's attitude against unionization, led by Isaac Kandel, made a sensible resolution of the conflict impossible. Russell met with Childs on November 7 and wrote a follow-up letter immediately. In it, he separated the issues clearly between the particular case and the general policy. Childs' committee was to look at only "the justice or injustice in the failure to reemploy certain workers in the Dining Halls."[8] Childs then accepted the assignment and made a public statement to the effect that his committee would hear from both sides of the dispute alternately and that its meetings, by agreement with all parties involved, would be closed, an item not supported by the student Continuations Committee. Immediately Childs received from George Counts and James E. Mendenhall a statement affirming the stand of the teachers' union and the AFT "that workers of whatever category should have the right to organize themselves into unions without discrimination on the part of employers."[9]

Things were now heating up, and Childs was thrust into the limelight. On November 20 he gave a partisan address at Milbank Chapel, Teachers College, entitled "Education and the Social Conflict." He called Karl Marx "one of the greatest intellectual giants of the nineteenth century."[10] He stated that "the immediate educational task is to construct a new social philosophy appropriate to this active alignment with the workers which will include, among others, the doctrine of interdependence and socialization as opposed to economic individualism and competition." And he mentioned three points that must be considered in the formulation of a concrete educational program:

1. A concrete basis upon which criticism of the existing social order should rest.

2. The direction in which social improvement lies, and in which social reconstruction should move.
3. A recognition of the obligations and related rights of the individuals to be educated.[11]

His old hero William Randolph Hearst, whose editorial policies Childs had admired as an undergraduate, got into the act and roundly criticized Childs and Counts in an editorial in the *San Francisco Examiner* entitled "Columbia Communism."[12] By this time, following the red-trap, which closely involved Counts and others, Childs was fully aware of Hearst's tactics.[13]

Meanwhile, Childs' five-person committee had been meeting four times a week in four-hour sessions since November 11. On December 7 it presented its unanimous report to the dean, who acknowledged its receipt two days later. In a special issue, the *Teachers College News* reported the four major findings.

1. "The severe and discriminatory wage-cuts imposed upon the full-time employees, not the dismissal of the four workers, constitute the central fact in the disturbed dining halls situation."
2. "The four workers who were not rehired were discriminated against because of their Union membership and activity."
3. "The conflict between the open shop practice of Teachers College and the desire of the men to be represented by a Labor Union of their own choosing is the basic cause of the problem."
4. "The Independent Hotel, Restaurant, and Cafeteria Workers Union of America to which these dismissed workers belong is a bona fide Labor Union devoted to the interests of its members."[14]

The report was well received from all sides. Several commentators used phrases such as "fair and courageous." The left-wing press, including the *Nation* and *New Republic,* noted that the situation had revealed a contradiction between the public educational policy of Teachers College and its private exploitation of its own manual workers. The *New York Times* merely reported the incident without comment, so in the scrapbook he kept at the time, Childs added his own, "The Capitalist Press Plays it Down." Harry Elmer Barnes in the *New York World-Telegram* summarized the episode and praised the

Childs committee for its "thorough-going study of the controversy."

The committee unhesitatingly confirmed the charges that the workers who had been fired were dismissed because of their union affiliations. The policy of the direction of the dining halls was frankly declared to be "open shop."

The committee did not charge the direction of the dining halls with callousness or indifference to the welfare of its employees. Rather, it paid a high tribute to the direction in this respect, and stated that it was about as satisfactory a type of paternalism as is likely to exist anywhere. But arbitrary paternalism is no solution. The laborer can find proper protection only as a member of a strong union.

"The basic cause of the dining hall's problem lies deeper than the personal shortcomings of individuals on either side of the controversy. . . . No possible personal limitations of either the employees or the members of the management can alone account for the present situation. The deeper source of the difficulty lies elsewhere. It is found in the conflict between the open-shop practice of Teachers College and the desire of these men to be represented by a labor union of their own choosing. Unless this aspect of the problem is dealt with adequately and effectively, it is likely that further trouble will be experienced."

This report is of more than local and passing significance for the following reasons:—First, it reveals what are in all probability conditions that are widespread in American colleges and universities. Second, it demonstrates the inherent weaknesses of paternalism, even when operating under the most ideal conditions. Third, it challenges one institution of higher learning to take the lead in developing an enlightened and forward-looking labor policy.[15]

The unions were, of course, delighted with the report; Childs received complimentary and grateful messages from the Hotel and Restaurant Workers Union of America, the Hotel and Restaurant Employees' International Alliance, and, significantly, the Teachers Union of New York City, Local 5 of the AFT. Childs' former teacher George Coe, to whom he had sent a copy of the report, responded enthusiastically from California and mentioned its educational value. Coe also wrote a discussion piece for *School and Society*. Although Coe raised questions, it is clear that he supported the Childs report, which noted that Teachers College should, "as a consistent part of its total educational program, illustrate in its relations with its employees the same democratic principles which it advocates for the school world."[16] Coe stated his belief that neutrality on the issues was impossible and that "education should initiate and guide social changes."[17] The editor of *Teachers College News* was more succinct: "Liberalism upstairs, autocracy downstairs, stand in damning contradiction."[18]

Russell responded to the report sensitively and promptly. Childs then wrote to the dean, "I . . . appreciate more than I can express the fine spirit in which you have received the report of our Committee and large-minded way in which you have sought to deal with the difficult situation it defines." He added, "This close contact with you during the past six weeks has meant much to me personally."[19] The dean, however, delayed action until he had met with the trustees. The four workers were reemployed in a minor clerical capacity, and back wages were paid out of a special two-thousand-dollar fund, which had been set up for the purpose, and to which Childs himself contributed fifty dollars.

But the matter did not rest there for Childs, for Russell, or for the four cafeteria workers who were, according to the campus communist pamphlet, the *Educational Vanguard,* let go the following summer.[20] Childs had regained his missionary zeal and continued to urge unionization for teachers. Of Russell's view, Cremin wrote, "[H]e did not see a role for them [unions] in the conduct of education. The tactics of labor, he noted, did not benefit a profession, and the teacher is a member of a profession, not a worker. The whole effort of the union to introduce policy management by faculties into American schools was pictured as abortive and conducive to the worst possible autocracy. Complete rule by the faculty was far more likely to be harsh than mild, for inevitably a few of the more vocal would get control and lead in the name of the group."[21] On July 23, 1936, the dean told an audience of one thousand students and faculty that, while he did not oppose organized labor, he maintained his view that teachers were professionals and not workers. Childs disagreed on all points. In a rebuttal a week later, Childs said that "teachers belonged to the working class, and that their interests were directly tied with organized labor."[22] Childs also suggested that by affiliating with labor, teachers and educators "restore many of the curtailments that education has suffered during the depression."[23] He held that the economic struggle between workers and owners clearly puts teachers in the same camp as the workers and makes teachers' unions mandatory. A few days following Childs' address to that audience in the Horace Mann Auditorium, Charles Hendley, president of Local 5 of the AFT, asked Childs for permission to print that address, together with one by Hendley himself, and then to have them distributed around several colleges, including Teachers College.

During this heated public debate, it was said that Russell bore animosity to Childs and his ideological allies. This was not altogether untrue, and Russell did get extremely irritated by Childs' political involvements in the 1940s. However, they held each other in high regard and continued to do so, even though they disagreed on the fundamental issue of unionization and the extent of the shared power between workers and owners, between administrators and teachers. In late 1943, Childs, together with Counts, sent Russell an inscribed copy of their small book, *America, Russia, and the Communist Party in the Postwar World*. Russell congratulated the authors on their "wonderful book." His careful reading of it is made apparent by his numerous, specific comments. He added that he considered the volume "to be one of the outstanding contributions of our time."[24]

In September 1951, Childs forwarded to Russell a copy of an article by George Axtelle, "Teacher Organization and Democracy in School Administration."[25] In it, Axtelle discussed the benefits to be gained from the teacher-labor relationship. Russell was completely unimpressed with Axtelle's position, in fact, he went so far as to call it "criminally wrong." This particularly personal letter, which was from "Will" to "Jack," reveals in a very human way some of Russell's feelings about administration. "Real administration consists of making heartbreaking decisions, ulcers, sleepless nights, choice of unpleasant alternatives, and accepting criticism which often belongs to someone else;—as well as accepting undeserved honors. Why share that? In fact, the concentration of that in one individual constitutes a social saving."[26] The paternalistic tone of the letter was not lost on Childs, who in reply restated several of Axtelle's arguments. More importantly, perhaps, Childs pointed out that that was not how Russell himself had acted as dean and president. "Surely you do not want a faculty composed of people who keep their mouths shut because they feel that if they were to speak what is on their minds they might lose their jobs."[27] As early as his 1936 rebuttal to Russell, Childs had admitted freely, "During my years at Teachers College no one has made any effort to curb my freedom of expression as a teacher. I think my experience at this point is typical of all others on our staff."[28] Childs' position was one of principle, not narrow self-interest—the missionary at work.

In response to a congratulatory letter from Russell on Childs' 1953 article on Bode, Childs, reaffirming his regard for Russell, wrote, "I am grateful for all you have done to keep Teachers College open to inquiry, to diversity of points of view, and to the free-play of ideas."[29] A year later Russell had to give Childs official notice of Childs' forthcoming retirement: "I want to tell you how much it has meant to me to be able to work with you during this past score of years. I don't suppose that two colleagues ever agreed more on what we were trying to do, and by what rules to play the game, and at the same time differed more widely on where we came out. With you away I shall miss the stone on which to whet what little edge I have and I won't be able to count on the wise word of caution to keep me from rushing headlong into hidden pitfalls and ambushes."[30]

In reply, Childs wrote,

It has been a real privilege to be associated with the men and women who have made up our faculty during this period of your leadership, and it has also been a privilege to have the opportunity to work with young people committed to American democracy and education.

As I recently told one of my classes, I often feel like a famous center-fielder of the early New York Giants who used to remark after an exciting game: "To think that they pay me for doing this!"

I was touched by your friendly personal reference. It is true that on a number of occasions I have been a member of "his Majesty's Loyal Opposition." But a "loyal opposition" can only manifest itself and function in a genuinely democratic environment. So you can think of me as a significant symbol of the free and democratic order that you were able to maintain at Teachers College.[31]

Russell, who was born a year later than Childs, had succeeded his father as dean of Teachers College in 1927, the same year that Childs entered the doctoral program. In 1949, the position was changed to president. He, too, retired in 1954, but he died suddenly on March 26, 1956.

For Childs, in the middle 1930s, there was a hiatus in union controversy. This was the time of his European sabbatical. John and Grace Childs left New York in September on the *Queen Mary* and spent most, if not all, of the nine months in England. His intention was to complete work on a book in the philosophy of education. It had been in the planning stages for some time, and Dana Ferrin of Appleton-Century was eager to publish it, even to the point of asking Childs whether his firm should accept another book in the same field. We have no information concerning the sabbatical or what was accomplished. The book itself presumably was never completed, although much of the material may have been used later in *American Pragmatism and Education*.

On his return to New York in the spring of 1937, in time to teach summer school and to speak at a dinner on May 14 in honor of Kilpatrick at the Faculty Club, the union situation among the city's teachers, which had been brewing for a time, slowly came to a boil. In the events of the following months, which have been described well by William Edward Eaton and Robert W. Iversen, Childs was to play a pivotal role.[32] In April 1938, he was nominated for the presidency of Local 537, the college teachers' local, for the forthcoming academic year. By this time he had been thoroughly disquieted by the activities of many of its members, even though he remained throughout the period hopeful about the benefits of unionization for the teaching profession. He therefore declined the nomination. Local 5 and Local 537, which, until it was chartered in January

1938, had been the College Section of Local 5, had been infiltrated by Stalinists, who were in fact a minority, but who, largely on account of the vagaries of the balloting system, exercised considerable control.

Childs himself had been troubled by communist influence right from the start, and it was this that had caused Dewey to resign his membership in 1935 and to become actively involved in the founding of the New York Teachers Guild. Later Childs stated that "every crucial issue was discussed on the basis of political sects which stemmed from Russia's tragic divisions. I was puzzled by the trend of meetings sponsored by the Union. The favored interests of the Stalinist group would always emerge in frequently wholly irrelevant resolutions. Soon I and others were filled with grave doubts on union trends."[33] Childs stopped paying his union dues after December 1937 but took no steps to publicize his withdrawal for a year, at which time a scurrilous article by James Wechsler, entitled "Twilight at Teachers College," was published in the Nation. It was essentially an attack on Dean Russell and mentioned the forced retirement of Kilpatrick, the dismissal of Elizabeth McDowell (a faculty member for seventeen years), and the closing of New College as examples of his authoritarianism. The decision to close New College at the end of the 1938–39 academic year was made for financial reasons. Cremin reported that in November 1938 the Teachers College faculty voted its approval of the closing, 55 to 29, with many abstaining. As far as Kilpatrick's release was concerned, he had reached the mandatory retirement age of sixty-five. Kilpatrick, at any rate, believed the rule to have been invented by Russell and largely aimed at him. As for Childs, he had been described by Wechsler as "a thorn in Russell's flesh at the time."[34] In the margin of his personal copy of the article, Childs wrote, "What is the source? Why this kind of characterization?"[35] Wechsler reported the rumor that had circulated of Russell's intention to fire Kilpatrick, Counts, Childs, Goodwin Watson, and Roma Gans. Again in the margin, Childs noted, "I was out of the country and had no means of checking this." The article was a shabby piece of work to which Counts responded strongly in the Social Frontier.[36]

In the December 24 issue of the *Nation,* Childs joined ten of his colleagues in deploring Wechsler's article.[37] He also wrote an independent letter in which he gave his reason for quitting the union. "I withdrew from Teachers' Union for one reason and one reason only—the present domination of the New York locals by left-wing political sects."[38]

The Joint Board of Teachers Unions of New York City, under the chairmanship of Edwin Berry Burgum, immediately issued a lengthy statement critical of Childs. Apart from disavowing any Stalinism within the union, the statement casts aspersions on Childs' activities and commitments to the cause.

It is important to note that Professor Childs was never an active participant in the work of the American Federation of Teachers. Shortly after he joined local 5 he was elected Chairman of the College Section Educational Policies Committee, but refused to serve. Although he was invited to speak at several important union conferences on education, he never participated. When the College Local was formed in January, 1935, he refused to be transferred on the ground that his interests were more definitely allied with those of the elementary and highschool teachers than of college teachers.

At the same time, although he asserted disagreement with the policies of the College Local, he refused a special invitation to confer with the executive board on the matter. More recently while asserting a genuine regard for the American labor movement he has questioned the need for teacher union activity on [or] college teacher union activity on college campuses. When the college local was considering a program of democracy in college administration, he appeared at a general membership meeting, although he was presumably no longer a member, and was the sole individual to voice opposition to the program—the main principles of which have since been embodied in the recent democracy by-law adopted by the Board of Higher Education.

All of these developments, capped as they are by his present belated explanation of his withdraway [withdrawal] from the American Federation of Teachers, indicare [indicate] that Professor Childs' interest in the labor movement ceases when educational problems on his won [own] campus are concerned.

Moreover, we are compelled to regard him as a very peculiar friend of education since his attack on the New York teachers local comes at a time when Local 5 is fighting to reduce class size and to defend progressive education as embodied in the activity program; when Local 453 is struggling to prevent wholesale dismissals from WPA and for the extension of free public educational facilities and when Local 537 is concerned with establishing at the private colleges democratic procedures of the type now functioning in the public colleges.

That Professor Childs has seen fit to drag in the question of "Stalinism" instead of sticking to the issues of New College's dissolution and Professor McDowell's dismissal on which he is at present opposed to the union, suggests that he does not wish to appear as an open defender of academic autocracy. We lament the fact that an educator, who was himself once among a group "exposed" by Hearst as a "Communist" is now using Hearst methods in behalf of the administration of Teachers College.[39]

The Columbia Chapter of Local 537 immediately issued a statement in response and called on the body "publicly to withdraw such attacks, and to present its apologies to Professor Childs."[40] The union officials were correct that Childs had not paid his dues for a year, but they also criticized the press for drawing attention to such an old matter. The editors of the New York Post responded immediately, "When a noted liberal educator such as Dr. Childs says a teachers' union is dominated by Communists it is news; it is doubly important as news when he is supported by so noted a liberal educator as Dr. George Counts. The date of his resignation had no bearing whatever on his REASON for resigning."[41] The joint statement is also suspect in face of Charles Hendley's enthusiastic response to Childs' July 1936 speech at Teachers College.

The joint statement and its treatment of Childs caused yet a fourth union member of the Columbia faculty to resign. Louis M. Hacker following Childs, Raup, and F. Ernest Johnson, wrote a strongly worded letter in support of Childs.

I am resigning from the New York College Teachers Union because I resent the attacks on Professor Childs's integrity and good faith. He and I, among a few others, were deeply interested in the sound establishment of a section of the Teachers Union on the Columbia campus. We drew up the "Statement of General Principles" upon the basis of which the section was organized and which Local 5 of the American Federation of Teachers printed and widely circulated. For two years I served as vice-chairman of the Columbia of the Columbia [sic] University section and sat on its executive committee along with Professor Childs. We tried, with a real measure of success, to recruit new members among the professorial and permanent instructional staffs for the purpose of giving the Columbia University section authority on the campus and to make possible consideration of serious educational and administrative problems. The feeling of Professor Childs and myself was that our real work lay on the Columbia campus because of the unique situation that confronted us there. And as one who was actively in charge of that work I know how unstintingly Professor Childs gave of his time and energies.

But the factionalists were hot for political activity before even they had a union on the Columbia campus. Meetings therefore were constantly given over to political debates and resolutions—the Spanish question, the Chinese question, the child labor question, fascism, participation in May Day parades, and the like. There never was any serious preoccupation with the basic problems of trade-union life on a university campus: the formulation of educational and personnel policies.[42]

The issue was, and continued to be until the matter was finally resolved in 1941, the communist influence and not the discontinuation of the New College or Kilpatrick's retirement.

Not all of the liberal wing of the Columbia Chapter did resign. Some felt it was important to try to expunge the influence from within. This they eventually did under the AFT presidency of Counts. Early in 1939, some that remained formed the Independent Group and announced an address by Counts to be given at Steinway Hall on January 19. The flyer supported Hacker's position and unequivocally stated the Counts' position.

THE ADMINISTRATION of the college local has precipitated a crisis fraught with danger not only for the New York locals but for the entire national movement. The methods of work and the character of the administration of Local 537 (similar to that of Local 5) have resulted in widespread criticism and even the resignation of prominent educators who have rendered great service to teacher unionism. A leadership that cannot hold within its ranks such liberal and prolabor educators as Professor[s] Childs, Hacker, Raup, and others, and that provokes the sharpest criticism from educators who have been a source of pride to our Union, such as Professor Counts, is to be condemned. Such a leadership must be held responsible for a development that may well result in a serious organizational setback for the Union.

THE INDEPENDENT GROUP, from its inception, has criticised policies of the Administration when it considered these policies harmful to the Union. Evaluation of proposed policies from the point of view of Union welfare has always been our first concern. We have never hesitated to point out, however, that the evil of arbitrary control is present in our local, as indubitably as it is present in the college local. Behind the superficial forms of democracy, the manifestations of this arbitrary control are clearly to be seen: our highly specialized network of affiliations; the peculiar prejudices of invited speakers (Spain meeting, Union courses); sudden outbursts at Union meetings against certain political groups in various parts of the world; the strictest censorship on the *New York Teacher*, whispering campaigns directed against loyal Union members, the strange opposition to the defense of such an outstanding worker victim of boss frame-up as Fred Beals, the removal of Mr. Mazen as chairman of the Legal Aid and Grievance Committee—incident upon incident testifying to an authoritarian grip on the Union, ill-concealed by the show of democracy.

IT IS AN UNHEALTHY condition of that type which underlies the present crisis in the college local. It is too much to ask us to believe that the resignation of Childs and the critical attitude of Counts stem from a drift to reaction.

OUR TASK IN LOCAL 5 is clear. There must be an overhauling in our methods of work. Regardless of differences of opinion on specific issues, here is a task on which it is the duty of all of us to unite: to secure the return of a healthy, critical approach to all the problems confronting us; to revive that eager, constructive spirit that seeks to build upon the collective experience and judgment of the entire membership; above all, to eradicate every sign of arbitrary steering of the Union, in the interests of a special group. In these days of growing authoritarianism, we must exercise the greatest caution lest we bring similar methods into our own Union. The Majority leadership, because it is the majority, has a special responsibility in this regard. Not only must it give consideration to the opinions and arguments of minorities; it must also be mindful of the vast number of Union members who do not regularly attend our meetings. It must be mindful, too, of the tens of thousands of teachers who have not yet been won over to unionism. The leadership does incalculable harm when it acts in such a way as to open the Union to the charge of being the auxiliary of a particular political group, and as to drive from its ranks prominent educators who have done and still can do much for the cause of unionism.[43]

The officers of Local 537, sensing that things were getting out of hand, requested an early meeting with Childs himself to discuss their "differences," to which Childs wrote a curt response.

The officers of the Joint Board of the Teachers Union of New York City have stated publicly that I am not a genuine supporter of organized labor, that I have never been an active participant in the Teachers Union, and that I have resorted to Hearst methods on behalf of the administration of Teachers College. If these charges are true, there is no valid reason for the leaders of the Union to meet with me. If they are false, they should be publicly withdrawn as an evidence of good faith on the part of those who now ask that I confer with them.[44]

On January 20, 1939, Childs had issued a statement reaffirming his faith in the labor movement, and in an interview with the *New York Jewish Daily Journal* he was at pains to make it absolutely clear that he remained a staunch trade unionist in spite of his resignation, which was due entirely to the growing Stalinist influence in the College Teachers Local. Childs' resignation, as well as Counts' nonresignation, received full coverage not only in the radical presses but also in the leading papers in New York City, Washington, D.C., Chicago, Los Angeles, and Philadelphia.

Union matters at Teachers College were now left in the capable hands of George Counts, who, after an unsuccessful attempt to win the presidency of New York Local 537, went to the AFT convention in August 1939 fully determined to gain the national presidency. Events played into his hands, for his strong anticommunist platform was supported by the surprising announcement of the German-Russian Nonaggression Pact immediately prior to the election. Counts won the post easily. He was to serve three terms as president of the

AFT, and they turned out to be critical. His first major task was to purge the union of communist influence; it took eighteen months. Public support for Counts was vigorous, and Childs was among the most outspoken. His interest in unionization was unwavering, in spite of those who questioned both his motives and his commitment. Among those who took an opposing view was Childs' leftist former professor Harry F. Ward, who believed that much of the fuss was aimed at bringing the country into the European war.[45] Those who sided with Childs were urging him and other former members of Locals 5 and 537 to sign a petition asking "the Executive Council of the AFT to charter a new local in the City of New York," but Childs did not sign immediately; he believed that the AFT could not "prosper either in New York City or in the nation until it comes to grips with the issue of Communist domination of these Locals in New York City."[46] An investigation of these locals was under way almost immediately, and by the end of May 1941 ballots had been counted and the offending locals, which included Local 192 of Philadelphia as well as the two New York locals, were expelled from the AFT. Counts himself commented, "It has been a bitter fight, but I think it was necessary. We must do whatever we can to root out of American democracy every vestige of the totalitarian pattern, whether it is on the so-called right or on the so-called left."[47]

At the 1942 AFT convention, which was held in Gary, Indiana, Counts stepped down as president but continued to serve as one of the vice presidents; he was succeeded by John Fewkes. The Executive Council, of which Counts was still a member, was instructed to set up a commission "to deal with the relation of public education to the problems of the war and the peace"; they did so and issued specific charges.

(1) To make analyses, to define issues, and to formulate statements of policy on questions arising out of the present emergency. Such pronouncements, upon approval of the Executive Council, shall be presented for public distribution.
(2) To consider from time to time what changes in emphasis and content in the school curriculum are desirable to further the winning of the war and the peace.

(3) To devise means of assisting the American Federation of Teachers to share in a vitalized adult educational program designed to develop an enlightened citizenry so essential at this critical juncture in the life of our country.

(4) To cooperate with other departments of the American Federation of Labor; with appropriate governmental agencies, including the National Office of Education; and with various national educational organizations, in the development of an educational program for adults, youth and children adequate to the demands of this dynamic situation.

(5) To cooperate with the Educational Policies Committee of the American Federation of Teachers in devising means by which the members of our locals may exchange experiences, and meet in regional conferences to develop programs to further the war and peace purposes of our country, and to safeguard the interests of the schools.[48]

Childs was named, along with Counts, Fewkes, Selma Borchardt, and Irvin R. Kuenzli, to this Commission on Education and the Postwar World and was appointed its chair.

Early in 1943, Childs and Counts produced their small volume, *America, Russia, and the Communist Party in the Postwar World,* under the auspices of the commission. It was this book that was praised by William F. Russell. Kilpatrick called the volume "detailed, vivid, strong," and "an important and a timely book."[49] It was widely reviewed nationwide, and most of the reviewers and commentators were equally favorable. President of Brooklyn College Harry Gideonse wrote, "This is an honest and courageous analysis, well-written and, in this best sense of the term, a tract for the times. I believe its answer is sound and constructive, and unless we wish to risk a third attempt to muddle through, it seems the only promising channel designed to prevent World War III"; and, in the same issue of *American Teacher,* Reinhold Niebuhr commented, "It makes precisely the kind of discriminations which ought to be made if we are to find our way through the very difficult problem of establishing a partnership with Russia in the postwar world without making any concessions to international communism, insofar as it represents a threat to the democratic institutions of the West."[50] Norman Angell of the

Saturday Review wrote that the two authors "have done a first-class job: competent, objective, thoroughly honest, and fearless."[51] Carl S. Joslyn, in the *Book-of-the-Month Club News,* echoed the comments and described the book as "a frank, sane, and realistic discussion of a question much on the minds of the American people today."[52] William C. Bagley, in *School and Society,* praised the commission for dealing with the relationships between the democracies and the Soviet Union "in a keenly competent fashion and in a context so broadly informed and so thoroughly consistent with American idealism as to be a source of gratification and pride to the profession of education in the United States." Bagley reminded readers that both authors were particularly qualified to write the book, Counts because of his expertise on the Soviet Union, Childs because he "has a realistic view of world problems, acquired in part from eleven years' residence and travel in the Far East."[53]

The book, which actually reads more like the work of Counts than that of Childs, and it was Counts, as Bagley pointed out, who was the authority on the Soviet Union, emphasizes the urgent need for accommodation with the Soviet Union following the end of the war. Childs and Counts mentioned many of the difficulties that would soon become readily apparent and held that rapprochement with communism would be extremely difficult. The authors stated that the "entire argument of this book is based on the assumption that we must modify this historic policy of isolationism."[54] It would be necessary for Americans at home and abroad to remove "the weaknesses, injustices, and failures of contemporary American society," otherwise communism will be seen as the more attractive system to the downtrodden peoples of the earth.[55] The authors had three underlying convictions: "first, that the present global War can and must conclude in a just and lasting peace; second, that the United Nations constitute[s] the most promising, indeed the only available, agency for laying the foundations for such a peace; and, third, that within the United Nations the most crucial and important of the many problems faced is that of the sincere, vigorous, and enduring collaboration between the United States and the Soviet

Union."[56] In fact, the book is an urgent call for accommodation between the Soviet Union and democracies. "The statesmen, the workers, and the educators of the two countries should make every effort to use every opportunity to surmount all obstacles and to develop the positive means of achieving such collaboration and understanding. The fate of the world hangs upon the consummation of this purpose."[57]

At the 1943 AFT convention, Counts and Childs participated in a panel discussion devoted to the book. By that time, it had sold a respectable thirty-four hundred copies and had been published serially in the *New York Post*. By that time, too, the commission members had supervised an issue of the *American Teacher* to celebrate Thomas Jefferson's two hundredth birthday.[58] It was widely distributed and was even mailed to labor leaders in Europe. Other publications by the Commission on Education and the Postwar World were planned.

As for Childs, the involvement in political activity was to prove enormously time-consuming. He had anticipated this and, as far back as December 1942, had written to Counts, then director of Division 1 at Teachers College, requesting that he be granted leave without salary for one term of each of the next two academic years. He offered the following reasons:

1. I am concerned about the critical financial problem now confronting the College and want to do what I can to help us get over this difficult war period.

2. Since we do not have children, we do not have the financial responsibilities which many of our colleagues are obliged to carry. While Mrs. Childs and I each have certain family obligations, they are not as large as those borne by many others of our staff.

3. I have certain other work, particularly in connection with the American Federation of Teachers Commission on Education and the Problems of the War and the Peace, which could easily take a great deal more time than I am now able to devote to it. There are also certain other projects which I have been obliged to delay during the past few strenuous years. This would give me a chance to get at them.[59]

In fact, the arrangement worked out was that Childs would be put on half pay for the entire year and would teach a half load each term. This was probably just as well, for the commission was soon merged with a new and enlarged commission set up by the AFT.

At the 1944 AFT convention, this time held in Chicago, a Commission on Educational Reconstruction, to be chaired by Floyd W. Reeves, was formed. It is possible that the AFT Executive Council thought, although there is no evidence of their having done so, that Childs' commission had wandered too far away from a strictly educational focus. However, the charge to the new commission was directed toward youth.

1. To provide educational services for the thousands of young people who have left school and will be out of work during the transition from war and peace.
2. To study all proposals for a national service act for the youth of the nation and to assure sound educational provisions when and if such a program is enacted by Congress.
3. To muster and organize the forces which are necessary for the enactment of federal aid to equalize educational opportunities for all the children of the nation.
4. To assist in inducting American youth into the life of our industrial society, with particular reference to vocational training and guidance and to work experience.[60]

During its first year, Reeves' commission largely devoted its efforts to "(1) developing a program to provide federal aid for education and improved services for child health and welfare; (2) improving the legislation designed to aid veterans; [and] (3) studying universal military training."[61] Members met in Washington, D.C., in December 1944 to undertake an analysis of federal aid to education. The following April, Reeves attended congressional hearings on behalf of the commission to support the passage of U.S. Senate Bill 717, which made federal aid available to schools, including restricted funds to private schools. On this issue, the members were not unanimous. While there was no disagreement about federal support for public schools, the sticking point was aid to nonpublic and sectarian schools. Childs himself must have spearheaded the opposition to this part of the bill, for he was adamantly opposed to government aid to religious schools. This was a theme he hammered home throughout the 1940s and 1950s.

Childs' first mature article on religious education appeared in 1938. It clearly lays out his experimentalist convictions about morals, education, and authority. Childs rejected dualisms and consequently held there to be no separate realm for morals and values apart from human experience. He stated a theme that was to form the basis of his 1950 book, *Education and Morals: An Experimentalist Philosophy of Education:* "We encounter a moral situation with its demand for ethical reflection and judgment whenever we are compelled to choose between a better and a worse in our ways of conducting and organizing human affairs."[62] He did not, however, reject the past but recognized the cumulative nature of experience; he noted that "the roots of transcendental notions are traced to their sources in ordinary experience."[63] Knowledge, too, he said, is a product of human experience, but it only has intelligible meaning when it is translated into action.

Turning to education itself, Childs noted that "learnings are never single," and that even when a child learns to spell words or recite a poem or work a mathematical problem, that child is also "learning a good many other things which have to do with the shaping of abiding intellectual and emotional dispositions."[64] We cannot be neutral or indifferent. Knowledge and values do not spring up spontaneously; some molding is inevitable. Thus, education is "a comprehensive experience in which values, attitudes, and basic dispositions are developed in one and the same process in which skills and knowledge are acquired."[65] Hence, he stated, there is no difference between public education, and specifically religious education, as far as both have concern for values and moral character. Both are grounded in experience; both are, therefore, moral undertakings. Childs concluded, all education is necessary character education.

This theme is reiterated and expanded in Childs' chapter in the Seventh Yearbook of the John Dewey Society. There he surveyed the transition of America from a religious to a secular society, secular in its faith in the democratic way of living. He then stated, "I believe these so-called 'secular' developments are deeply spiritual in character. Taken together these changes have resulted in a movement more in harmony with the moral and spiritual interests of democracy than are the traditional outlooks and the political, social, and educational arrangements which they supplanted. . . . [T]o return to the former would be to lower, not to raise, the spiritual quality of American life and education."[66] A few years later, he wrote in the same vein, "Nothing that degrades the life of the individual can be considered spiritual; nothing that enriches it can be considered unspiritual."[67] To Childs, as indeed to Dewey and his followers, secularization was not at all antithetical to the spiritual and the moral; these needed to be construed in a new context within a culture that honored the method of science and a democratic way of life. Childs realized only too well that his views were "in deep conflict with older authoritarian and supernatural presuppositions." But he was unabashed. Speaking of secularism, he wrote, "Its insistence on freedom of thought and the autonomy of the sphere of knowledge was the social and political counterpart of its insight into the conditions essential for gaining knowledge, and of the need of protecting the community of inquirers from outside interferences which would hinder or destroy the only process by which an uncoerced consensus can be attained."[68]

Childs believed that this view was in harmony with the contemporary temper of American society, even though he recognized that most people still believed in some sort of afterlife. Clearly, for him, this was an incongruity that time would resolve. But he explained his conviction that "the introduction of this non-authoritarian, experimental, co-operative procedure into the school was an ethical action. It has strengthened, not weakened, the spiritual life of our people."[69] We now had access to knowledge "no longer subordinated to the alleged requirements of life in another world."[70]

The consequences of this secularizing of our thought were important to the public schools. Not only were the emphases within school programs changed and subject matter no longer primarily drawn from religious and literary classics, but "[g]radually it became recognized that the primary work of the school was to equip the young to take their full part in these ongoing affairs of the community, not to introduce them to the beliefs of supernatural religion or to the ceremonies of the church."[71] Childs concluded that "the spiritual life of American democracy will not be enriched, but impoverished, if the public schools are compelled to give up their allegiance to freedom of thought and to the scholarly study of whatever subjects they are asked to bring within the range of the experience of the young."[72]

Childs continued to voice strong opposition to federal aid for private schools. He felt keenly that such aid would seriously weaken the principle of separation of church and state, as well as the schools' commitment to democratic principles and free inquiry. He made his reasoning clear:

According to the democratic conception, individual human beings are the only centers of experience and value, and all institutions—civil and ecclesiastical—are considered means for helping these individuals attain the most significant experience. Since our country is committed to this morality of democracy, we are justified in measuring the spiritual worth of our educational institutions by their fruits in, and for, this democratic way of life. Both public and private schools should be judged by this criterion. They can be considered positive forces in the spiritual life of the American people only to the extent that they strengthen the democratic community.[73]

Then he stated, rather as a prophet of old, "He who weakens the public schools weakens American democracy. . . . He who opposed federal aid for public education weakens the spiritual resources of our country."[74]

At a conference on Jewish education held in Atlantic City in May 1948, featuring Mrs. Eleanor Roosevelt and Cardinal Francis Spellman, Childs spoke about "American Democracy and the Common School System." The talk was subsequently published in *Jewish Education*. In the interim, Childs delivered an expanded version at Teachers College in October. In Atlantic City, Childs again stressed his opposition to aid for parochial education. He also made the suggestion that *all* children should spend at least half of their "compulsory school period in the common or public schools."[75] Not surprisingly, this view was scathingly rejected in the Catholic press. In his Teachers College address, Childs referred back to some of the incidents surrounding the proposed U.S. Senate Bill 717 and criticized the provision in the bill that provided federal funds for educational services as well as for social services to public *and* nonpublic schools.

Religion continued to be a topic of great interest to Childs, although the bases of that interest were quite different from what they had been in his YMCA days. He collected (and kept) clippings and journals and even gave some addresses about the matter. Childs always believed that sectarian education had to be kept out of the schools, although he clearly understood that, and even valued, the country had profound religious traditions and liberties. As he was to write later, "Religion will survive. Its roots are so deep that it can adjust to new methods, new values, and new knowledge. Faith is in those who are seeking necessary reconstructions. It is through these reconstructions that we shall re-enact all that is precious in the experience of man."[76]

As the decade of the forties progressed, Childs modified his views slightly. For example, although in 1947 the Commission on Educational Reconstruction unanimously endorsed a statement, which had been years in the framing, on federal aid to education, Childs appended a minority report. In essence, he felt that funds for welfare services to all children should not be joined with legislation that seeks to equalize educational opportunity through federal aid. He reiterated this view at the AFT convention on August 18, 1947 in Boston. An editorialist in the Catholic newspaper *Tablet* wrote that Childs "assailed the religious public schools and snobbishly indicated they were just tolerated and not, as should be the case, accorded their constitutional and traditional rights to exist and increase."[77] Childs felt that federal aid to sectarian schools was *not* a constitutional right.

Meanwhile, the work of the Commission on Educational Reconstruction continued. In 1948 Childs coauthored with Counts and Reeves a short pamphlet that pointed out in strongly worded terms the threat from the Soviet Union and suggested a program to counteract it. They also spoke against compulsory military service because they believed that an emphasis on mass armies was misplaced in the postwar era, that conscription reinforces "a horse-and-buggy military policy in an atomic and missile age." Rather, they suggested that "the interests of the nation require an enlarged and improved program for the education of the children and youth of the nation."[78] They proposed a five-pronged advance that called for

1. health, including basic medical care, diet, and work with the physically handicapped;
2. recreation as an end in itself, but also as an antidote to delinquency, and pools, playgrounds, summer camps to be operated by the public schools, and be free from segregation;
3. work-study projects, which would include forestry and the development of state and national parks;
4. domestic travel, which would help to wipe out prejudices and provincialism;
5. schooling, where, "[j]ust as Britain's Empire was said to have been won on the playing fields of Eton, so the democracy of the United States will have to be saved and strengthened in the classrooms of its public schools."[79]

The tenor of the pamphlet is summed up on its last page: "The simple conception of national defense in narrow and traditional military terms can serve only to lull us into a false sense of security. The safety of our country—and of democracy throughout the world—demands a sweeping and comprehensive defense, on many fronts. It calls, . . . above all, for an educational system that will give all our children an abiding belief in democracy and the willingness and ability to defend it—physically, morally, and intellectually."[80]

   In 1950, Childs himself became chair of the AFT's Commission on Educational Reconstruction. As late as 1955, it published a volume entitled *Organizing the Teaching Profession*.[81] At that time, Arthur A. Elder was serving as chair, while Childs, Counts, George Axtelle, and others, were listed as members. Although the volume purports to be a history of the

AFT, neither Childs nor Counts seems to have contributed much from his own experiences.

A couple of months after the appointment of the AFT's earlier Commission on Education and the Postwar World, Childs had got wind that the AFL, at its annual convention held in October 1942 in Toronto, had called on its president, William Green, to appoint a Postwar Planning Committee of its own. He, therefore, sent a letter to Matthew Woll, a vice president of the AFL and an acquaintance, outlining the work thus far of the AFT commission. Childs expressed the hope that the AFL commission would work "in the closest understanding and cooperation with our parent organization."[82] He also sent a copy of the letter to William Green. Green was most interested in the content of Childs' letter and on December 10 invited him to serve as the AFT representative on this AFL committee. Childs was "happy to accept the invitation to be a member," and he was pleased to learn that it was to be a "working committee."[83] Green called upon the committee to investigate and report on four topics: a plan for labor representation in the peace conferences that would follow victory; specific proposals, which the labor representatives should seek to have incorporated in the peace treaty; a broad program of postwar reconstruction to prevent a disastrous depression; and expansion of social, economic, and political security for all American and world citizens. Work on this nine-person committee was very close to Childs' heart, and it also gave him the opportunity to form friendships with Matthew Woll, who was named chair, and David Dubinsky, the respected president of the International Ladies Garment Workers Union (ILGWU).

The committee met in Washington, D.C., in April 1943 and passed a unanimous statement supporting "the participation of the United States in the responsibilities of the post war period and in the organization and maintenance of some form of mutual security program."[84] The following year Matthew Woll joined the AFT representatives in pushing for the passage of U.S. Senate Bill 717, which was not, in the end, passed.

Childs was understandably anxious to achieve as much overlap as possible between the work of the AFT and AFL committees. In this way the importance of both would be enhanced. Woll asked Childs to organize a subgroup to address the problem of education and social welfare and in time used his AFT committee as the subgroup. He was also asked to chair another subcommittee to report on racial discrimination and minority groups.

Childs took an extremely active part in the proceedings and frequently sent Woll statements and suggestions that might be of use to him. In April 1944 a small pamphlet entitled *Post War Program [of the] American Federation of Labor*, which had been prepared by Woll's committee, was put out by the AFL. This seems to have concluded the work of the committee, which is not mentioned at all in Dubinsky's autobiography or Max D. Danish's biography of Dubinsky. In 1970, A. H. Raskin, the cowriter with Dubinsky of the autobiography, wrote to Childs at Rockford asking him to pen some memories of Dubinsky's activities in the Liberal party. Childs responded that he had destroyed most of his papers when he moved and consequently could not comply with the request. He noted, however, that he and Dubinsky were on the subcommittee that drafted the report. Two years later he did send Raskin two papers, one on the work of the AFL Postwar Planning Committee and the other on the founding of the Liberal party. The former gives some idea of Childs' attitude towards the work of the AFL committee:

Although I had long known of the statesmanlike leadership of David Dubinsky in labor and public affairs, it was through our work on this Postwar Planning Committee that we became personally acquainted.

We soon found that we were at one on the fundamentals, and that our views were in line with those of the Chairman, Matthew Woll. Organized labor was giving full support to the war effort and we spoke for the Federation when we declared that "the complete defeat of the Axis Powers is essential to clear the way for democratic international reconstruction." But we were also voicing the view of the Federation when we went on to state that "to stop with that alone would not furnish us with any permanent guarantee of security."

Along with many leaders both within and outside official government service, the members of our Committee were convinced that scientific and technological developments had made the historic war system so destructive that human welfare, possibly even human survival, itself, required the elimination of that system. Our report begins with the declaration that "war is the enemy", and its opening paragraph concludes with the judgment that "the elimination of war as an instrument of national policy is a condition essential to the perpetuation and the further development of our democratic way of life."

Our Committee was aware that any determined effort to get rid of the existing war system carried far reaching implications for traditional American thought and practice. Having been involved in two world wars in a period of less than thirty years, we perceived that it was sheer sentimentalism to suppose that the American people could continue "to rely on our favored geographical position to maintain our national safety." In sum, our Committee recognized that the day for our historic policy of isolationism had passed beyond recall.

We also recognized that real commitment to the development of a substitute for the war system involved, in the second place, the refusal to engage "in that rivalry for power which is inherent in any sustained effort to make ourselves secure through a program of national expansion and militarism." We knew that on this crucial point we spoke for organized labor, because "all working people realize that unilateral militarism produces not security, peace, and a rising standard of living, but increasing suspicion, mounting military expenditures, imperialistic adventures and war." Thus our Committee concluded that, in spite of all the difficulties, the road to "safety from war is in the international organization of peace," and we united with other groups in the demand that "the United States should do its full part to develop a general system of mutual security." The position of our Committee was approved by The Executive Council of the American Federation of Labor, and by this action organized labor further made political purposes and political activity an inherent part of its basic program.

In the context of this historic decision, it is important to note that the leaders and members of organized labor are not utopian dreamers. Indeed, their own organized labor movement has been developed and sustained by workers who did not ignore, but rather took account of harsh realities, and who struggled in the midst of actual conditions to develop the concrete means by which their needs and aims could be met. Better than many peace-seeking groups, organized labor realized that the development of a viable "general system of mutual security" defines a critical human need, not a ready-made human capacity.

Our Post War Planning Committee, for example, was aware that nations are stubborn facts, and that they would persist after the close of the Second World-War. It realized that nations are the products and the substance of history. Nations have their age-old traditions and their distinctive modes of life, thought, value and aspiration. Many believe that the cultural and political pluralism inherent in the existence of nations is an element of value worthy of preservation. But national groups also have memories, age-old ambitions, rivalries, and antagonisms, and frequently these inherited and cultivated national drives are in conflict with the interests and drives of other nations. Recognizing the reality of nations, our Committee was careful to distinguish an "international movement for mutual security and peace" from a system of world government. It considered that the development of an international agency designed to supplant the historic war system delineated both a possible and a desirable goal, but it rejected as both utopian and undesirable the movement to create an all-inclusive system of world sovereignty and authoritative control over the life affairs of the various peoples of the world.

Our Committee recognized, for example, that freedom of thought and expression are values that should be safeguarded, and that "tyrannical governments which would crush out freedom of thought in their own lands endanger spiritual freedom everywhere. In the world community of today, we cannot be indifferent to cruelty and oppression because such indifference strengthens the arm of the oppressor. Mere verbal protests are not enough, and yet we must be careful not to interfere in the domestic affairs of other peoples which are properly their own concern."

. . . The report of our Post War Planning Committee was completed and approved by The Executive Council of The American Federation of Labor more than a year before the Charter of the United Nations was adopted.

. . . In line with this general labor orientation, our Postwar Planning Committee gave great attention to proposed functional departments in the program of the United Nations. It called for the enlargement and the further strengthening of the International Labor Organization as an agency "for raising the standard of living of peoples in all countries and for the safeguarding the rights of the working people." Our report also stressed that "in order to maintain international peace, political and military programs must be associated with a far reaching *economic program* which will be designed, not to advantage certain nations at the expense of others, but to organize and utilize the new productive powers of industry and agri-

culture for the advancement of the standard of living of all peoples.["]
In sum, our report held that world-wide economic improvement is
an essential of security.

The labor report also gave specific support to such functional
agencies of the United Nations as the projected Food and Agricultural
organization and The Economic and Social Council. The recommendation was also given that permanent welfare agencies be nurtured
by the United Nations in the fields of health, education, and human
rights.

The report also characterized "free enterprise as an essential part
of the democratic way of life." It held that "free enterprise and free
labor are interdependent. Neither can last without the other." But
the report also declared that organized labor "means by free enterprise bold initiative for the increase of the range and efficiency of
production, not the disregard of the needs and rights of others." The
Postwar Planning Committee farther defined its interpretation of free
enterprise in the following paragraph:

"We want a regime of economic freedom, but our enterprise system must
demonstrate that it can function so as to husband and utilize, not to waste
and dissipate our natural resources. We want free enterprise, but our productive system must be committed to the progressive raising of the national
income and the maintenance of full employment. Such a system is necessarily
opposed to all tendencies toward monopolistic restriction. We want free
enterprise, but we also want an economy which will provide ample support
for the health, educational, recreational and similar public services so essential
to the welfare of the working people in our industrial society. Finally, we want
a program of economic enterprise which will not be repressive, but will
support the free exercise of civil and political liberties."

. . . It is now 28 years since the Report of the Postwar Planning
Committee was completed, unanimously endorsed by the Executive
Council of The American Federation of Labor, and made the basis
for the discussions of a two-day Conference of labor, professional,
business, agricultural, and church leaders held at the Hotel Commodore in the City of New York. It is also more than 25 years since the
Charter was adopted at a representative international conference,
and the United Nations was formally established.

. . . One concluding word about David Dubinsky and the Postwar Planning Committee. Sometime following the conclusion of the
work of the Committee, I received a phone call from Professor James
T. Shotwell, Honorary President of the American Association for the

United Nations, inviting me to have lunch with him at the Faculty Club of Columbia University. During our luncheon he reviewed the work of the A.F.L. Committee and its important and timely contribution, and then went on to speak of the great personal satisfaction he had derived from the opportunity to serve as a consultant for the Committee, and his high regard for the mature and able leadership that Matthew Woll and David Dubinsky had given to the work of the Committee. He added, you may be interested to hear that when I informed certain business leaders of my plan to work with the labor group on postwar problems, they warned me against it, and assured me that "I would certainly get my fingers burnt." "Actually," he continued, "I consider it one of the finest and most fruitful experiences I have ever had."[85]

Childs' other important political activity during the 1940s, activity which would thrust him onto the front page and the editorials of the *New York Times,* was his work with the Liberal party. For several years, the American Labor party (ALP) had been threatened by communist domination, as had the AFT. Dubinsky and A. H. Raskin reported, "They might well have succeeded as early as 1940 if the signing of the Stalin-Hitler pact had not forced the New York members . . . into what was the politically suicidal position of opposing a third term for President Roosevelt."[86] George Counts had been elected chair of the ALP in 1942 and was faced with the task of another communist purge. The party broke into two parts, with Counts and allies again spearheading the right wing. The communist pressure increased, so that by early 1944 when national election preliminaries were under way, a break was inevitable. Thus, in May a call went out "for the formation of a Liberal Party around which all genuinely progressive liberals and trade unionists could rally."[87] Like all third parties in this country, it had great difficulty getting a foothold and remained largely confined to New York State. Dubinsky stated that only once did he believe there might have been a real possibility of forming a national Liberal party. This was at this time when Thomas Dewey was chosen over the liberal Wendell Willkie as the Republican presidential nominee.

So in May, not long after he failed to win a single convention delegate in Wisconsin, out of the blue I got a call from Willkie saying he would like to get together with me and some of our people to talk about the future. I called [Alex] Rose and we arranged to meet with Willkie for a private dinner at my apartment on West Sixteenth Street. We invited the three principal intellectual leaders of the Liberal Party—Professors John L. Childs and George S. Counts of Columbia University and State Supreme Court Justice Samuel Null—to join us for a discussion after dinner.

Willkie lost no time in telling us the idea that was burning inside him. It was time, he said, to get started on building a national third party—not for the 1944 Presidential campaign, but for the years to come. In his estimation, both the Republican Party and the Democratic Party were moribund. Once F.D.R. died—and no one could doubt that his health was failing—the Democrats would be as much a prisoner of the reactionaries as the Republicans. That was the way Willkie saw it, and he made it plain that he was more than eager to volunteer to lead a liberal coalition under a third-party banner.

. . . For the Liberal Party, it could mean a marvelous start in local politics. Willkie was at the top of his prestige with progressives. He would be a great asset at the head of our municipal ticket. As for him, the more he saw of the 1944 campaign, the more contempt he developed for the Republican Party machine. He had very idealistic expectations of what the world could become when the war ended, and that made him more anxious than ever to be part of a movement with imagination and inspiration. He even discussed his thoughts in a general way with F.D.R. and came away convinced that he had Roosevelt's good will for what he had in mind.

Then it all ended as suddenly as it began. I picked up a newspaper in October 1944 and read of Willkie's death of a heart attack. It was a crushing moment. The national third-party project died with him. So far as I was concerned, it died for all time. No similar Mr. Right ever came along as a potential rallying center.[88]

The Columbia connection with the Liberal party belongs as much to Counts as to Childs, for the former would eventually run under its banner for the U.S. Senate in the 1952 election. He lost handily, but it was an experience he never forgot, and it gave him "the opportunity to speak both personally and through the media to thousands of people on a variety of issues."[89] Childs himself was chosen initially to head the Liberal party's Committee on Platform and Program. He was described in the *New York Herald Tribune* as "one of the

Right-Wing leaders of the American Labor party who led the
bolt of the Right-Wingers when the Communists and the Left-
Wing faction won control of the A.L.P. in the recent primary
contest."[90]

At the first convention of the embryonic Liberal party,
which was held in New York on May 19 and 20 and attended
by fifteen hundred people, Childs was elected state chairman.
Childs himself believed this was because of his work on the
AFL's Postwar Planning Committee. Joseph V. O'Leary was
elected the first secretary; Harry Uviller, treasurer; and Alex
Rose, chair of the administrative committee—all three were
also defectors from the ALP. A *Declaration and Platform* was
adopted, and the new party pledged to support Roosevelt's
reelection, with Henry A. Wallace for vice president and Robert F. Wagner for U.S. Senator. The party subsequently
switched its support from Wallace to Harry S. Truman, when
the latter became the official nominee of the Democratic party.
Childs wrote the foreword to the *Declaration and Platform,*
which totaled thirty-six pages. The last section of the forward-
looking *Platform,* "Cultural Foundations of American Democracy," gives a taste of the whole and reflects the dominant
interests of the Columbia University group.

I. Public Education
An authentic aim of American democracy is to give all of
its children an equal start.
Hence we hold that, in addition to universal public education, it is the responsibility of the public, operating through
government at federal, state and local levels, to supply any and
all deficiencies whenever a family cannot provide its children
with adequate care, food, clothing, health services, recreation
and other cultural opportunities.
While we believe education to be a function of the state, the
inequality among states of tax resources, as well as of population
in relation to such resources, makes it necessary for the federal
government to cooperate with the states. Hence we advocate
federal aid to the states for public education. Such federal funds
should assure to all equal opportunity for educational and allied
services, without discrimination on the ground of race, creed or

color. They should assure a cultural minimum wage to the teachers so as to provide properly qualified teachers.

Within each state we advocate the widest possible expansion of facilities in nursery schools, kindergartens, health services, guidance, recreational facilities, adult education and an expansion of the system of college scholarships. Classes should be no larger than educationally advisable. Schools should be staffed adequately with properly qualified personnel. To attract proper personnel and keep them at their maximum efficiency, they must be appointed and promoted on the basis of merit and fitness, receive a cultural wage, be assured of tenure and proper pension protection.

The system that has grown up in the army and navy of college education for promising men should find its counterpart in peacetime. The government should provide college education for qualified youth of both sexes through federal payment of the cost of subsistence as well as tuition.

II. Civil Liberties

The program of our party is grounded in two fundamental convictions. We believe, first, that the general welfare now demands basic readjustments in our domestic and international relationships and institutions. We believe, second, that these readjustments can be made by peaceful educational, economic and political means. This peaceful transformation can be achieved only if the rights to associate, to investigate, to discuss, to listen, to criticize, to learn, to teach, and to publish are maintained unimpaired in the postwar period.

The extension of governmental functions need not abridge these rights guaranteed in the Constitution. During the past decade the exercise of these liberties has been actually strengthened even though peacetime functions of government have grown, and we have had to endure the severe strains of total war.

Another threat to these rights, however, has steadily grown. The concentration of control in industry and finance has been paralleled by a concentration of control over the major means of communication. Today five companies dominate the motion picture market and own the theatres that receive seventy percent of all that is paid at the movie box offices.

Four radio networks dominate the air of America. Moreover, most of the important listening time is limited to one hundred giant business corporations, because of the prohibitive cost. In addition, one-third of the radio stations are dominated by the newspapers. The number of daily papers is steadily contracting; within the last few years they have declined from 2300 to about 1700, and of those that remain, many are syndicated. This "boiler-plating" of the American mind constitutes a major peril to our democracy.

We are opposed to this cartel of the information-disseminating and opinion-making industry of our country. We consider it one of the most dangerous of all concentrations in private hands.

Our party will seek to unite all liberals to develop means by which a free competitive market in opinions and ideas can be restored and maintained. We consider these freedoms, and the independent mind which they make possible, the very foundation of our democracy.[91]

During the months before the 1944 election, Childs not only spent a great deal of time in the party headquarters at the Claridge Hotel but also addressed assemblies and spoke out on a variety of issues—always commanding the attention of the press. One of the first of these speeches was to the delegates at the annual convention of the ILGWU on May 31. In it, he gave his definition of a *liberal:* "By 'liberal' I mean anyone who is engaged in socially useful work and who wants to join with other workers to develop a free society of, by and for workers."[92]

Childs realized that the chairmanship was going to be enormously time-consuming, so he requested once again to be placed on half-time appointment at Teachers College. It was granted, but what he did not know is that William F. Russell drafted a long and testy letter to him that, on reflection, the dean decided not to send. In part it read:

My guess is that you have a very practical mind. You see your role as one of direct action,—more than thru the minds of thousands of TC students. You think that development of the Union (I am not opposed) and development of a political party (again I am not opposed) are your major contributions.

I know that you are on a half-time basis. This arrangement is a recognition on your part of the area of your effort. However, I want to say to you that you were employed by TC in the hope that you would be a leader in philosophy of education; that you would make your contribution mainly in the education of your students and in leadership in your field. I am coming to believe that you have failed; and that you will fail, unless you change.

Of course, you have tenure and will remain on active status until you are sixty. You can continue to use your efforts as you like. You can make your post a springboard for union or political organization. It would go better with me if you would also do your main job; and give to all of us the vision and inspiration of which you are capable, and which we expected when we appointed you; and which we hoped to stimulate by the constant succession of improvements in status and position which have come your way.

I want to make quite plain that I have said everything in this letter that is on my mind. This is no covert action on my part to control you as to activities or thoughts; to discourage your association with any group or organization; to redirect your line of political or social thinking. In all this you have my full support. My only purpose is to ask you to reflect upon what it was Teachers College invited you to do.[93]

With his customary zeal, Childs threw himself into the preelection foray. On August 2 he was at the Commodore Hotel addressing an audience of eighteen hundred. Mrs. Roosevelt was the main speaker. Childs and Counts "expressed their beliefs that neither the Republican nor Democratic parties could fulfill 'the promise of a land for common people' and asked support of the Liberal party as a force that could."[94] A preelection rally of twenty thousand people was held in Madison Square Garden on October 31. The speakers included Henry A. Wallace, then Roosevelt's vice president, as well as Senators Harry S. Truman and Robert F. Wagner. It was considered quite a coup to have rivals Wallace and Truman appear together. Entertainment was provided by Ethel Merman, Victor Borge, and opera star Jan Kiepura. The headline artist was Frank Sinatra, who not only made a speech in support of Roosevelt but also sang and danced ("feebly"). Childs chaired the huge meeting and called on the audience to stand for a minute in tribute to Wendell Willkie. Childs gave a radio address just prior to the election in which he urged "the re-election of President Roosevelt to prevent the forces of privilege, race prejudice and patronage from getting control of the national government."[95]

The Roosevelt slate was elected, and the New York Liberal party contributed 329,235 votes to that victory. In a few weeks, however, Childs addressed an audience at the Hotel Victoria urging the president to withdraw his appointments to the State Department. This request elicited a somewhat scathing editorial in the *New York Times,* inquiring about the difference between *liberal* and *Liberal.*[96] In an immediate response, Childs stated the principles of his Liberal party.

The leaders of the Liberal party believe that it is an authentic expression in our period of the democratic liberal tradition. We share many of the historic faiths and ideals of liberalism. The Liberal party believes that government is a means which has no good or aim other than the good of its citizens; that government should rest on the consent of the governed; that the right to inquire, to know, to publish, to associate, to discuss, to criticize, to agitate, to propose and to write is essential to the life of freedom and that in a changing world institutions must be changed to meet new conditions, but that in the United States all necessary reconstructions can be brought about by peaceful processes of education and organized economic and political action. . . . We believe in cooperative planning and the coordination of public and private enterprise.[97]

Roosevelt died on April 12, 1945, just weeks after his inauguration, but his positions continued to be supported by the Liberal party. At its first anniversary dinner, the party "rededicated the organization to support the policies" of the late president. Childs addressed the audience and decried the policies of both the Soviet Union and Great Britain. "Nor are these imperialistic tendencies absent from the policies of our own country. The growing demand for immediate universal military training, for an all-powerful navy, for strategic naval and air bases, for the right to trade where we want without regard to consequences for other countries, as well as demands for oil and air imperialism, all indicate that there are powerful interests in our country which would seek to us make this the Century of the America rather than the Century of the Common Man."[98]

For most of 1945 the interests of the party were focused on New York and its opposition to William O'Dwyer, who was supported by the former mayor, Fiorello La Guardia. As it turned out, O'Dwyer, who was the nominee of both the Democratic party and the ALP, won the election. Nineteen hundred forty-five was also the year that marked the end of World War II. Even so, the grim lists of casualties were printed daily in the *New York Times*. When Childs heard of Winston Churchill's defeat in the British general election, he immediately sent a telegram to the new prime minister, Clement Atlee. He might have exaggerated the importance of his party's significance when he wrote, "The liberal-labor forces of America will cooperate to the limit with your Government as it strives to substitute the ways of collective security, rising standards of living and peace for the discredited patterns of imperialism and war."[99]

In 1946 the Liberal party held its third convention, and Childs was reelected unanimously as state chairman. O'Leary and Uviller also retained their positions. Vice-chairmanships went to David Dubinsky, Reinhold Niebuhr, and George Counts. Childs was not in good health at these meetings and turned the chair over to Counts. He continued to speak in public and was frequently quoted in the news. The Liberal party also had a weekly radio program, and Childs addressed the airwaves on several occasions. He opposed certain policies of the AFL and called for "a planning economy administered in the interests of all."[100] He supported the government's posture concerning control of atomic weapons, he urged Prime Minister Atlee to work towards India's independence, he approved the hanging verdicts at Nuremberg because they represented "a step forward in international law," and he complained when the party was denied air time on the White Plains, New York, station WFAB.[101] Never had he had such a large and ready platform.

Again, the main focus of the year was the off-year elections. The party supported the democratic nominees for governor (James M. Mead) and senator (Herbert N. Lehman), as well as Counts for lieutenant governor and O'Leary for controller. It did this in spite of Childs' concern "'about the sterility of progressive thought' in Republican leadership and 'the timidity of mind' in Democratic leadership."[102] Three issues were stressed in the Liberal campaign: the party urged (1) American participation in "a world organization strong enough to save us from the horrors of an atomic war"; (2) "a firm price control and a labor-management accord"; and (3) adequate housing for all, subsidized if necessary.[103]

During this period, Childs again shared the speaker's platform with Mrs. Roosevelt and, at the party rally in Manhatten Center just a few days before the election, also with her son, FDR, Jr. In spite of these efforts, Thomas Dewey and Irving McNeil Ives won the election; the *New York Times* noted that the trend ran decidedly against the Democratic, Labor, and Liberal alliance. Nevertheless, the Liberals had gained around two hundred thousand votes, well over the fifty thousand necessary for it to achieve legal status as a party. As Childs said, "Under the election laws of this State, the Liberal party now becomes a legal party. In view of the strong Republican trend, we consider these results satisfactory. They provide a solid basis for building in the future a progressive, non-totalitarian political movement in this State."[104] Moreover, in a sense justifying its independence of both the two main parties, the Liberals had helped send Republican Jacob K. Javits to Congress as Representative from the Manhatten Twenty-first District.

A few weeks following the elections, Childs sent an official letter to Dubinsky tendering his resignation as chair of the party.

I write to present my resignation as State Chairman of the Liberal Party, to take effect not later than the end of this year. I have delayed taking this step for a month since the election in order to be sure that my decision was well grounded, and did not come as a result of fatigue growing out of the strenuous fall campaign.

. . . The time and manner of announcing this action to the public I shall leave with you and the other leaders of the Party. I am hoping the adjustment can be made so as to arouse no misunderstandings, for the case is exactly as I have outlined it above.

My heart is with the Liberal Party, for I am as deeply convinced

as ever that we need a re-alignment in American politics, and that
the new labor-liberal party should not make a united front with
totalitarians, Communist or Fascist.

If I can be of any service in working out further plans, please feel
free to call upon me. If later I am needed in some less exacting post
I shall be more than ready to serve.

The Party has made a real contribution in the three years of its
existence; properly led and organized it has much greater things
ahead of it. I have a high regard for my colleagues of the Party and
I deeply appreciate the loyal way in which they have supported me.
I am still an "amateur" in the political field, but I have learned much
from my associates during this period.[105]

In fact, Childs was not replaced until the following spring.
On May 9, 1947, Childs, together with Dubinsky, Rose,
Uviller, O'Leary, and Counts met with the distinguished
Adolph A. Berle, Jr., who had been assistant secretary of state
from 1938 to 1944 and more recently U.S. ambassador to
Brazil, to confer with him about becoming the new chair
of the party. He was ready to do so and took over almost
immediately. Childs himself was named one of the vice-chairs
and continued to speak out on public issues, both domestic and
international. For example, he joined his colleagues Counts,
Axtelle, and Berle in making a statement in support of the
Marshall Plan for European postwar relief. He urged the members of the Teachers Guild to take a strong anticommunist
stand by attempting to shatter some of its kindlier myths.
Occasionally he was called upon to address issues as the former
state chair and to write short pieces for the party broadsheets.
In April 1948 on radio station WNBC, New York, he responded vigorously to Thomas Dewey's assertion that the
Liberal party was an ally of the communists. "It is because
Dewey and the reactionary forces back of Dewey are against
this basic task of democratic reconstruction that they tend to
take shelter in shrill and underground attacks on authentic
liberals. But the public will not be long deceived. It is beginning
to recognize Governor Dewey for the superficial political op-
portunist that he is."[106]

Childs remained a vice-chair of the Liberal party for several years. In 1952 he was among those who supported George

Counts' bid for the U.S. Senate. Counts was defeated, although he did get a half million votes. Again Childs thought he should step down and expressed the conviction that younger people should be brought into leadership positions. In 1954 he headed the recruiting drive for new members in anticipation of the 1956 elections. In 1955 he chaired the nominating committee that put Counts into the state chairmanship for what turned out to be four terms. He also wrote a statement of principle on behalf of the party.

> The Liberal Party is grounded in the principle that a democratic government and program must be representative of all the component elements in American life including organized labor, the farmers, white-collar workers and small businessmen. The present national administration repudiates this principle and assumes that the welfare of everybody will be automatically promoted when big business dominates our government. In 1956 there will be a national referendum on these conflicting conceptions of the general welfare and the means by which it should be promoted. The Liberal Party will do all in its power to make it possible for President Eisenhower to retire to his farm at Gettysburg, Pennsylvania.[107]

In 1956 the people were not ready to send Dwight Eisenhower to his farm. As late as 1959, Childs spoke at the fifteenth annual Liberal party dinner, where the principal speaker was Senator Hubert Humphrey.

Several things probably conspired to slow down Childs' political career. In the first place, in his resignation to Dubinsky, he wrote:

> I must now make a decision about the main direction of my future life-work. The University authorities have been most generous in arranging for me to carry for the last five years the outside work with the A.F. of L. and the Liberal Party. They have been interested in what I have been trying to do, and they have considered it important.
> On the other hand, the University authorities rightly are concerned to have the work of my field—Philosophy of Education—given the best possible leadership during the postwar period, both in its teaching and its research and writing aspects. My conclusion is that I should now make these professional interests primary.[108]

He certainly would have needed time to work on his most important book, *Education and Morals* (1950). In the second place, his mother, to whom he wrote clearly but left-handedly a single postcard every day after her husband's death, died early in 1950. Third, his own health was not good. He was just sixty, and in 1952 he was suffering from what was described as "coronary thrombosis." In 1953, for example, he refused an offer to speak to the Young Liberals: "My doctor requested me to refrain from taking on additional engagements for the time being."[109] From this time on, Childs took care to conserve his strength, and his daily regimen included an afternoon nap. As is so often the case with those who have an early warning of a serious health problem and take heed of it, he lived to an advanced age.

Childs remained on one committee until 1963, probably because it demanded less time than had the others. In 1939 "a permanent research body, sufficiently independent of other associations and of any government" was formed "to engage in a thorough and comprehensive study of all aspects of the problem of international peace, with special emphasis on plans for a future world organization to maintain peace and to promote the progress of mankind."[110] The chair of the Commission To Study the Organization of Peace was James T. Shotwell, the distinguished historian who had taught at Columbia since the turn of the century until his retirement in 1937; he served as chair until 1955. Shotwell's continuing efforts on behalf of peace brought him into close contact with the world's leading politicians. Members of the commission were "selected from various sectors of the intellectual and academic community, not merely on the basis of their technical competence but also taking into account their concern for a world community based on law and justice." The "Shotwell Commission," as it was popularly known, took particular interest in the establishment and work of the United Nations, and John Foster Dulles stated that it "made an indispensable contribution to the creation of the United Nations."[111] It is easy to see how the work of this commission appealed to Childs. It issued regular reports, of which Childs was a signer to most from 1943 through 1963.

It was Childs himself who insisted that pragmatism demands action: "Its emphasis on experience, on experimental activity, on the creative role of intelligence, and on the values and procedures of democracy brought these elements in the life of the American people into fuller consciousness and thereby enhanced their influence in public affairs, including the enterprise of education."[112] This position, similar to his missionary commitment of earlier years, led him to participate enthusiastically in a variety of political activities from the middle 1930s until his retirement. These activities afforded him the opportunity to teach or even preach far beyond the walls of his classroom. He put his beliefs to the experimental test and thought them proven. Actions do make a difference. There can be little doubt that Childs' political activities did detract from his writing, yet he was enormously prolific throughout the political period. Moreover, in the long view, more was probably gained than lost by these efforts. He demonstrated, as did many of the experimentalists, that theorizing does not preclude tough activity.

6.
The Great Debate

As Childs' political activities began to taper off, he concentrated his energies once more on the philosophy of education. Indeed, it is suggested that these public activities were an extension of that philosophy and the need he felt to translate his beliefs into action, as he had done in China earlier. The return was made more smoothly than it might otherwise have been on account of his colleagues at Teachers College and elsewhere. True, George Counts and George Axtelle continued to be more active in politics, but Childs himself, with retirement only a few years away, had other priorities. William Heard Kilpatrick had retired, and Childs played a major role in his birthday celebrations. John Dewey was in his nineties, and Childs was to devote many of his later writings to Dewey. Their relations were professionally close, but one could guess that both Dewey and Kilpatrick were former teachers; indeed, Childs always addressed Kilpatrick as "Professor Kilpatrick," who responded, "Dr. Childs." George Counts, another former teacher, became a close friend. Childs' association with Boyd H. Bode also moved from a professional to a more personal level. As with Counts, the intellectual journey of the two men was somewhat similar: both were midwesterners with intensely religious backgrounds, and both came to pragmatism somewhat late in life. Bode had actually taught at Madison while Childs was there but had moved on to the University of Illinois in Urbana in 1909, just as Childs enrolled in his first undergraduate course in philosophy. Bode went to Ohio State University in Columbus in 1921 and remained there until his retirement in 1944. It was during this time that he self-consciously moved from philosophy into philosophy of education and became one of the main spokesmen for experimentalism outside of New York. He wrote a warm letter to Childs on the publication of his dissertation, and then the two men came into closer contact with writing, under Kilpatrick's editorship, *The Educational Frontier,* which also involved Bode's ardent disciple H. Gordon Hullfish.

At that time Childs had associated himself with the liberal wing of the experimentalist camp, as has already been indicated. Writing in 1933, the same year of *The Educational Frontier,* Norman Woelfel placed Bode in the conservative wing of the movement and criticized him for failing to include in his thinking the "social forces operating decisively on the contemporary American scene."[1] This was a criticism that Childs also directed at Bode for the remainder of the decade. It is hardly surprising, therefore, that Childs and Bode carried on a dialogue of disagreement throughout the 1930s, which was conducted mainly in the pages of the *Social Frontier.* It began in 1934 with Childs' enthusiastic review of *Conclusions and Recommendations,* the summary volume of the AHA's Commission on the Social Studies in the Schools, which was actually coauthored by Counts and Charles A. Beard. Bode held some reservations about the book, and these centered around its posture that teachers should not only assume a leadership role in social reconstruction but that they should go so far as to indoctrinate towards rather clearly defined goals. The report tried "to combine an authoritarian 'frame of reference' with cultivation of effective and independent thinking."[2] "This is hopelessly self-contradictory," wrote Bode. "The insistence on independence of thinking becomes an empty pretense if the conclusions to be drawn are determined in advance." Bode stated his position clearly: "The basic 'dogma' of a democratic philosophy of education relates to method, of reliance on intelligence, and not to conclusions;" it is a risk-taking enterprise, for the outcome may not be what the writers of the *Conclusions,* principally Counts and Beard, had hoped for. "To dictate conclusions betokens a distrust of the common man, even though the dictating be done for the avowed purpose of promoting democracy and the liberation of intelligence."[3]

The debate heated up, really around this one issue. Childs believed that an appropriate education must take into account the social realities of the day (economic depression), and it should play an important role in ameliorating conditions by describing the desired society and indoctrinating the young in the values of the new order. Bode, on the other hand, believed that the first obligation of an educational program was to develop intelligence while promoting the *processes* of democracy. In Childs' words, "Professor Bode challenges on educational and ethical grounds the suggestion of the Commission on the Social Studies that the schools should serve as an agency for the development of a particular social outlook. ... To Professor Bode the deliberate formulation and introduction of such a social *frame of reference* into educational procedures signifies a return to dogmatism and authoritarianism."[4] Bode liked the tone of the article but objected to Childs' characterization that his conception of education was extremely individualistic; Bode thought the point at issue was "whether the pupil is to do his own thinking, or to have it done for him."[5]

In 1938, after the publication of Bode's *Progressive Education at the Crossroads,* the issue resurfaced in Childs' review of the book, again for the *Social Frontier.* Childs noted that, as fundamental as experiential intelligence is, it does not supply an adequate base for an educational program: "No democratic society can or should attempt to become neutral about educational outcomes." Childs also rejected the contention that the development of a child's beliefs and outlooks in certain directions is antithetical to the development of intelligence, for "the development of creative intelligence necessarily involves that selecting and guiding of experience which is education."[6]

In a letter to Childs, Bode rightly pointed out that the heart of their disagreement seemed to be over the question of indoctrination.[7] The debate continued in the *Social Frontier*. If the school is to be a place where the democratic way of living—"[k]indliness, consideration for others, . . . and voluntary cooperation"—is to be maintained it must not indoctrinate. "We must aim at a democratic social order and we must avoid indoctrination."[8] Bode was afraid that "the schools will be just as seriously wrong if they become agencies for promoting a specific type of reform."[9] They must not mount "a campaign for a specific scheme of ownership and distribution."[10] Bode himself hoped they would develop loyalty to the principle of democracy. But there is a sense in which Childs hit the nail right on the head when, in his response to Bode, he wrote that the error lies in assuming that "concern about *method* can substitute for concern about *objectives*." Childs believed that Bode had confused ends with means. "[H]ow adequate is it," he asked, "to allow our interpretation of democracy to simmer down to a generalized formula of 'reciprocity' and 'the continuous expansion of common life'?"[11] Rather, "no statement of the meaning of democracy can be considered adequate which fails to recognize that the reconstruction of our economic system . . . necessarily becomes one of the controlling *ends* of democratic effort for our generation." So Childs boldly made his statement of faith that "democracy is no longer compatible with our historic laissez-faire profit system, and that the present supreme technological, political, and *educational* task is the construction of a *planning society* that can provide the means for the continued development of our democratic values [italics added]."[12]

The men had hoped for an opportunity to meet and discuss their differences, and Bode was invited to address the Teachers College Philosophy of Education Club on December

2, 1938, but he was unable to accept owing to a prior commitment. Relations, however, remained very cordial as both, in their ways, attempted "to get progressive education to think in terms of a social ideal."[13] And indeed, this was no mere intellectual issue, for it was at the nub of one of the problems facing progressive educators. George Hartmann, since October 1937 editor-in-chief of the *Social Frontier*, felt that the debate was sufficiently important to be continued in the pages of the journal, and over the next months, H. Gordon Hullfish, Kenneth Benne, William Stanley, James Skipper, and John Dewey entered the lists. As with the discussions preceding the publication of *The Educational Frontier*, the lines were drawn between the Teachers College group on one side (Childs, Benne, Stanley) and the Ohio State group on the other (Bode, Hullfish, Skipper).

Dewey tried to mediate the discussions by restating areas of agreement; first, "all education takes its direction from a social aim"; and second, "the social aim is set by the democratic principle."[14] Dewey did not think that it was useful to view democracy as an abstract concept but that it would serve better to see whether "the economic structure of society bears, under present conditions, an inherent relation to the realization of the democratic idea."[15] He seemed to side with Childs. The debate continued with Bode emphasizing the individual more than Childs liked; Bode wrote that "the supreme test of progress lies in the development of individual capacity."[16]

Bode had a deep dislike of authoritarianism, and his fear was that the program of education proposed by Childs would result in yet another form of authoritarianism. He wryly noted that "[o]ur whole American life has been an unedifying mixture of authoritarianism and democracy from those earliest days down to the present time." So, the school must become "the institution or agency which has the special obligation of providing for the continuous reinterpretation of democracy." For Bode, "the central educational problem in our democracy is the problem of reconstructing our way of life."[17] Childs did not disagree, only he found Bode's commitment too undefined, too vague; Childs was adamant that it was the economic situation that defines the moral obligations of the present. It would seem that the difference was merely one of sequence. Childs accepted Bode's as an appropriate first step, but beyond that it was necessary to look at contemporary life. Childs did so and concluded that it was precisely the economic situation that was antithetical to the democratic ideal, hence the schools must have in mind a new social order compatible with democracy. Childs wanted action at once, but as the future he envisioned was not cast in stone, he recognized that any plan was always subject to inquiry and possible revision.

The debate once engaged passed from its two chief protagonists to the other partisans at New York and Columbus. Childs mentioned the possibility to Hartmann of putting the discussions into book form with additional articles by Jesse Newlon and Counts and summary comments by himself and Bode. But matters were brought to an abrupt end by the overriding issue of war and peace. In August 1939 Childs sent to Bode a copy of a manifesto that had been drafted by him and two colleagues and endorsed by almost one hundred forty members of the Teachers College faculty. It was entitled "Democracy and Education in the Current Crisis."[18] Bode was complimentary in his response but was concerned that its approval was too nearly unanimous at Teachers College: "It is my conviction that not one in fifty of our school population ever gets any intelligent notion of what democracy really requires of him. If our students saw what it meant they would not be much at ease in Zion." If Bode did not actually call the manifesto vague, he did suggest that its tone was too general—too general, that is, for anyone, certainly any American, to take offense. In the manifesto, democracy is referred to as a way of life. For Bode democracy was not merely a way of life but "an overarching principle by which conflicts among values are judged and adjusted."[19] By the same token, Childs, in a generally enthusiastic review of Bode's recent book, *How We Learn*, wrote that Bode himself was too vague concerning democracy.[20] Bode admittedly found democracy an unobjectionable slogan ("the presidential candidates of *all* the parties make their appeal to 'democracy'.") and stated that by itself the word *democracy* forms little basis "for distinguishing between sentiments or slogans and principles or guides for action."[21]

But Bode thought that democracy's greatest attraction lay in its appeal to intelligence. This assertion was not satisfactory to Childs, who called Bode to task for his opposition to "all education that seeks the deliberate nurture of a particular social outlook," that is, to all forms of indoctrination.[22] Nevertheless, Childs described Bode's book as "the best comprehensive treatment of the educational implications of modern psychological and philosophical thought now available."[23]

In 1942, John S. Brubacher, president of the Philosophy of Education Society, tried to enlist Childs as chair of the Program Committee for the 1943 meetings. In fact, the meeting did not take place; neither did the 1943 St. Louis meeting of the National Society for the Council of Teachers of Education, whose president was Grayson Kefauver of Stanford University. An unscheduled 1944 yearbook of the council was published under the general title *Adjustments in Education to Meet War and Postwar Needs.*[24] Seven areas of education were discussed, with the lead chapter being devoted to philosophy of education. Brubacher essentially drafted the chapter, and he was joined by Childs and Bode as coauthors. Childs made numerous but minor alterations; Bode thought the article did not come out strongly enough for democracy and made some substantial additions. Brubacher acted as go-between; there seems to have been no direct communication between Childs and Bode on this matter.

Bode retired from Ohio State University in 1944 and spent the next academic year at the Graduate Institute of Education in Cairo, Egypt, followed by summers at the University of Tennessee and University of British Columbia. He then moved to Gainesville, Florida. On November 10, 1947, he was the recipient of the William Heard Kilpatrick Award for Distinguished Service in Philosophy of Education. As was Bode, Dewey, Kilpatrick, and Hullfish were on hand for the presentation. The proceedings were chaired by Counts, who expressed the thought, probably held by many that day in the Horace Mann Auditorium, that they would "never again hear these three giants of educational thought . . . speak from the same platform."[25] In his address, entitled "Education for Freedom," Bode returned to his recurring theme, the cleavage in our culture that impedes our search for moral standards: "Either the controls for moral conduct are derived from non-scientific theories regarding the cosmic structure of things, or they come to us from empirical observation and controlled inquiry into the physical and social conditions of modern life."[26]

That evening, a dinner was held in Bode's honor at which Kenneth Benne and Childs replied to the afternoon address. Childs raised some questions (as did Benne) that hint at some of the differences that they had disputed earlier. First, "what role . . . do adults have in the process of education?" Second, does Bode's commitment to scientific procedures disbar theists from the process and also "inevitably commit the young to a naturalistic outlook?" Third, would the effort to communicate "knowledge" to the young concerning social, moral, economic, and political affairs that had been determined scientifically "be a form of imposition and enslavement in absolutes?"[27] We do not have Bode's reply, but R. Bruce Raup noted that it was "sharpened with the wit for which he is famous."[28]

In his speech, Childs mentioned two areas where he thought Bode had made the greatest contribution to American education. First, "the field of the psychological analysis of human behavior and learning" in which Bode held that the mind is "a kind of purposeful functioning in the environment through which means are consciously developed for the attainment of anticipated outcomes." Second, Bode's conviction that "democracy and experimental science are organically associated, and that taken together, they demand a new orientation to the educational enterprise."[29] The Childs-Bode debate was really no further to resolution, although it did face head-on the problems that reconstructionism presented to other experimentalists. It had also laid the foundations for what was probably Childs' closest intellectual association of his mature years, as it was carried out in a rich and extensive private correspondence between the two men. The tone of the letters between them, their warm consideration and frankness, is rare for Childs.

Dewey's influence was far and away the most pervasive intellectual force on Childs. Other major influences were Kilpatrick, Bode, and Counts. It is the work of these three men that Childs examined at length in his 1956 book on American pragmatism. The Kilpatrick connection has already been discussed, and the association with Counts was to continue into retirement. Of Bode, Childs wrote, "I consider him one of the most generous men I have ever met, and he was ever ready to encourage the rest of us and thus help us to do better than we otherwise might have done."[30] Their relationship was significant beyond the personal level because it throws light on some of the disagreements among Dewey's closest followers. These disagreements were not in themselves divisive, and Bode took pains to point out that they should not divide: "We must not start any fights just now in our own circle."[31] The differences do demonstrate that, even among those who understood Dewey best, his work needed interpretation. It was during the last few years of Bode's life that he and Childs tried to iron out and clarify some of those differences.

Bode believed that Childs correctly stated his views in his, Childs', contribution to Sidney Hook's volume in honor of Dewey's ninetieth birthday. In his essay, Childs focused on two points made by Bode: first, the "fundamental characteristic of democratic education . . . is the central place that it gives to the cultivation and the liberation of the intelligence of the individual"; and second, "the development of the understanding of the individual must never be subordinated to a desire to commit him to a particular program of social change or reconstruction."[32] Bode's two points did not suggest to Childs that the educator should avoid committing the child to definite patterns of life and thought. Certainly, he would not use authoritarian methods, but he found it insupportable that a child could "use the experimental method of inquiry for a period of years without at the same time developing habits of thought and methods of analysis and verification that are consonant with the procedures of science."[33] At this point Childs was much closer to Counts than he was to Bode. Counts, in spite of the force of Dewey's own arguments, and to a lesser extent Childs, called this a form of indoctrination. Childs wrote, "The democratic way of living is more than a process of intellectual inquiry, and education in and for democracy in-

volves the introduction of the young to many additional values. ... A democratic society has every right to require its
schools to cultivate its young in those common appreciations
and behaviors that are the ultimate ground of its health and
security."[34] Bode was more bothered by this imposition, and
so the argument of the late 1930s was taken up again by both
men in the 1950s.

Bode wrote a congratulatory letter to Childs on his chapter
in Hook's book in honor of Dewey's ninetieth birthday and
thought that the summary of his own thinking as presented was
"made with an enviable clarity and simplicity and basic correct-
ness." However, to impose a certain value system on children
remained for Bode objectionable, even if done in the interests of
democracy. He wrote, "We cannot, I think, protect democracy
by cultivating loyalties to such abstractions as 'respect for personality', voting, security, and what not. We can have a lot of
that without any of the spirit of democracy."[35] In a subsequent
letter, Bode stated his point of view more specifically, "Why
not say instead that our cultural heritage is full of conflicts and
contradictions and that these are to be handled by the method
of 'inquiry.' ... In terms of this procedure, the principle of the
dignity and worth of the individual gets translated into the doctrine that the continuous extension of common interests and
purposes is the test of morality and progress."

That reference to morality reflected in part Bode's receipt
of a copy of Childs' new book, *Education and Morals,* which
some consider his most important and original contribution
to educational literature. Bode liked *Education and Morals*
and in the same letter stated, "I can't recall when I have read
anything with so much unrestrained enthusiasm. ... And I
don't know of any discussion which even approximates the
simplicity and effectiveness of your presentation. It is unques-
tionably a major contribution to the concept of democracy as
a way of life. I have read it through with undimmed enthusiasm
and with a renewed faith."[36] Childs himself summed up the
basis of the book:

The conceptions set forth in *Education and Morals* were evolved
as I struggled to define and formulate the implications of develop-

ments in American life and thought. I consider that Dewey was both penetrating and valid in his conviction that the democratic way of life and the experimental mode of inquiry tend to combine in the support of a basic method of thought and education. One of the perduring problems of deliberate education is to achieve a procedure in which that which is necessarily the communication of meanings from the perspective of the teacher will at the same time be a process of the discovery of meanings by the pupil or student.[37]

Education and Morals, which is dedicated to Dewey and Kilpatrick, is a rich book—particularly in its wide and balanced grasp of the principles of pragmatism as they had come to be applied to education. Not surprisingly, the work of Dewey is referred to many times. Save for its central theme, Childs did not make in it any novel contribution to pragmatism, but he argued its position eloquently and intelligently. He adopted, in a more extended fashion, the form that Counts used in *Dare the School Build a New Social Order?* Childs spelled out important fundamentals in the first two chapters, and in the following three he pointed out the fallacies in the three other dominant educational philosophies or positions. First, he took on the supernaturalists and religious groups, not for the first time, as has been seen. Second, he attacked the naturalists, who believe that education is a natural unfolding and therefore tend to ignore the environing conditions. Third, he went after Robert Hutchins and the great books. The arguments are precise and telling. This first part of the book grew out of his belief that education itself becomes confused and uncertain at a time when "the society of which its program is an expression is also confused and uncertain."[38] Like Counts, Childs knew he lived in a period of profound and organic societal change; this was made even more evident by the dominant postwar concern with the frightful potential of atomic war.

Childs' major insight, and perhaps his most lasting contribution to pragmatic thought, was his conception of the *moral*—which was a topic of great interest anyway to the one-time missionary. Morality is brought into play in the making of choices; morality is thus taken out of the realm of the transcendental and is brought into the realm of the everyday. Schooling is a matter of doing things to human beings, and it is deliberate. It involves "definite modification in the habits, the appreciations, the skills, the knowledge, the attitudes, the allegiances, and the dispositions of individual children."[39] Thus it is required of us that we make choices among what Childs called, "genuine life alternatives."[40] It is in the making of these choices that education becomes at root a moral enterprise. Childs stated this clearly early in the book. The moral interest "is involved whenever a significant choice has to be made between a better and a worse in the nurture of the young. The moral factor appears whenever the school, or the individual teacher or supervisor, is *for* certain things and *against* other things. The moral element is preeminently involved in all of those selections and rejections that are inescapable in the construction of the purposes and the curriculum of the school."[41]

Early in the book, Childs lay down four important points, which formed the basis of the remainder: (1) "man achieves his human attributes through a process of experiencing and learning"; (2) "all organized education is in the nature of a moral undertaking"; (3) "the development of the program of the school inescapably involves an evaluation and interpretation of the ways of life and thought of its society"; (4) "the realization that the process of cultural interpretation and evaluation inherent in the work of the school becomes both more important and more complex and difficult in a period of cultural transition."[42]

Childs' vision of the world in transition was very much in line with that of his colleague George Counts, and both were the front men of social reconstructionism. Both visualized a new order "marked by global interdependence, by control over the energies of the atom, by a disturbing and expanding scientific method and mentality, and by a more socialized and cooperatively planned system of democracy." Consequently, "the schools must educate the young in an altered conception of social welfare and in a reconstructed pattern of human rights, responsibilities, and loyalties if they are to be equipped to share in the preservation and the further development of our democratic civilization."[43] For Childs, this suggested six necessarily moral imperatives into which the young must be enculturated. Here Counts might have used the word *indoctrinate,* but Childs was a little more cautious.

It is these six moral imperatives that comprise the second part of *Education and Morals,* and they are as follows. *Morality of primary experience:* children must be treated as ends, not as means. Knowledge and intelligence have to be based on direct doings and undergoings, or put another way, on firsthand or primary experience, not on abstract materials handed on without reference to the children themselves. *Morality of inquiry:* meaning "universalizing the community of inquirers, by confronting and utilizing doubt to test and expand beliefs, and by employing empirical and public data and methods that foster uncoerced cooperation in the search for knowledge and standards. Through the use of these procedures, experimental inquiry has socialized the process by which man comes to know."[44] *Morality of an open society:* suggesting the centrality of democracy, not as an end for its own sake but because "it provides the conditions necessary for the growth of mature human beings."[45] Freedom of inquiry for students and teachers is thus assured; it must be recognized that, and here Childs drew on his political involvements, the morality of communism is in deep conflict with the morality of democracy. Teachers should not protect communists in their ranks. *Morality of function:* wherein schools are torn between the morality of individualism on the one hand and that of the general welfare on the other. The 1987 Wall Street gangsters are examples of the former, and they would have disgusted Childs. On the other hand, said Childs, American democracy "will recover meaning and vitality as it succeeds in reorganizing an economy in which all find security and opportunity in cooperatively planned functions that are recognized to be socially useful."[46] *Morality of community:* here Childs echoed Dewey's belief that school is not preparation for life but life itself. He stated that "a school can be a consistent and effective moral agency of democracy only to the extent that its ways of organizing and conducting its own affairs are in harmony with the democratic ideals it seeks to foster through its modes of instruction."[47] It therefore follows that "schools have a real responsibility to do their share in turning our country into a society in which *all men* have a living experience of equality."[48] *Morality of patriotism:* Childs' vision of patriotism is not narrowly nationalistic, it is broadened to include all humanity. "The development of an America that will have the strength to take her full part in the struggle for a democratic world civilization defines the deepest purpose of our system of education. . . . It is from the perspective of this world need and purpose that education of the American citizen should develop its concrete meanings. There is no conflict between this broadened conception of the meaning of American citizenship, and the need of humanity for a world organized for security, peace, freedom, and social progress."[49]

Childs' patriotism did not stem from a narrow jingoistic perspective, that should be clear enough already, but from his total commitment to democratic social arrangements. This commitment became his gospel after he came under Dewey's tutelage. Democratic social arrangements were at base morally good, not because they served narrow patriotic interests but because they treated individual human beings as ends in themselves and not as mere means. Thus education is an essentially moral enterprise because real life alternatives are "inherent in the construction of all programs of organized education. These selected and weighted educational programs inevitably have consequences in the behaviors and dispositions of the young. Hence the most basic problem of education is the moral problem of determining the patterns of life and thought in which the young are to be nurtured. Educational selections are grounded ultimately in value judgments; these value judgments become less arbitrary and more significant and responsible when we are aware of the moral preferences implicit in our educational activities."[50]

Education and Morals was published in April 1950 by Appleton-Century-Crofts, and, on the whole, it was well received. The senior editor, Dana Ferrin, told Childs that the firm was "proud to be your publishers."[51] Paul Hanna, professor of education at Stanford University, had read the book in manuscript form and thought it "the most important general work in the philosophy of education since John Dewey's *Democracy and Education.*" This comment must have pleased Childs enormously. Hanna admitted that the education proposed in the book was "neither for all nations, nor for the inhabitants of the City of God," but he did believe it was "for the American people during the present troubled epoch."[52] William F. Bruce, teaching at the State Teachers College, Oneonta, New York, made perceptive reference to Childs' political experiences: "We seriously doubt if this book could have been written with such courage and balance unless the author had been able to merge a rich public experience with a penetrating understanding of the extensive literature of experimentalism. In other words," and here Bruce supported Childs' position, "the book itself is a demonstration of the quality of personal morality made possible through primary experience, which is one of its central themes."[53] Childs' old union associate Irvin R. Kuenzli, still secretary-treasurer of the AFT, also saw the book as an extension of Childs' political activities and made reference to his "outstanding courage and unrelenting support in the battle for democracy in education." He added, "To my mind that, in itself, is a moral principle of the highest order."[54] William W. Brickman's review for *School and Society* was somewhat halfhearted, and he rather laconically commented that it was fortunate that Childs did "not suggest, as he did over a year ago in an address, that all children be made to receive part of their education in public schools."[55] Brickman also thought the book was a cautious form of progressivism. This view was echoed more positively by Harold Soderquist in a full-length review for the *American Teacher.*[56] He noted that Childs stopped short of challenging teachers to build a new social order and suggested that Childs was now more conservative than he had been in the 1930s. Soderquist also commented on Childs' excellent writing but regretted that there was no touch of color or humor. And, it must be noted, this earnestness characterizes all of Childs' work. He is on a serious mission and this must never be doubted. In contrast, Counts, equally serious but lacking missionary zeal, always managed to incorporate lighter touches.

Perhaps sensing the same lack, Ordway Tead, then chair

of the New York Board of Higher Education, suggested that Childs had omitted those "over-beliefs," as William James had called them; that Childs had neglected those concerns that "lend poetry and meaning and graciousness to the human career." Consequently, Tead noted, some might find Childs "deficient in a total philosophy or outlook which would inject the necessary and rightful emotional warmth and evocative spiritual maturity into the educational process itself."[57] This is a justifiable criticism of Childs, whose zeal and sense of imminence led him to ignore the arts in his work and, in spite of a fine sense of literary style, to keep his eye focused perhaps too much on intelligence. Childs took the unusual step of writing a letter to the *Survey* to clarify the point raised by Tead.[58]

The reviewer for *America,* a Catholic weekly, also noted "the coolness and detachment of Dr. Childs' writing," although his concern was not so much with style but with content, as he decried Childs' secularist position, along with those of Horace Kallen, Brand Blanshard, and Sidney Hook.[59] In an extended article in the *Harvard Educational Review,* Peter A. Bertocci took issue with the chapter on religion and supernaturalism.[60]

As was his wont, Childs gave copies of the book to a number of friends and colleagues, and he received many flattering responses. His old teacher Arthur I. Gates, then current director of Childs' department at Teachers College, was enthusiastic and suggested that *Education and Morals* "may well be the book which provides the leadership during the second half century so obviously and seriously needed."[61] Robert King Hall, also a Teachers College colleague, wrote to Childs that he "was struck by the strong patterns of similarity between the content of this book and your offerings in Education 200Fa."[62] Ruth Streitz sensed this and thought the book an excellent one for graduate students particularly, for she found it "a book which must be studied deeply, discussed critically and evaluated continually in the light of additional experience."[63] George Axtelle was already using the book in classes that summer at New York University and noted that the students were enthusiastic about it. By the fall the book had been adopted by more than a dozen colleges. And a few years later, Childs received a request to have the work translated into Japanese, in fact, two Japanese scholars were trying to get the work done. The book appeared in 1958 with a new preface by Childs. There was some discussion, too, of translating the book into Korean.

At the time of publication of *Education and Morals*, Bode's illness took a turn for the worse, although he recovered from his stay in the hospital in early April. The doctors felt that he still might have a few years left; Hullfish wrote more cautiously, "He is apparently sliding down-hill but has a sufficient reserve and strong recuperative powers."[64] In spite of ill health, Bode was able to continue a fascinating and stimulating correspondence with Childs. As the friendship and admiration, as well as trust, developed, they elaborated on their respective differences—which were in fact more a problem of emphasis. There was also some accommodation. Childs wrote, "I believe that we also have a responsibility for the kind of intellectual and emotional dispositions that are developed as the process of inquiry is carried on. This does not mean that values are to be cultivated apart from inquiry, but it does mean that we who guide the process of inquiry should be clear about the kind of attitudes and loyalties that we want to see develop in and through inquiry."[65]

The gap closed slightly in Bode's response, which alludes again to one of his main themes—the cleavage in our culture— the cleavage between inherited dualistic traditions that reveal themselves most clearly in modern times in our relying on supernatural interventions while relying also on naturalistic, or scientific solutions.

Now that I am writing, I may add a few remarks on my own approach to this business of educational theory. Not that this approach has any inherent novelty or significance, but it may serve to explain why I have, as I suspect, sometimes given the impression that the thinking process, as Dewey expounds it, is the whole of education. I was through college before I began to sense, without understanding it, the cleavage in our culture. My home training was fundamentalist and this involved all kinds of collisions. The immediate purpose of education, as I see it now, is to prepare for membership in the social order. What I did not see was that our cultural patterns had both a supernatural and a naturalistic source. A liberal education requires that we see this conflict and decide which side we are on. But this is not for infants, who must be brought up, first of all, in those ways of living which give a measure of unity to our cultural patterns. We thus require truth telling, decent manners, respect for property, etc., etc., if we are to live together at all. But if we adhere to the Dewey philosophy, we try to make these standards grow out of *social* relationships and not out of an authoritarian scheme. The insight into the cleavage in our culture is cultivated as we come upon the inevitable conflicts and gradually sharpen the contrast between the underlying philosophies. Dewey's philosophy is distinctive, first, in that it makes the school an embodiment of democratic living, and secondly, that it provides for the progressive transformation of this democratic living through intellectual reconstruction. It does not try to provide a fixed pattern or content for democratic living, but trusts to progressive reconstruction.[66]

In 1951 Childs was awarded the Butler Silver Medal by Teachers College. The citation reads: "In recognition of his contributions to the philosophy of education, and particularly his studies of educational problems relating to spiritual values and public morality, culminating in the publication during 1950 of his important book, EDUCATION AND MORALS."[67] In congratulating Childs, Bode once again referred to the cleavage in the culture: "It is high time for us to cultivate the insight that the most basic problem in education is the moral problem—or to put it differently, the problem of heightening our awareness that our cultural patterns require loyalty to two different and incompatible systems of moral values."[68] On this point, Childs and Bode were in full agreement. Childs proposed that they should engage by correspondence in a detailed exploration of the points where they actually differed. Bode thought that these differences were not actual differences per se but variations in emphasis or modes of approach. And so Bode laid out a summary of his philosophy of education, at least some of the main points of confusion. They center, not surprisingly, around the cultural cleavage; that is, the cleavage between those who hold an antecedent commitment to those customs that make appeal to the nature of things, and those who appeal to consequences, to changes in social relationships. Bode believed that a "basic obligation of education is to focus on this cleavage in our culture." Insightfully, he added, "It is this confusion, not Russia, that will lick us eventually if we don't watch out."[69]

In his reply, Childs noted that the cleavage raises a basic moral problem: "Whether we agree to make an *empirical* approach to social and moral questions." With great precision, Childs then gets to the heart of the pragmatic dilemma—discussed twenty years earlier in his dissertation—and one of the main points of criticism from its opponents:

1. Does the wholehearted acceptance of pragmatic method involve metaphysical consequences? More specifically, is the full use of the experimental *method* necessarily associated with a naturalistic orientation? By naturalism is meant the rejection of theism, that is, the rejection of the belief that there are *purposeful* forces, other than human, concerned with the development and the conservation of values. By naturalism is also meant that morality is viewed as "not transcendental but social in its origin and validity", and that all sanctions and standards for conduct are to be derived from within the context of social relationships, and from no other source whatsoever.

2. If the consistent use of experimental method has these naturalistic presuppositions, can we, then, hold that its adoption in the work of the school does not also entail a *commitment* to the naturalistic position? In other words, is there a naturalistic metaphysic implicit [here?][70]

Bode somewhat sidestepped the issue in his response, "*Sharing* is the key to a rich, satisfactory life. When conflicts begin to emerge, the road to sharing is blocked. We can't share by whole-hearted identification with both sides to the dispute. This just breeds paralysis. But the situation provides a clue to the remedy. Society needs to be continuously reorganized in such a way as to facilitate sharing."[71]

In a ten-page response to Bode's letter, Childs cleverly summarized the issues that had arisen thus far. With regard to the metaphysical point already discussed, Childs continued:

In conclusion, a word about the metaphysical implications of the method of pragmatism in education. Your last letter helps a lot, and our positions now come very close together. If I understand you, a student can be thorough-going in his commitment to scientific and democratic method and at the same time hold to a theistic interpretation. In other words, the method, as method, determines the ways we arrive at beliefs, test and hold them, but it does not determine automatically the content of our beliefs. Those of us who are naturalists in metaphysics must hold our position open to review in light of further evidence and interpretation; those who are theists would likewise have to make their theism a finding, not a presupposition, of their experience, and also hold it subject to the results of further inquiry.[72]

In spite of his deteriorating health, Bode replied immediately and at some length.

Let us first take a look at this concept of "metaphysics." If I remember correctly, you used this concept quite a bit in your Ph.D thesis. I'd like to have you clarify this concept, since it seems to tie in with the subject in hand. As long as we rely exclusively on "scientific method", the term *metaphysics* is out of order. It refers to a kind of knowing which cannot be achieved by scientific method. How then is this done? If we hold to metaphysics, we must also supply an appropriate epistemology. Plato seems to have relied on immediate *Anschauung*. "A straight line is the shortest distance", etc. This was convincing to me until I learned—much later—that the straight line is probably not an indestructible feature of "reality" but a tool devised by mathematicians. Paul, Marx, Stalin—all have their own forms of Anschauung, independently of scientific method. I would have to deny that their insights are insights into the immutable structure of "reality." Nix on that. This kind of knowing thus becomes a form of bootlegging. So we should throw it out (I mean the term), unless we are prepared to state and defend this alleged form of knowing. The big issue in educational theory is whether scientific method is the only form of knowing; but this issue is hardly ever stated clearly.

. . . As to theism, I like to escape from the appearance of dogmatism! Theism is irrelevant unless we go back to some kind of metaphysics, which means some form of authoritarianism. If metaphysics is needed, then it must be included in our school program, which means goodbye to democracy. Our program should start with the recognition that our cultural heritage is a mess, and that a truly liberal education is one that liberates us from the tyranny of tradition. To see the conflicts in our tradition is a long step towards *freedom*. If I believe in democracy, this belief will indeed be reflected in the organization of my school, etc. But all this is already a part of our tradition, and nobody objects to this except insofar as this conflicts with other parts of this tradition.[73]

The issue is so central to any deep discussion of pragmatism that the continuation of this dialogue between two of its leading proponents makes important reading. Childs, therefore, responded to Bode a few days later.

I now turn to your second major point, namely, the bearing of a commitment to scientific attitude and method on metaphysical interpretations. It may be that the difference here is *verbal*, or it may relate to something of genuine importance. If the term "metaphysics" is taken to refer to the characteristics of a deeper order of reality which cannot be known through ordinary experience, but only through supernatural revelation or through some process of intuition or immediate mystical apprehension, then, the subject of metaphysics is necessarily beyond the interest and the reach of those who believe that all knowledge is gained through empirical, scientific procedures. If reference to this other world is what you mean by the term "metaphysics", then, I am in full accord with your proposition that "as long as we rely exclusively on 'scientific method', the term *metaphysics* is out of order."

But there is good ground for another interpretation of the meaning of the term "metaphysics." I find it difficult to accept the following passage on Dewey's view in your last letter: "The one great and let us hope redeeming meaning is that it avoids entangling alliances with metaphysics. This latter is the basic meaning of 'pragmatism' or 'Deweyism' as it seems to me." Dewey, for example, states in *Experience and Nature*, p. 51: "If we follow classical terminology, philosophy is love of wisdom, while metaphysics is cognizance of the generic traits of existence. In this sense of metaphysics, incompleteness and precariousness is a trait that must be given footing of the same rank as the finished and fixed." Or, again, on Page 47, he states: "As against this common identification of reality with what is sure, regular and finished, experience in unsophisticated forms gives evidence of a different world and points to a different metaphysics. We live in a world which is an impressive and irresistible mixture of sufficiencies,

tight completeness[es], order, recurrences which make possible pre-
diction and control, and singularities, ambiguities, uncertain possibilities, processes going on to consequences as yet indeterminate." Here
Dewey seems to make a real place for metaphysics. But I take it
neither of us wants to settle this point by an appeal to Dewey as a final
authority. We are more interested in the implications of experimental
science.

As Ratner indicates there is a basic difference between saying
that as pragmatists we can know nothing of a theory of nature or
existence in general, and asserting that we cannot have a general
theory of nature. Indeed, many pragmatists hold that a number of
metaphysical elements are involved in the resolve "to rely exclusively
on scientific method." If we are confident that our method is *the*
method to be used whenever we are concerned to get knowledge,
then our confidence in our method must rest on some view of the
nature of the world in which we live. In some respects it is all of one
order.

Sidney Hook in his doctoral study, written under Dewey, begins
his discussion with the following: "The title of this study (The Metaphysics of Pragmatism) has been selected with malice prepense. It
conjoins two terms whose connotations are generally regarded as
opposite in order to make more emphatic the belief that 'method' is
dogged by a pack of metaphysical consequences; that a 'pure' method
which does not make [involve] reference to a theory of existence is
as devoid of meaning as a proposition which does not imply other
propositions. . . . Unless [But unless] pragmatism is to experience
the same fate which has befallen the positivism of Comte and the
phenomenalism of Mach—philosophies proudly and avowedly anti-
metaphysical—it must analyze the implications of what it means to
have a method and examine the generic traits of existence which
make that method a fruitful one in revealing them."[74]

Yes! I want to follow the method of experimental inquiry and
no other method in all situations in which I am concerned to get
knowledge. But I want to use that method with my eyes open, not
closed. Does the use of this method mean in practice the acceptance
of a particular theory of existence? If so, I want to know as much as
I can about what that theory implies. Dewey and Hook seem to agree
that it implies that we live in a world which is characterized by process
(or processes), and that nature is an affair of affairs—a world in
which novelty, contingency and uncertainty are ultimate traits—and
a world in which situations are so determinate that we can deal
with them in their concrete singularity without taking the whole of

existence into account in any particular inquiry or experiment. Now if any such view of the world is bound in with our use of experimental method, and we are against "bootlegging" in education, we should take responsibility for the world-view that is the correlative of the method by which we secure knowledge and control. I am confident that you are with me in this full opposition to bootlegging of all kinds.

When I said in my last letter that I thought science and democracy had a grounding that was broader than the mere fact they were accepted in our own country, I did not mean to imply that this deeper grounding was to be found in some non-experiential sources. My point was the simple one that many peoples other than Americans have been led to the use of experimental science and to the effort to organize a democratic mode of living. It seems to me therefore that our emphasis on science and democracy has a right to take account of this wider experience, and not confine itself to the mores of the American people.[75]

Bode replied a week later.

Let me add a word or two about "metaphysics." I don't get the point here. Historically, as we know, metaphysics meant a distinct realm, which could be explored only by reliance on a distinctive method—mystical insight, or intellectual apprehension. Pragmatism means, first of all, that we reject this view, this "two-worldism". But what does it mean positively?

I get no help from the suggestion that it means a "general theory of nature". What is there in this that it needs to be designated by a term which invites all the errors of the past to return and make themselves at home with us? For example, we assume that if anything happens anywhere, it is theoretically possible to determine a set of causes. This is an assumption involved in all scientific research. So what? Are we therefore justified in labeling this kind of thing "metaphysics"? Or am I using the wrong kind of illustration here?

Perhaps I should study this business more extensively before making comments. But I have tried for many years to teach this unfounded "metaphysics" without arriving at anything but a sense of frustration. At present I am pretty well convinced that it is much more important to see that "scientific method" and metaphysical inquiry cannot be harmonized and that many of our troubles arise from the fact that we give lodging to both (e.g. "growth" and "metaphysics"). Perhaps I am all wet. I do not, however, gather from your quotes what is meant by metaphysics.—Must stop now, however, I think we stand a chance now to strike pay dirt. Let me hear from you when you are good and ready, though you are no invalid, as I seem to be. I feel more and more that "pragmatism" needs to be extended at such points as these, or the whole movement will be deflected by its enemies. Bear with me if I seem to ramble occasionally.[76]

At this point the exchange stopped as Childs became preoccupied with preparing his chapter for the twelfth yearbook of the John Dewey Society, which was edited by Bode's disciple H. Gordon Hullfish, who was urging him to get it completed.

This perceptive essay summarizes the situation in the postwar world, with the Soviet Union on one side and the United States on the other. Childs also looked at the ways in which America might adjust to the situation both intentionally and drastically. It is a luminous discussion that highlights the differences between Bode, and to a greater extent also Max Otto, and Childs, who reveals himself as extremely tough minded.

Otto believed that the method of democracy is the method of creative bargaining and listed its distinguishing characteristics:

1. "An honest attempt to appreciate the aims in conflict and their relation to the circumstances responsible for just those aims."
2. "The search for a new set of aims in which the conflicting ones may be absorbed."
3. "The invention of a workable program through which the new set of aims can come to fruition."

But such bargaining failed in America's dealings with the Soviets because it was not "buttressed by the development of other modes of power—military, industrial, and political."[77] And it was clearly, according to Childs, doomed to fail in the face of the intransigent opposing views in educational matters, not to mention political and economic ones. Indeed, he was convinced that "we shall have to move from conference and creative bargaining to determined political action and legislation."[78]

While Otto and Bode held that conflicts could be resolved by the extension of common interests and purposes, Childs went further when he wrote that "we misconstrue the meaning of democracy when we view it as an alternative and substitute for the social struggle. Democracy should rather be viewed as a movement to make the struggle between rival groups and conflicting interests more rational and less arbitrary."[79] Childs did not say who was to do this, but his answer would have been through the democratic processes society has developed, through democracy as a means, as both Otto and Bode suggested. However, democracy for Childs was also a controlling end, a moral value in and of itself. Or, as he said in this essay, the concept of democracy has "both ethical and political implications."[80]

Robert V. Bullough, Jr., in his sensitive book on Bode, recognized the importance of the early debate on democracy and indoctrination between Bode and Childs. He believed that it was in part colored by their geographic difference, between the smells of grass and overalls and the smells of the big city. On most aspects of the case there was agreement, but, as Bullough stated, "Bode could not countenance the specificity with which *The Social Frontier* group was willing to prescribe the end toward which social reconstruction should be directed."[81] Bullough's partly imaginary discussion between Bode, Childs, and Norman Woelfel, one of the original assistant editors of *The Social Frontier,* is essentially accurate. What Bullough did not know was that the debate had been taken up in somewhat different form after the war. However, he correctly identified Childs, together with Counts, as the leading voices of social reconstruction.

In the spring of 1952, Childs had a mild thrombosis which laid him low for a short while. By June he was able to report that he was making steady progress but that his doctor recommended a month of complete rest. Therefore, he did not teach summer school as had been advertised in the Teachers College catalog, although he did receive his salary of $1,667 as indicated in the budget. John Dewey died at the age of ninety-two on June 1, 1952. Childs wrote a letter of condolence to his wife, Alice; the loss of his intellectual mentor did not improve

Bode's own precarious health. "Dewey's death has hit Father," wrote Bode's daughter, Eleanor, "more than any of us would have expected. He hasn't been able to do work or writing since the news came."[82] Bode recovered slowly and wrote an article about Dewey for the October issue of *Progressive Education*.[83] It was clear that Bode's energies were being seriously sapped as the cancer took its inevitable course. "I have stretches when I am no good. . . . and there is no cure for old age."[84]

Childs himself recovered, but he took great care of himself for the rest of his life. He had long gone to bed at 11:00 P.M. and got up at 6:30 A.M. He tried also to get a fifteen-minute nap in the afternoons. Childs had little idea that Bode was as ill as he was. Bode, always generous to others, expressed concern about his friend, "Take care of yourself. We can't spare you." He went on to suggest to Childs that they work on a volume which would attempt to show how completely Dewey broke with philosophic tradition and how revolutionary that was. "The issue is simple of course—scientific method is a method which everyone uses on occasion or in certain areas or else it is the only final court of appeal. In the latter case it of course rules out every form of authoritarianism. It then becomes the basis for a distinctive set of standards—morality, esthetic values, truth, etc."[85] Childs was intrigued with the idea of writing such a volume, among whose proposed authors would be Hullfish and Counts. It might take roughly the form of the essays in honor of Max Otto which had been edited by Frederick Burkhardt and just released.[86] Dewey had contributed one essay; Bode had written the lead essay, "Cleavage in Our Culture," which was also the title of the book. Childs thought that Bode's understanding of Dewey's "psychology and logic, as well as of his conception of values" was most penetrating and hoped that this same essay could be included in their proposed volume.[87] Childs felt it to be "the time for a militant statement of the democratic-scientific position."[88] The volume was never written, but Childs pursued the idea in his 1956 book, *American Pragmatism and Education*, which contained a lengthy chapter about Bode. In the preface to the book, Childs stated a twofold purpose, both halves of which echo views he and Boyd H. Bode discussed at the beginning of the decade.

It seeks to set forth the view of the pragmatists about the deeper elements involved in this cleavage in our culture, along with their proposals for intellectual, moral, and educational reconstruction. It also seeks to define certain difficulties and ambiguities in the original philosophic and educational formulations of the pragmatists, indicating the kind of revisions that are required if these weaknesses are to be overcome. We are convinced that pragmatism negates its own basic principles whenever it takes the form of a completed, closed system, and that it will fail to enjoy the support that it deserves if it refuses to take account of demonstrated inadequacies in its own patterns of thought and education.[89]

As 1952 closed, Bode's illness was making it increasingly difficult for him to concentrate: his letters became shorter and less focused. Childs did not see it as he replied at length to Bode's last letter of December 15. Or, if he did see it, he chose not to make it apparent. It can hardly have come as a surprise to him, however, when, at the beginning of February 1953, Hullfish informed him of the seriousness of Bode's condition: "Indeed, I am amazed that you have had the correspondence you have enjoyed this past year. He has slipped far these past months and I do not believe he can last much longer."[90] Childs responded, "I thought that the opportunity for Dr. Bode to write informally about the things that have become the deepest part of his life was on the whole a good outlet during this period of confinement. I also realized that the time was approaching when it would have to end. I shall send him a personal note, for I have an affectionate regard for him and I want him to know how much his life, his books, and his letters have meant to me."[91] That is about as personal as Childs ever let himself get.

Boyd H. Bode died on March 29, 1953, at his home in Gainesville. Hullfish spoke the eulogy at his funeral. Childs wrote an article for the October issue of *Teachers College Record*. It is a fair summary of Bode's views, even of those that were at odds with Childs' own. At the end, Childs wrote, "Even when we have differed from Dr. Bode, we have learned much from the man and the values that he was ever concerned to keep alive and controlling in the work of education. . . . In him, intelligence and morality, science and democracy, found a superb embodiment."[92]

7.
Retirement

John Childs left Teachers College on July 1, 1954. He had reached the mandatory retirement age of sixty-five in January of that year. It had been a grand career spanning twenty-six years. He did not seem to resent retirement, as his close colleague Counts or as his old mentor Kilpatrick did. In fact, he soon received invitations from both the University of Buffalo and the University of Illinois to teach the following summer, but he turned them down to take time to complete his last book, *American Pragmatism and Education*, which was contracted to be in the hands of its publisher, Henry Holt, by September 1, 1955. Shortly thereafter, John and Grace Childs left their Long Island home in Manhasset and moved to Princeton, New Jersey. The choice of Princeton seems odd, but

Childs apparently had reason to hope that he would be asked to teach at the university.

American Pragmatism and Education was Childs' last full-length book, and few people were better able to lay down the main tenets of the philosophy as it bore on education and to deal with its subtleties as well as with its limitations and ambiguities than he was. It is virtually impossible to do the volume justice in a short summary, for it is packed with well-reasoned argument. Suffice it to say it is probably the clearest and best-written survey of American pragmatism and its implications for education.

At the beginning, Childs presented the principles of pragmatism:

[T]hought is intrinsically connected with action; theories and doctrines are working hypotheses and are to be tested by the consequences they produce in actual life-situations; moral ideals are empty and sterile and apart from attention to the means that are required to achieve them; reality is not a static, completed system, but a process of unending change and transformation; man is not a mere puppet of external forces, but through the use of intelligence can reshape the conditions that mold his own experience; ordinary people can develop from within the context of their own on-going activities, all necessary institutions, and regulative principles and standards.[1]

All systems of philosophy are culturally based and grow out of the ideas that preceded them. Childs thought that pragmatism was distinctively American; it should not be overlooked that it developed out of conditions that were common to most of the Western world—the growth of experimental science, the wide acceptance of the theory of evolution, the spread of democracy or the democratic temper, and the emergence of an industrial order, which challenges both economic individualism and the self-sufficient nation-state. For the remainder of the first part of the book, Childs elaborated on these four fundamentals, as they were discussed by C. S. Peirce, William James, George Herbert Mead, and, of course, John Dewey.

Of particular interest, in light of Childs' own moral philosophy, is the chapter on "Democracy and Pragmatism," for which he drew heavily from the work of Dewey. Childs explored Dewey's conception of the interrelation of the scientific method of thought and the democratic way of life, examined the adequacy of his empirical interpretation of the nature of the good and the morally right, and looked at the implications for the conduct of education that Dewey derived from the major meanings of democracy. He concluded that the right "is that which is in harmony with personal and social good" and which must be judged in terms of consequences.[2] "This principle of the evaluation of acts by their consequences in subsequent conduct and experience necessarily brings the whole range of human activity within the domain of the moral, because all these varied activities tend to modify those who participate in them."[3] Ethics are not derived from supernatural activity; Dewey rejected "ethics from above" in favor of "an ethics that is simply the development of the intelligence implicit in human experience."[4]

In the second half of the book, Childs moved to the work of Kilpatrick, Bode, and Counts—the three thinkers to whom he remained close until each died. He drew out the differences between them and proponents of mainstream pragmatism. Because of his association with all three, Childs brought substance and information that would be hard to recover now without his book. He then looked at that group of progressive educators (Raup, Axtelle, Kenneth Benne, and B. Othaniel Smith) who coauthored the book, *Improvement in Practical Intelligence.* They are, said Childs, "convinced that indeterminate or problematic situations are of two main types, and that the young should be specially prepared to deal with each of them."[5] First, there are the actual conditions, requiring the discovery, the analysis, and the descriptions of facts. Second, decisions must then be made about what should be done— what ought to be rather than what is. Childs, not surprisingly, thought this was a false dichotomy for "both democracy and science rest, in the last analysis, on certain moral foundations," although he thought the authors focused attention on an important problem that had too often been overlooked.[6]

After a bold discussion of pragmatism and religion, Childs

concluded the book by looking at pragmatism and the future of education. He reiterated his own deeply held view that "organized education is inescapably a *moral* undertaking."[7] He reviewed the chief contributions that pragmatism had made to education. First, that education is now looked at from the perspective of the children, their interests, abilities, and stage of development. Second, that habits and attitudes are formed through adjustment to surroundings and that the consequent reconstruction of experience occurs when children act upon the environment, which also acts on them. Third, that children learn not just the subject matter—however presented—but also a host of accompanying intellectual and emotional dispositions.

Childs did not shrink from examining some of the difficulties of pragmatic educational theory. He debunked the notion that the research function of the school (inquiry) is synonymous with its educational function; there are many aspects of the culture that, in spite of change, are functioning well and are not problematical in any vital sense. This led to the second difficulty: "the inquiries of the young for the most part relate to areas in which the teachers are already in possession of most of the meanings," they are not genuine research situations. Thus the teacher knows "the best means of communicating to the young that which is already known."[8] He then made a bold statement (not so far from the position of Counts relative to indoctrination): that the supreme test of an educational experience is not primarily what new knowledge has been uncovered but rather what changes have taken place in the habits, appreciations, meanings, and attitudes of the young. This might be surprising to those who see the problematic situation as the sole basis for learning. Childs' own actions as a teacher demonstrate the point perhaps more clearly. Following World War II, Childs believed the quality of students, even at Teachers College, had declined, and he took some rather drastic steps in his own classes. He introduced regular true-false tests, which have been described by at least two of his students as "horrible." In an exchange of letters many years later with Raymond E. Callahan, the issue was discussed at length. First, Callahan recalled the situation.

I think of you often and I use one of my experiences with you to make a point in my classes. The situation develops as students challenge the use of grades on exams or indeed the very idea of any *required* reading. They want *freedom* and they want to follow their own interests. I say O.K., fine, but let me tell you a story of my own experiences. I say that I am with them—that I am really a *Summerhill* man and that I did my graduate work at the great Mecca of progressive education, Teachers College, Columbia.

It happened (I tell them) that I was taking a graduate course in philosophy from one of the great leaders in progressive education, John L. Childs. We were reading C. S. Peirce, William James, and John Dewey among others—not very light reading. Dr. Childs would give a heavy reading assignment and then, in order to assure that we had done the reading, he would open each class by giving us a short true and false test. I tolerated this for about six weeks and then one day after I had done rather badly on one of the tests, I went storming into his office to inform him that I was dropping his course. Why, he asked? I replied that I had come to the Mecca of progressive education only to find my study of Dewey being handled in a most traditional way. He thought awhile and then asked me three questions:

1. Was I doing the reading? Answer, of course, because of the damned tests.
2. Would I have been doing the reading and reading as carefully if it were not for the tests? I had to answer in all honesty no—I had been reading Dewey line by line.
3. (The final question.) Are you learning anything worthwhile? I had to admit that I had, that Dewey especially had opened new worlds for me.

The moral of the story (I tell them) is that external pressure to learn is O.K. if what is being learned is worthwhile![9]

A few days later, Childs responded to Callahan's letter.

As you will know, I have long believed that guidance is ineradicable from the enterprise of deliberate education. The problem therefore is not one of guidance versus no guidance—it is rather one of becoming responsible about the way in which we do actually guide the activities of others. Teachers can be responsible only when they know what they are about when they are about the education of its young.

Dewey had a penetrating insight when he observed that *acquiring* comes best when it is a function of *inquiring*. Many of his followers, however, fail to recognize, as Dewey clearly did, that authentic and fruitful inquiry, may be initiated and directed by those with special knowledge and competence in a given field. This is, indeed, the basic presupposition of all organized education.

Take my course, *American Pragmatism and Education*. I was confident that Peirce, James, Dewey and Mead had pioneered in their situational interpretation of the nature of thinking as well as in their emphasis on the intrinsic relation of meaning and action. The problem of the course was to get graduate students to probe into these seminal meanings on their own. My true-false tests were means for *directing study* fully as much as they were means for *checking* on the kind of reading that was being done. I also learned much from the response of students in the class discussions.[10]

Childs wrote three major books, and all have now been reviewed. It is clear that he was an interpreter of pragmatism and its educational implications and that he did not "invent" anything totally new, as did Dewey, or even as other associates, such as Kilpatrick and Counts. But that is not to say he was merely a disciple; he was, in its best sense, a critic. Childs himself said that "the function of educational criticism and discussion is to examine and to appraise; it is not irresponsible fault-finding. Criticism seeks to distinguish the warranted from the unwarranted, the desirable from the undesirable, and the viable from the dead and obsolete. *Hence criticism can confirm as well as disconfirm.*"[11] In *Art as Experience*, Dewey pointed to the role of the critic in art, who has the twin tasks of analysis and synthesis. The critic for Dewey was neither friendly nor unfriendly. The role is to reveal what is there (to analyze it) and then to put it together or to reformulate it in a novel or at least in a revelatory way (to synthesize it). Looking at it from this very Deweyan perspective, it is clear that Childs performed the critical role extremely well and nowhere better than in *American Pragmatism and Education*. He traced the history of pragmatism, confronted its ambiguities, broke down its parts, identified its problems, answered its critics, then put it back together. His synthesis was formed by tracing the moral nature of a pragmatic education. This is found in *Education and Morals*, but it is perhaps most sensitively put in this last book, where the moral aspect is not so much the leitmotiv but

the ground bass. For that he earns a place in the roll of important philosophers of education.

   American Pragmatism and Education was out by the end
of March 1956 but was not widely reviewed in journals or
newspapers. H. Gordon Hullfish did an extensive report on
the book for the *Teachers College Record,* in which he summarized the main points made by Childs. He noted two important
achievements of the book: "The uncritical educational practitioner should be brought to realize the commitments of his
actions; and those critics of pragmatic educational proposals
who blandly announce that here is an educational philosophy
devoid of directing ideals should find a pathway to graciousness smoothed for them."[12] Irving Robbins of Queens College
wrote to Childs, "You have done a masterful job of integrating
the diffuse writings of so many giants and presented a clear
picture of a point of view that is mistakenly being discussed
by small people hoping to become king by rejecting giants."[13]
President Hollis L. Caswell of Teachers College was high in
his praise of the book, while Raymond Callahan called it "a
tremendous contribution not only to educational thought but
also to American intellectual history."[14] Callahan actually used
the book in a seminar he had conducted that summer at the
University of Cologne. In fact, by the fall of 1956 it had been
adopted in college courses at thirteen institutions. Nathaniel
Champlin at Wayne State University decided to structure a
graduate seminar around it.

   B. Othaniel Smith and George Axtelle, coauthors of the
book about which Childs had made some critical comments,
both wrote letters to Childs. Smith called the book a "definitive
analysis of American pragmatism," while Axtelle commented,
"It is amazing how clearly you have developed what is com-
monly found as 'difficult' ideas." Axtelle agreed with some of
the criticisms Childs had made of him and of his coworkers
and ended by saying, "I think we were mistaken to belittle the
role of compromise, and should have emphasized its practical
necessity."[15]

   The work on the book finished, Childs accepted an invitation to teach at Madison. While he was there he visited Max
Otto to whom he gave a copy of the book. Several months

later, Otto wrote a lengthy letter to Childs commenting on the book in glowing terms. "If there is a better over-all presentation of the educational philosophy of pragmatism it hasn't come my way. . . . It's comprehensive, informed, generous-spirited, straightforward, penetrating in its analysis, and honest—*positively* honest, taking care to have a reason for saying what you do. I cannot but think that *American Pragmatism and Education* will be read for a long time for its illumination and candor." Otto also felt that Childs had discussed Dewey, warts and all. "That's exactly what's called for, a pointing out and supporting certain shortcomings by someone who *appreciates* Dewey fully for the great philosopher he was, but who cannot write from the assumption that genuine appreciation is blind appreciation."[16]

Childs sent Kilpatrick a copy of the book, receiving in exchange a cordial note: "I am inclined to say that it is the best discussion of John Dewey's educational ideas that I have ever read."[17] This was high praise indeed. It was this book, the culmination of Childs' work in clarifying and illuminating pragmatic thought in its educational context, that occasioned the honor of the William Heard Kilpatrick Award for Distinguished Service in Philosophy of Education.

Childs' relations with Kilpatrick had remained warm throughout and beyond their joint years at Teachers College, even though they still addressed each other respectfully as "Professor Kilpatrick" and "Dr. Childs." It had been Kilpatrick himself who had telephoned Childs to offer him an assistant professorship at Teachers College, and it was also Kilpatrick who wrote to Childs informing him that he had been awarded, by unanimous recommendation of the committee, the 1956 Kilpatrick Award. It is perhaps some indication of the importance of this award that it had not been given to anyone since Boyd Bode received it in 1947. The award occasioned many letters from friends, colleagues, and former students. Childs, who had not been well earlier in 1956, was extremely pleased and proud to have been selected for this distinction. He wrote to Kilpatrick, "I have been deeply moved by this action on the part of the Committee of which you are Chairman. Indeed, you have been a party to a number of the

high moments in my life experience. . . . I am of course much
honored to have an award that bears your name for it is a
name that stands for the best in American education and it
has long been identified with the most progressive tendencies
in philosophy of education." Then in an unusual burst of self-
disclosure he added, "To have this recognition from you and
other colleagues in the field I so dearly love is one of the most
meaningful things that could have happened."[18]

The award was presented to Childs on November 9 in
the Horace Mann Auditorium. Hollis L. Caswell, William F.
Russell's successor as president of Teachers College, presided,
and R. Bruce Raup and George Axtelle made remarks. Following the presentation Childs delivered his address, "The Future
of Our Common School," which was reprinted in substantially
altered form in the *Educational Forum* the following January.

Childs' tribute to Kilpatrick was not elaborate, but it was
sincere and reveals a little of his thoughts both about his old
teacher and about Teachers College, from which he had so
recently retired.

Personally, I have learned many things from Dr. Kilpatrick.
Tonight, I have time to mention only one of them. It was through his
suggestion and encouragement that I developed the conviction that a
philosophy of life and of education does not have to be a formal,
second-hand thing, taken either on authority or on faith. On the
contrary, as a consequence of our ordinary encounters with the world
of persons and things, all of us have embedded in our own experience
the primary materials from which philosophies have always been
developed. Dr. Kilpatrick has emphasized that as human beings, and
particularly as teachers, we have the responsibility to make the data
provided by these everyday experiences both the source and the
criterion of that which we shall regard as reasonable, worthful, and
desirable in human thought and conduct. It is indeed a pleasure to
receive this Award from a Committee of which Dr. Kilpatrick is the
Chairman.

I am gratified, in the second place, that this Award meeting is
sponsored by Teachers College. I served for twenty-six years—from
1928 to 1954—as a member of its staff in Foundations of Education.
Those were eager, challenging years, and I am honored to have been
associated with the effort of this institution to strengthen the cause

of liberal education in our own country and throughout the world. During that quarter of a century of depression, World War, and postwar adjustments, I often wished that I were better qualified to meet the responsibilities and the opportunities of my post, but I never had any doubt about the endeavor of our College to make a searching scientific and moral analysis of the ends and the means of democratic education. Teachers College has its problems, but I know of no other institution of higher education which has better understood the imperatives and the possibilities of our age, or which has done more during this transitional period to help our country preserve its democratic heritage.

Students and faculty members come and go, but colleges and universities span the generations. They have a double function: to preserve, on the one hand, the best that man has achieved in science, art, religion, and human relationships, and, on the other, to enrich the realm of meaning and to extend the powers of human control. I am confident that Teachers College will continue to lead in this dual role of conservation through transmission, and of discovery through research and invention.

I am happy, in the third place, that this Award is associated with the cause of public education. Although Teachers College is, in the main, private in its pattern of support and control, it has always found its supreme purpose in the strengthening of the program of the common school. It regards the common school as one of the finest products of our democracy, and it also regards it as one of the foundational agencies for the preservation of that democracy.[19]

A few days following the presentation of the Kilpatrick Award, Kilpatrick himself was honored by the League for Industrial Democracy (LID) on his eighty-fifth birthday. Childs remained in New York and was among those taking part in the celebration. Counts presented the award to Kilpatrick. The March 1957 issue of *Progressive Education,* edited by George Axtelle, was devoted to Kilpatrick and his work; it included a short piece by Childs. Kilpatrick wrote Childs that he did "not see how it could have been possible to write a more appropriate opening article."[20] Childs had also been present five years earlier at Kilpatrick's eightieth birthday celebrations, which were also sponsored by the LID and held at New York's Commodore Hotel on November 17, 1951. The tributes of that evening, and Kilpatrick's own address, were published in the February 1952 issue of the *Teachers College Record*. Childs wrote the lead essay in the issue.

Dr. Kilpatrick has lived the philosophy which he has taught. . . . He early perceived that a child is a person, and that in the ethic of democracy a person is a being who is to be treated as an end and never merely as a means. Accepting this basic moral principle, he has worked to create a school which would have no good other than the growth of actual children, and which would view all else as a means for the promotion of this growth. He recognized that fundamental to all of the various kinds of human growth is growth of mind, and by growth of mind he has meant growth in capacity for reflective thought.[21]

One of the more intriguing results of this period was a project that produced five recordings devoted to panel discussions of Kilpatrick's educational philosophy. They were known as the "Kilpatrick records." Several of Kilpatrick's colleagues participated in this project, and the fifth record featured Kilpatrick discussing "Civilization and the Good Life" with a group of children. Childs, Kilpatrick, Axtelle, and Eduard Lindeman were featured on the second record, for which the topic was also "Civilization and the Good Life." Childs and Kilpatrick, also with John Dewey, were to have been the discussants on a sixth record, "What's on My Mind." It was noted that the trio would discuss certain aspects of Kilpatrick's life's work and thought.[22] However, this sixth record was never made.

Childs, when he was seventy-five, was able to pay yet another tribute to his former teacher and mentor when Kilpatrick's ninety-first birthday was celebrated at Teachers College. The printed program contained a short essay by Childs entitled "A Recollection." Childs was unable to attend. When he later sent the piece off as a contribution to a proposed *Festschrift,* which does not seem to have been published, he changed the title to "An Interpretation."

Retirement brought several honors to Childs in addition to the Kilpatrick Award. In March 1955, both he and Counts were presented with the John Dewey Award by the New York

Teachers Guild. It was a most appropriate coupling. In 1959 Childs was elected to the Laureate Chapter of Kappa Delta Pi. That same year he was presented with the LID's Citation for Distinguished Service to Democracy. Childs felt he could not travel from Urbana, where he was teaching at the time, to New York to receive the award, which commemorated the one hundredth anniversary of Dewey's birth, but it pleased him that it was presented to him in absentia by Kilpatrick. In his official response to the award, Childs wrote, "Three of my deepest life interests—organized labor, organized political action, and organized public education—are comprehended in the program of the L.I.D." He also noted that Dewey "rejoiced in the steadfast way that the L.I.D. championed democracy both as social and political *end*, and as social and political *means*."[23] In 1962 the LID elected him to membership in its National Council. In 1957 Wayne State University gave him an award for leadership in public education, and in 1971 he received the Education Day Award also from Wayne State. His former student Frederick C. Neff taught at Wayne and not only used Childs' books in class but encouraged his own students to contact Childs personally. In commenting on *American Pragmatism and Education,* Neff thought that it was the "single most cogent book on the subject" and that, even in 1971, "it is now more timely than ever."[24] In 1965 Childs was honored with the the John Dewey Society Award "In Recognition of Distinguished Lifetime Service to Education in the Spirit of John Dewey." The American Humanist Association presented him with the John Dewey Humanist Award in 1978; but he was not up to making the journey to Florida to receive this honor.

Upon completion of *American Pragmatism and Education,* Childs felt free to accept some of the invitations that he had received to become a visiting professor. His first assignment was for summer teaching at the University of Wisconsin in 1956. He spent the entire 1957–58 academic year at the University of Michigan. During his time there he delivered a lecture entitled "An Evaluation of Dewey's Theory of Education." He also suggested that the university pay tribute to its great former faculty member with a centennial celebration.

The financial situation at Michigan in the late 1950s was not good, and the decision was made to keep any Dewey centennial plans modest, and arrangements were made to have Childs return to Ann Arbor to deliver, under the auspices of the Department of Social Foundations, a celebratory address. This he did on October 5, 1959, under the title "Enduring Elements in the Educational Thought of John Dewey."

Claude Eggertsen was particularly pleased to have had Childs spend the year at Ann Arbor and made some plans to have him return in the fall of 1960 to help in the formulation of policies in relation to the international commitments of the School of Education, a topic always of great interest to Eggertsen. As it turned out, Childs was far from well, and at the last minute the doctor advised him to cancel the trip. However, by March he was better and returned to Michigan, where he delivered an address entitled "Education as a University Discipline."

During these early retirement years, Childs spoke at a number of institutions and for a number of occasions. Many of these pertained to interpretations of the work of Dewey in particular or of phases of pragmatism. These included the Scarsdale [New York] Adult School ("Whither America"); the Metropolitan Museum of Art ("Challenge of Science to Education"); Goucher College, Towson, Maryland (where he shared the platform with Brand Blanshard); the New York Teachers Guild (where he spoke on the occasion of the presentation of its first John Dewey Award to Senator Herbert N. Lehman, whom the Liberal party under Childs' chairmanship had supported for the U.S. Senate, and where, a few months later, he himself was also a recipient of the award); New York University ("Education and Politics in a Democracy" and later in 1959, at the Dewey centennial); State University of New York (SUNY) Oswego ("Education in a Multi-Religion Society"); Ohio State University (where he gave the Bode lecture); Wayne State University ("Education and the Ethics of Democracy"); Rutgers University (again for the Dewey centennial); Boston University ("Genesis of an Educational Point of View"); SUNY Albany (for a curriculum workshop); University of Florida ("Experimentalist Theory of Education");

Michigan State University ("American School and the Disadvantaged"). This last lecture was one of Childs' final public addresses. It is in many ways a succinct summary of his educational viewpoint at the end of his career and is worth reproducing in its entirety, particularly as it, till now, has remained unpublished.

The American School and the Disadvantaged

I have been asked to sketch in this paper my view of "the problem of the disadvantaged and education in America." Two terms—"education" and "the disadvantaged"—are fundamental in this assignment. I begin, therefore, with a brief consideration of these terms.

Education, as I conceive it, has two main dimensions. In its primary form, it begins whenever a child commences to develop *expectations*. These expectations do not unfold from within as the child matures; they are generated by environmental transactions in which the child relates what he does with what he undergoes. Thus education is transactional in nature, and both environmental conditions and the living creature are involved in it. It follows that habits, skills, techniques, sentiments, meanings and attitudes are literally functions of environmental affairs—physical and social—as well as of the human being who lives in and by means of them. Breathing, for example, is a function of both air and lungs, in like manner the skills required to ride a bicycle are properties of both the bicycle and the biological organism. What holds for physical skills also holds for intellectual abilities—we have the meaning of a thing, or situation, when we grasp its potentialities, that is, when we know what to expect of it, the various ways in which it can be used, and have acquired the art of responding effectually to it. Intelligence develops as this kind of distinctive functioning develops in which directly experienced things are taken as *signs* of absent and future things. As Charles Peirce observed, "all thought is of signs". The signifying value of things is strengthened and liberated as symbols which stand for the actual characteristics and potentialities of existential things are developed and utilized.

Education, however, has another significant dimension: we learn not only through direct involvement in the world of persons and things, but also from what we are told, what we read, and what we attain through deliberate study of the activities and achievements of others. The school necessarily has to do with both of these forms of learning. This means that a good school deliberately plans its own program in terms of the experiences that its pupils are having at home, in their neighborhood groups, and in the established ways of the larger community to which they belong.

One of the never-ending problems of deliberate, organized education is to provide for the most effectual blend of these two types of learning. The program of the school easily degenerates into a routine process of verbalization and memorization whenever its emphasis on book-learning excludes significant opportunity for learning through that direct process of doing and undergoing which many designate as "primary experience". On the other hand, as the record shows, an "activity" or "experience" curriculum may become so dominated by the immediate interests of the child that it fails to mature him adequately in those developed systems of meanings—historical, scientific, institutional, and philosophic—which are the marks of a mature and resourceful mind. From what we now know of individual differences—both native and acquired—it is probable that one important way in which the school can serve all its pupils, including those that are considered disadvantaged, is to provide a blend of these two modes of learning that is sufficiently comprehensive and diversified to take actual account of the individuality of each of its pupils. Learning in a school requires grading and grouping, but neither age factors, nor I.Q. scores, should be permitted to over-ride what actual achievement record each pupil discloses about his interests and learning potentialities. One of the leaders of the Intelligence Testing movement has stated in a recent article that all "attempts to create 'culture-fair' or 'culture-free' tests have failed." He adds: "I do not believe it is possible to find support for the pure genetic I.Q. concept in any text book written in the past thirty years." The life children lead in city slums and deprived rural areas conditions the I.Q. scores they get on standardized intelligence tests.

I turn now to consider the second major term included in this assignment, namely, "the disadvantaged." From the standpoint of any program of education that makes the welfare and the growth of the child its supreme objective, the concept of "the disadvantaged" is both important and complex. Although the founders of the American public school movement did not employ the term "disadvantaged" in their educational discussions, the essential meaning of the concept pervaded their educational thought. They believed that the American way of life, grounded in the principle that government is an agency of the people and should rest on "the consent of the governed," required a new kind of school system devoted to the ideal of equality of educational opportunity. Hence the educational pioneers of the young Republic boldly abandoned the dualistic European system of education—a system with one set of schools designed to provide a limited kind of education for the children of the "masses," and another segregated set of schools planned to provide an education of quality for the children of the aristocratic ruling class. They emphasized the central feature of the American school by calling it "a common school". It had three main purposes: (1) education to meet the needs of everyday living, (2) education for literacy and social competency, and (3) education for citizenship in a nation in which ultimate authority is lodged with the people. Dr. Lawrence Cremin whose doctoral study was on the development of *The American Common School* has given the following summary of Horace Mann's conception of the nature of this school:

"Mann's school would be common, not as a school for the common people—for example, the 19th Century Prussian Volkschule [nineteenth-century Prussian *Volksschule*]—but rather as a school common to all people. It would be open to all, provided by the state and the local community as part of the birthright of every child. It would be for rich and poor alike, not only free but as good as any private institution. It would be nonsectarian, receiving children of all creeds, classes, and backgrounds. In the warm associations of childhood Mann saw the opportunity to kindle a spirit of amity and respect which the conflicts of adult life could never destroy. In social harmony he located the primary goal of popular education."[25]

It was the existence of this common school system that gave me an opportunity for education, and which bred in me a sense of the meaning of community. Both the elementary and the secondary school branches of my home town, Eau Claire, Wisconsin, enrolled children from all parts of the city and the surrounding country side, and they came to this public school system irrespective of the occupations, the religious institutions, or the wealth and the social and nationality backgrounds of their parents. Through these early school experiences we developed the understandings and appreciations that disposed us to believe that the things we had in common were foundational. Our school system had certain courses that were required of all, but it also had its fields of specialization, and the doors of the University of Wisconsin were open to those who satisfactorily completed these various specialized programs. Neither the common school system of Eau Claire, nor the University of the State of Wisconsin, believed that there was any intrinsic opposition between cultural and vocational interests, or between the world of thought and the world of the practical arts. I also learned of the value of the common school during my thirty years as a member of the faculty of Columbia University. During this period I had opportunity to participate in New York labor, social, educational, and political action groups. Often the able and devoted leaders of these progressive movements were immigrants, and the children of immigrants, who had become devoted to the democratic patterns of social and political life through what they had derived from public school and college systems of the City of New York.

It must be admitted, however, that the common school pattern never became the universal pattern of American education. For generations in the South, and in certain other localities, we pretended that parallel racially segregated school systems were compatible with the democratic system of equality of opportunity. Even, today, some denounce the Supreme Court declaration that schools that are compelled to be separate for racial reasons cannot provide genuine equality of educational opportunity.

All along we also have accepted private schools for the children of the wealthy assuming that the existence of these private institutions did not seriously hinder the cultivation of "the social harmony" that Horace Mann regarded as the supreme goal of American education. Today, we realize the seriousness of this conflict. For the flight to the suburbs by the members of the upper classes has demonstrated that public schools can become in spirit private schools when they are dominated by privileged economic groups. Nor can we say that the residual slum parts of our urban centers provide the conditions that make possible authentic common schools, equipped to give an education of quality to all their pupils.

Committed to the principle of religious liberty, we have also permitted religious organizations to operate segregated church-related schools. Today, the burden of maintaining these separate religious educational establishments has become so great that their supporters are demanding with growing militancy that justice requires that public funds be allocated to them in view of the educational services they provide for large numbers of our children. Far-reaching decisions will soon have to be made about this phase of our national educational program.

In sum, the struggle to establish the common school system still continues. New interpretations of the nature of this school system, and new ways of providing for its vitality must be developed. To resolve these problems will require more than resolute action by teacher organizations working independently—once again the American public will have to define what education, devoted to equality of opportunity, and opposed to the perpetuation of groups of disadvantaged children, means under the transformed conditions of life in which we now are involved.[26]

By the time of that speech, as Childs was moving into his late seventies, his engagements tapered off; he was being very selective. He had turned down one engagement that others would eagerly have accepted. In a letter to Eggertsen he expressed his views clearly.

I share your lack of enthusiasm about the two presidential candidates. From what I hear our attitudes are those of many others. I was asked to sit on the dais the evening that Kennedy accepted the nomination of the New York State Liberal Party, but I did not accept. On the other hand, Grace and I are both quite clear that we shall not vote for Nixon. Kennedy has gone far to make his own position clear in words on the state-church question. The problem, however, is more than one of *individuals,* and it is also more than one of *words.* I am quite sure that the "Church" will bring its influence to bear on public officials whenever its policies are involved. Nor do I want our world position integrated with that of the Vatican. I think much is at stake in our country making its own distinctive approach to the fateful world problem.[27]

Another visiting appointment was undertaken by Childs for the spring term of 1959 at the University of Illinois. His extensive class notes are extant and it is clear that he continued to challenge his students. A more lengthy association with the state of Illinois was, however, in the offing.

Towards the end of the 1950s, Delyte W. Morris, the aggressive president of Southern Illinois University, Carbondale (SIU), still only emerging from being little more than a state teachers' college, introduced the idea of elevating the reputation of the institution by hiring, at reasonable salaries, distinguished faculty recently retired from more prestigious schools. Luminaries such as Katherine Dunham the dancer, Marjorie Lawrence the opera singer, Henry Nelson Wieman the philosopher, and R. Buckminster Fuller, architect and general guru, were among the group. The imaginative chair of the Department of Educational Administration and Supervision, Arthur E. Lean, with the blessing of the then-current dean, Douglas E. Lawson, seized the opportunity. The result was that the College of Education managed to attract a cluster of educational stars, including Childs, Counts, Axtelle, Harold Benjamin, Leonard Koos, and Nelson Bossing. Lean had received his doctorate from the University of Michigan and had written his dissertation under Claude Eggertsen. To mark the centennial of John Dewey's birth, Lean organized a yearlong series of lectures. The speakers selected were Benjamin, Axtelle, Wieman, William Brickman, George Geiger, and Childs, who happened to be teaching at the University of Illinois for the spring term. When Lean issued the invitation to Childs, he also inquired whether Childs would be interested in a temporary appointment as Distinguished Visiting Professor at SIU. Childs was interested and took up the matter with Lean when he traveled to Carbondale at the end of April 1959. The lecture was subsequently published, along with the others, in Lean's and Lawson's *John Dewey and the World View*. Childs' essay was titled, "The Civilizational Functions of Philosophy and Education," and it opened the volume. In it Childs defended Dewey against the charge that his empirical philosophy lacked any basis for moral guidance and recalled Dewey's faith "in the competency of ordinary human experience to develop from within its own movement both its governing methods and its guiding ideals."[28] To assign meaning, truth, and value to some transcendental realm, as generally done, is inevitably dualistic and has led to the serious cleavage in our culture, which is half empirical and half authoritarian. Childs recapitulated five basic tenets of Dewey's thought: (1) change is the pervasive aspect of existence; (2) reflective thought originates in a doubtful, problematic situation; (3) problematic situations have both intellectual *and* moral aspects; (4) a democratic society is a dynamic society; (5) the supreme human loyalty is to a shared process of discovery and reconstruction.

Having laid his groundwork, Childs turned specifically to Dewey's theory of education, for "the educational task, the philosophic task, and the social and political task are intimately interrelated."[29] Thus it follows that parents and teachers can only be intelligent about education as they are intelligent about the society that education serves. The connection becomes increasingly important as our society rapidly becomes a world society. This supports the contention that educators must make choices, for education does not spontaneously define itself. However, educators cannot rely solely on themselves, they must share the task with scholars in other fields that bear on human activity; cooperation between layperson and professional is essential. Nevertheless, teachers themselves must develop "understanding of the traditions, the institutions, the values, the trends, the problems, and the potentialities of their civilization."[30] It can perhaps be seen from this essay, as well as any other, the ease with which he could summarize and communicate without distortion Dewey's work to others, and it reinforces Kilpatrick's comment that he made following the University of Michigan lectures that Childs' was indeed "the best discussion of John Dewey's educational ideas that I have ever read."[31]

Following Childs' return to Urbana to complete the semester at the University of Illinois, where he had also been offered a temporary position, Lean made Childs the specific offer to move to SIU for the winter quarter of the following year (January to mid-March 1961), at a monthly salary of thirteen hundred dollars. The teaching schedule was to be fairly flexible, although Lean had proposed one section of the undergraduate course in philosophy of education and an advanced graduate seminar in the same area. On June 26, after consulting with his physician in Princeton, Childs accepted under the stated terms, adding that he proposed the graduate seminar be titled "The Educational Thought of John Dewey." George Axtelle and his wife, Margaret, had arrived in Carbondale for the fall quarter of 1960, and when they vacated the university apartment to move into their own home, John and Grace Childs moved into it in January.

Childs returned to Princeton following the term at SIU, and Lean moved from the departmental chair to become dean of the college. He immediately invited Childs back for the fall or winter quarter. Because of the press of work, Childs did not return until the spring of 1962. Through the offices of a former student, Morris (Mark) Berger, Childs was invited for the summer session at SUNY Albany. He taught two master's-level courses in the philosophy of education. On their return to Princeton in mid-August, the Childs put their home up for sale and made plans to move more or less permanently to Carbondale, where he was to be attached to the Department of Philosophy. He continued to teach the undergraduate section of philosophy of education but also assisted in a general studies philosophy course, as well as teaching a graduate course in ethics.

Childs moved back to the College of Education after one year in Philosophy Department and eventually resigned in 1965. There was talk that he should return for the winter quarter 1967 to assist with teaching the doctoral seminar in cultural foundations while Arthur Lean was on sabbatical leave, but Childs seemed genuinely relieved that the plan did not materialize, as he wanted to continue a writing project that he had under way—the proposed book on Dewey, which never materialized.

Of particular pleasure during his Carbondale years were his renewed associations with Counts, Axtelle, and Wieman. Childs and the latter two were enthusiastic members of the Unitarian Fellowship while they were in Carbondale. During the 1960s this was a place of stimulating intellectual debate. The Fellowship provided Childs the opportunity to engage in discussion on religion, although he always came back to the essential pragmatic connection to the human enterprise. "I propose two such overall commitments that seem to me to be empirically grounded and confirmed. One of these pertains to the realm of belief and knowledge, namely, commitment to the self-correcting and creative pattern of experimental inquiry; the other pertains to the realm of value, namely, commitment to the self-governing and self-reconstructing pattern of social and political life which we call democracy."[32]

After retiring from SIU, Childs accepted one last teaching assignment. The 1965 summer session was spent, appropriately, at the University of Wisconsin. The course he taught, also appropriately, was entitled "Education in the Philosophy of Experimentalist Outlook." The detailed syllabus is twenty-nine pages long and begins with an examination of Peirce's functional view of thinking and ends with the experimentalist conception of educational method. The required readings included Childs' own books, *Education and Morals* and *American Pragmatism and Education,* as well as Counts' *Education and American Civilization,* Dewey's *Democracy and Education,* Bode's *How We Learn,* James Bryant Conant's *Education of American Teachers,* and Robert M. Hutchins' *Higher Learning in America.* Suggested readings ranged a little farther but also included books by Sidney Hook and Kilpatrick. In addition to the syllabus, Childs' own lecture notes are extant, and show that, while he had a plan, he departed from it when change was called for, although he kept within the context of the course. For example, when he decided to move from Topic II directly to Topic IV of the syllabus, he noted, "in a changing, novelty developing, uncertain and precarious world that will depend upon events."[33] In this instance, the loss of class time had been occasioned by a discussion on Roman Catholic views on birth control. Childs laid down the facts of the matter as he saw them but did so in an objective manner.

I. Read Dewey's statement of the nature of the situation in order to show certain similarities in his thought and that of Freud.
II. Features of birth control problems as encountered by Roman Catholic Church.
   1. Received and operating beliefs, standards, and theological declarations about sexual family life:
      Sexual intercourse for married people is a normal and desirable experience, generally attended by deep personal satisfactions—both physical and psychological. Its basic purpose, however, is procreation, and thus intercourse should never take place unless those involved are prepared to welcome and care for children who may result from it. Hence all use of artificial contraceptives is immoral—contrary to both natural and divine law.
   2. Disturbing, challenging and rebellious factors.

a) The invention of simple and effectual contraceptives now used by many, including some who are Roman Catholics.

b) Marked decline in the mortality rate due to modern science, sanitation, imposed diets and the like.

c) The recent rapid increase in population in most parts of the world. Eisenhower asserts "this is possibly the most critical problem facing mankind today."

d) The organization of many groups—religious and secular—who approve of planned parenthood by use of contraceptives.

e) The increasing gap between the biological age for marriage and the present-day sociological age.

3. Preliminary response.

a) Discussion of problem by the Pope and other Church Leaders.

b) The appointment of Commission—lay and clerical—to study and make recommendations.

III. What, if any, continuity is there between the Christian ethic and the democratic ethic.

III.a. Is this an experimental procedure? If so, why? If not, why not?

1. What are the crucial features of experimental procedure.

IV. The correlated educational issue:

1. Shall we honor, proclaim and transmit the truth to the young and discipline them in it?

2. Shall we search for the truth, seek to *extend* it, and evaluate received beliefs we prepose [propose] to transmit them to the young.

V. According to the pattern of experimental inquiry where is authority located?

1. In the received beliefs and standards; in the facts and consequences of acting on existing beliefs; or in the procedures by which we modify all standards and beliefs in light of changing conditions and experienced consequences.

VI. The nature of responsibility.

1. According to the law, infants, the insane, and the sub-normal all have something in common; they cannot prefigure the consequences of their acts, hence they are not regarded as legally responsible for their acts.

2. What does this suggest about the relation of intelligence to responsibility?

a) Does anything that bars the exercise of intelligence in any field confiscate our opportunity to become responsible, mature, in that field?[34]

The topic interested the class sufficiently for Childs to have been asked to state his own personal views on the issue at the next class meeting. This he did, not as a tirade but as a logical exposition of the case in light of what he regarded as the "stubborn past":

II.   A number of you have indicated, that you want my own view of the question as to whether the Roman Catholic response to the problem of planned parenthood and the related problem of the relation of population to resources constitutes an authentic example of experimental inquiry?

1. I shall give it, but first I want to call attention to the educational principle that is involved in Dewey's conception of philosophy as a deliberate effort to develop "patterns of continuity which are required in effecting the enduring junctions of a stubborn past and an insistent future."

2. This educational view may be pointed up by asking the following two questions:

a) One: Shall organized education honor, proclaim and transmit existing bodies of truth and value to the young and nurture, "indoctrinate" and discipline them in these truths and values? Or,

b) Two: Shall we search for the truth, seek to extend existing bodies of truth and value, and evaluate and try to improve operating life practices as we formulate and organize them into a curriculum for the young?

c) In other words, shall we view the school as an agency for the conservation of the culture through faithful transmission of it to the young, or shall we view that school as an agency that seeks to improve the culture as it introduces the young to received traditions and values and to emerging life conditions.

3. The view of the founders of the American school system was that our democracy required a distinctive kind of education and that enlightenment should be one of its primary purposes.

a) If education is to enlighten must it deal with these life areas where a "stubborn past" has encountered an emerging, and insistent, future?

b) Are these areas, generally areas of controversy? Why?
   i.) Conflicting groups with alternative and conflicting patterns for dealing with them.
III. It is in this civilizational-educational context that I place the problem of planned parenthood and the deliberate effort to regulate the growth of population in terms of world resources.
  1. This clearly is a problem that involves fundamentals in the lives of individual human beings, but it is equally a <u>social problem</u> and involves the making of <u>public policies</u>. Thus Eisenhower states: "I am delighted that a committee is concerning itself with this subject, one that I consider constitutes one of the most, if not the most, of the critical problems facing mankind today.["]
   a) Eisenhower also recognizes that though the problem is in the social, moral field, it is also properly a governmental problem. He declares: "Unless something is done to bring an essential equilibrium between human requirements and available supply there will be not only a series of riotous explosions, but a lowering of standards of all peoples, including our own."
   b) He adds that it is both a domestic and a world problem and our government is concerned with both aspects; (I quote) "Ten years ago I did not believe it to be the function of the Federal Government to interfere in the social structures of other nations by using, except through private institutions, American resources to assist them in a partial stabilization of their numbers. I expressed this view publicly but soon abandoned it.["]
   c) One form these Federal funds will take will be to cooperate with governments abroad in the establishment of Public Health Clinics through which women will be given accurate medical information and trained help in the use of contraceptives that [are] making the spacing of the birth of children possible.
   d) Clearly ethical view[s] and principles of what is better and what is worse are involved in all of this.[35]

John and Grace Childs celebrated their fiftieth wedding anniversary during that summer in Madison, and the occasion was marked by a reception in the Round Table Room of the Wisconsin Union. In characteristic fashion, Childs told the guests, who included the members of his graduate class, that on no account were gifts of any sort to be given. He added, "This is a 'practical absolute' not open to modification or development or ethical evaluation, *yours* to obey, not to reason why or to defy."[36] Childs invited his students and their spouses, and other guests included their close friends Edgar B. and Fay Wesley, Donald and Barbara Arnstine, as well as the Merle Borrowmans and the William Hays. Striking a jocular tone, Childs did ask guests to bring along a four-line poem of their own invention on the roles of husbands and wives. He wrote his several versions in advance, none of them evincing much metrical success.

> "The Prayer of the Women—God Give Us Men"
> *As our wives so frequently say*
> *They are plunged into deep dismay*
> *As they struggle in the space of two score and ten*
> *To transform mere boys into responsible men.*[37]

For several years following his final retirement, Childs received many letters from across the country—some from grateful students—requests to write the usual letters of recommendation, to read and recommend manuscripts, to join a variety of organizations, to attend special functions, to write articles and essays, to talk with people from the media, to donate money. To most of these he declined. In the first place, following his final semester at Madison, he was in the hospital. His health had never been particularly good since the trouble in the early 1950s, but by dint of discipline and a fairly strict regimen, he remained active until well into advanced age. In the second place, he still planned to write the Dewey book, but his publications dwindled. One of his last pieces was written for Francis Villemain's *Studies in Philosophy and Education,* which shows no diminution at all of his interest in scholarly work. In it he took a hard look at Reginald Archambault's edition of Dewey's 1899 lectures on pedagogy at the University of Chicago and the ways in which they served Dewey's developing thoughts on education.

As the Childs aged they decided to leave Carbondale. It

is said that John wanted to return to Madison. Not only was the University of Wisconsin one of the great loves of his life, but his brother, Cliff, and his family were living there. It seems that he was not able to find a suitable retirement facility in Madison itself at that time, and so they decided to move to Rockford, Illinois, which is only an hour's drive from Madison. It is also well placed between the Childs' respective homes—Eau Claire, Wisconsin, and Kankakee, Illinois. In March 1968 they left Carbondale and made their last move to Rockford.

On his application for accommodation at Wesley Willows, a retirement community in Rockford, Childs listed his hobbies as fishing, gardening, and tennis. He had always been a keen sportsman, and both Grace and John spent time with the garden and became fond of growing roses. John also liked to play pool. He described himself on the application as a "lifelong Methodist," and "a church member since early childhood years." In fact, he never participated in the religious life of the community. He had good relations with Reverend Edwin Hunt, founder and administrator of the fine facility, who never even knew that Childs had been a missionary or that both his advanced degrees were in religious education.

The Childs were well liked by residents and workers at Wesley Willows. For thirteen years they occupied a two-room apartment on the second floor. Meals were served in the spacious dining room, and the couple at first sat at a table for four, which they shared with a retired businessman and his wife. Later they sought the company of some of the other retired educators. John Childs was rarely seen without his suit and tie.

The Childs bought into the Wesley Willows Retirement Community on very advantageous terms, and the fact that both lived into their nineties turned out to be no financial burden at all on their resources. "[W]e entered Wesley Willows Retirement Home at Rockford, Illinois, under a life contract that involved the down payment of what is called a 'founders fee.' We are now in our seventh year at Wesley Willows, and we consider the decision to move into a Retirement Home a wise one. *But* inflation has become severe, and it has meant

that the monthly charge for board, room, and household services has been increased each year. Today, it is 35 per cent
higher, than when we came here, and inflation has steadily
increased its pressure."[38] In the Childs' contract, their charges
could be increased by a maximum only of 5 percent a year.
(Later residents of Wesley Willows did not have such good
fortune.) Inflation, therefore, which was considerable during
the 1970s, affected them very little. In fact, their capital was
never touched during their stay there.

Childs had always been thrifty, although he was generous
for causes he found worthwhile. For example, over the years
he had given more than fifty thousand dollars to Teachers
College, where his annual salary (excluding summer school)
had never exceeded eleven thousand; and during the 1970s he
gave forty thousand dollars to the Wisconsin Fund. It was
hard for him to spend money on himself, and during the last
years, when his eyesight had failed too far to engage in one of
his favorite pastimes—reading the *New York Times*—he had
to be persuaded to pay for someone to read it to him. Childs'
concern with money did not grow out of meanness, for he had
been extremely generous throughout his life, but from great
carefulness. In the Christian tradition, money, as well as talent,
was a form of stewardship. But the Childs were quite well-to-
do during their final years. Much of their capital came from
the Fowler farm, which in 1972 was sold to the Monk family,
who had been tenants for years. Their urge to sell was hastened
when Mrs. Monk was burned to death from an explosion in
the basement of the farmhouse. At the time of his death,
Childs' estate was worth around half a million dollars. Generous bequests were made to all his nephews and nieces or to
their heirs, and the residue was divided between Teachers
College and the University of Wisconsin, which each received
over $160,000. At Madison it was to be used specifically to
support the liberal arts program of the university, the area of
Childs' own degree in 1911. His library was given to Rockford
College, and arrangements were made before his death for his
papers to be deposited at SIU.

For George Counts, 1971 marked the beginning of his
final retirement, and Arthur Lean invited Childs to write a

statement honoring his old colleague. Childs obliged. The letter is worth quoting in full, for no one better than Childs could
have focused on the most salient aspects of Counts' career.

Dear George:

A letter from Southern Illinois University reports that you have
decided to make this your last term of teaching. No one has ever
more fully earned the right to retirement, and I hope that the years
ahead will be marked by meaningful but not too strenuous activity.
One thing is certain—your social values and interpretations and
related educational ideas are not about to retire; they will continue
to function with increasing influence in the field of public affairs.

During the decade of the 'Thirties, American democracy and
education made a fresh demonstration of their power to deal with
elemental civilizational problems. Your bold and searching writings
contributed to the far-reaching reconstructions achieved during that
period. I have long thought that one of the best ways to grasp what
was going on in the 'Thirties is to read the works of George S. Counts.
I also believe that *Conclusions and Recommendations,*—the Report
that you drafted for the American Historical Association Commission
on the Social Studies, will live as a classic statement of fundamentals
in the educational enterprise.

Significant also is your work in the field of international education. All along you have been frank and penetrating in your interpretations of the strengths and the weaknesses of Russian, Communist
education. Today, the comparative or international study of education has become one of our foremost academic disciplines. Your
work, along with that of Paul Monroe and Isaac Kandel, helped to
create this discipline.

Thought and action were blended in a remarkable way in your
career. Your leadership as National President of the American Federation of Teachers helped to open the way for the solid growth the
Federation has experienced in subsequent years. By emphasizing that
teaching is a form of productive, social activity, and by uniting teachers with other workers, you contributed to the strength of both
organized labor and organized public education. It took courage to
expel three of the largest Locals from the American Federation of
Teachers, but by this resolute action you and your colleagues demonstrated two basic points: (1) that the teachers' right to inquire, to
conclude, and to communicate presupposes that teachers are free and
honest inquirers, controlled by regard for evidence and independent
in their thought and study, not political puppets disposed to shift

their social and educational positions in order to make them conform to the twists of a political line defined and imposed by external authoritarian, political systems and parties; (2) you destroyed the widely held dogma that "any splitting of the forces on the 'left' could only serve the forces of reaction." For both you and John Dewey academic freedom is a holy right because it is grounded in that rigorous, self-correcting "process of winnowing and sifting by which alone the truth can be found."

During the more than fifty years of your university teaching, you never regarded your classes and seminars as mere elements in a fixed routine. You have always considered that *interaction* with the lives and minds of students is a *transaction* of high potentiality. As a teacher you are also deeply respected for the many hours you gave each week to conferences with individual students about their personal and professional problems, and their educational interests and plans. Many students from foreign countries, having become acquainted with you through the reading of your books and articles, arranged to come to the United States in order to study with you. Today, your formal doctoral students are serving in our country and in many foreign lands as eminent leaders of public education.

So, well done dear friend! You have helped to nurture an educational tradition that will live as long as the American people retain their faith in democracy and the common school movement. Grace joins me in affectionate regard to you, and to Lois, that faithful and able woman who so devotedly shared in this service of, by, and for deliberate education.

Fraternally yours,
John L. Childs[39]

It will be noticed that Childs' usual reticence prevails through most of the letter; only at the end does a warmer tone emerge. Indeed, the feeling that the Counts tribute was public is reinforced by the fact that Childs sent copies of it to some of his old friends and acquaintances in New York. Carl J. Megel, a former president of the AFT, appended a laudatory final paragraph in his response. "However, John Childs, in your modesty you give credit to someone else. But in my opinion, in many ways, the contributions you made were far superior. Yet you have received scant praise or acclaim for your long and noble efforts. Between John Dewey, George Counts and John Childs, I would rate the contribution by John

Childs as far superior when we consider the 'nitty gritty' of AFT efforts toward growth and stature."[40]

This view was echoed by a doctoral student at Teachers College—William Burton. Burton was a student of Dwaine Huebner's and had been introduced to Childs by mail by Lawrence A. Cremin, who told Childs that Burton wanted to pursue "intellectual issues of the 1930s" with Childs.[41] As it turned out, Burton was more interested in other matters and asked Childs about those things in his life prior to 1931 that had shaped his life and work. Burton also asked some pointed questions about Counts and voiced his hunch that it was Childs who after 1937 continued to develop the "liberalizing notions" that had been initiated by earlier theorists, such as Counts.[42] Burton was willing to travel from New York to Rockford to get a taped interview with Childs, but Childs declined to be taped and, when he realized the direction of Burton's work, withdrew his cooperation altogether. Burton's questions were digging too deep for this very private man.

At Rockford, Childs continued to take an avid interest in the events of the day, yet he was, as is customary as one gets older, taking some steps back from the positions he held earlier. Reflecting on the events of the early 1970s, Childs grew uneasy with the disturbances on college campuses. He always believed accommodation to be more effective than confrontation, but particularly the events at Madison he held to be "gravely defective."[43] In writing to Delyte W. Morris, president of SIU, he stated, "In my opinion, some of our most militant student activists of this period do not add up. They have rigorous home work to do on both ends and means and the basic interdependence of the two."[44] As for union tactics, he simply drew back from the posture he might have taken during the 1930s.

As the strength of our Union increases our problems also become more difficult. One of them is the problem of inflation, for as long as it continues the AFT will be forced to give a primary place to bread and butter issues. Inflation is today a crucial problem for all organized labor. Here again, education, labor, and politics are all bound in together.

Another problem is that of the AFT and school boards and school administrative leaders. The traditional labor pattern of the union versus the bosses and the owners does not fit the structure of public education. Many of our crucial educational problems—both rural and urban—require more effectual cooperation on the part of these forces. Until pressing our independence we need, in my opinion, to create better means for consultation and cooperation. The solution is not given; it must be created.[45]

These modifications of his views obviously reflect the growing conservatism of age, as did the move to Rockford. But the moderations occurred in other spheres. For example, he had occasion to pay tribute to Eugene and Berta Barnett, old friends from the China days, on their sixtieth wedding anniversary. Barnett had served the YMCA in China from 1910 until 1936 and was the association's associate general secretary of the National Committee of the YMCA in China from 1923 until he returned to work for the association in the United States. He had also studied at Columbia for short periods in 1923 and 1931. In writing to the Barnetts, Childs said, "Over the years we have been identified with many groups, but the China group fellowship out ranks all the others."[46] He had also been in correspondence with James Sykes of the Madison YMCA who wanted to talk with him about his work with the association. Childs responded by sending a check and thus halted the probing.

In the middle 1970s Childs felt that the shadows from the west were lengthening, to use a metaphor he frequently employed. George Axtelle, the close colleague from the New York days and at SIU, died in August 1974. Three months later, on November 10, George Counts also died. In writing to Lois and Martha Counts the day following George's death, Childs could not quite get out of his pulpit: "Just as Horace Mann is identified with the creation of our common school movement, so will George Counts be identified with the preservation of that movement through pioneering reconstructions." But, he added rather ruefully, "the day of our generation is coming to an end. A great day it was!"[47] In 1977 he rewrote his will and bought two burial lots in Greenwood Cemetery in Rockford.

By the late 1970s, the visitors to John Childs in Wesley Willows had tapered off. He was no longer able to drive his car, and his wife's health was deteriorating. Grace Childs died on January 20, 1980, and it affected John greatly. In July the following year he left the apartment and was moved to the Health Center at Wesley Willows. This facility is for residents no longer able to take care of themselves. Each person has a small room with a hospital bed. Small items of furniture can accompany patients, and John Childs took his papers. He rarely complained at all and was always gentlemanly. He adjusted well to the move, and his judgment was described as good and his memory unimpaired. But his decline was such that Cliff Childs was appointed his guardian. Cliff died in September 1983.

John Childs had always been a very private person; he rarely revealed much of himself. He had secret corners. In old age he did not get abrasive or argumentative; he never forced his views on others. In a social update of July 1984, Childs was described as "very pleasant and polite most of the time. Does not socialize with other residents." It was also commented that he consulted the staff and that he had a "nice smile—appreciative—polite." But he was clearly going downhill and was sometimes disoriented. Yet even at the end of the year he could still shuffle around. John Childs died on January 31, 1985. The coronary condition of 1952 had caught up with him at last, and his death was noted as due to "arterial sclerotic heart disease." He was not buried until the summer. Grace's body was exhumed, and the two of them were interred in the family grave at Lake View Cemetery, Eau Claire. Childs had come home to the Wisconsin that in many ways he had never really left, "an indigenous American, a native son of one of 'those typical Western prairie states.'"[48]

8.
Conclusion

This book is essentially an intellectual biography, in which I have attempted to demonstrate the route John Childs took as he moved from prayer to pragmatism. There is little here of Childs' personal life. For a long while this troubled me. Was I not looking in the right places? Had I missed important sources? Did I neglect to talk to the appropriate people? Eventually, however, I came to believe that I had perhaps accomplished almost unwittingly the search for Childs the person. What I had found was what there was. Here was a self-contained, private, moralistic, intelligent man, whose commitment to his ideals was his life. There were few stories about him, as there were concerning George Counts. True, I found that Childs wore the same clothes, that he fished with intensity, that he gave up religion, but these details did not, I believed, constitute a portrait. Early in my research I labeled him a puritan, unaware at the time that Harold Rugg had also called him one. The couple of times I met Childs I found him somewhat remote and unsmiling, but later Robert E. Mason told me that for Childs life and living were extremely serious affairs. In writing this book, I found Childs thorough, systematic, organized—and nothing, not even the way he arranged his own papers, seemed out of place. This biography, then, is a bit dispassionate, unemotional, earnest, but then so, I have concluded, was Jack Childs. The lack of gossip, of anecdotes, of humor, in these pages, is a reflection of its subject, who, it seems to me, valued total commitment and privacy above all else.

Jack Childs had been quite an active sportsman in his younger days, and, until I uncovered photographs of him in his twenties, I found it hard to believe that, as his nephews related, he had once been quite "burly." Fishing was always one of his big passions; one suspects, however, that even his fishing was tempered with a certain intensity. Robert Mason recalls that Grace Childs told the story of her husband getting up early to fish during their annual holiday at Lake Chetek and finding that one of the boys (presumably a nephew) had taken an oar. Childs expressed disgust but went ahead with the single oar, rowing himself canoelike into the river. His nephews also mentioned that he used to make *them* do the rowing while he caught the fish. Rugg was somewhat disparaging when he referred to Childs as "that Puritan." Robert Mason, speaking more positively, also called Childs a puritan and commented that Childs believed grave issues were bound up in the positions people held. Childs certainly expressed distaste for people with whom he profoundly disagreed, and he would sometimes even leave the room if he saw one of his intellectual enemies present. However, this dislike was not exactly personal, it was rather that he was dealing, so he believed, with earth-shattering, momentous issues.

There was an air of solemnity about Childs that was certainly not present around George Counts. But Counts had not been a missionary and, although he used all the resources he could muster to pull people to his point of view, and indeed

rather sadly in later life felt that he had essentially been un-
heeded in his calls for educational and social reform, he always
had the light touch of the true gadfly. For Childs, life was a
more serious business.

Following his own retirement, R. Freeman Butts wrote:

> Jack Childs became my model of what a professor of foundations
> ought to be in relation to the administration of the College. He was
> always there to plague me because I could never live up to his style
> but always wanted to. It seemed to me that Jack was not only fearless
> in his criticism, but usually right; he always laid the issues out on the
> table with directness and candor—not to say a challenge to duel.
> In a faculty discussion he might sit back for a while—seemingly
> sharpening up his rapier—but would come into the fray at the critical
> moment to make the most telling blows.[1]

These few sentences catch the flavor of Childs the man
and reveal the respect in which he was held. His honesty
and his concentration were widely acknowledged. Raymond
Callahan deeply admired Childs' integrity and fairness. In fact,
for him it was Childs and not Counts who exemplified the
characteristics of a really first-class teacher. These included
tolerance for divergent ideas, so long as they are well argued
and well presented. Alice Miel, another former student, reinforced this opinion in a letter to Childs: "I remember rejecting
even your proposal of the French Revolution, but now I would
agree that all young people somewhere sometime somehow
should be taught the concept of revolution."[2] All of Childs'
former students with whom I spoke referred to his sharp mind
and his thoughtfulness. Those who knew him best perceived
a lurking sense of humor, but they saw also more obviously
his serious, intense air. Others thought him intimidating, and
they learned quickly not to say anything offhand. His debating
skills on important matters were never in doubt, although he
probably told none of his students that he had been on the
Madison debate team in his student days.

They all noted his dress, too: dark suit, white shirt, black
tie, well-polished shoes. Donald Arnstine once asked Childs
why he always dressed in such a drab fashion. He replied,

"Life is so full of choices, Don. I decided that this was one area in which I would not have to choose. No one can accuse me of dressing carelessly, and I can save my thinking for more momentous problems than 'what shall I wear today'." In Childs' last semester teaching at Madison, Arnstine asked him to talk about the old days at the university. He did "fondly recall his work as editor of the *Cardinal*, and his weekly interviews with President Van Hise, whom he considered, along with others on the Wisconsin faculty, a genuine progressive. But he would quickly bring conversation back to the present."[3] Childs believed his work was not mere speculation; certainly it was not recollection; it was a call to act. Carl J. Megel described Childs as "the practitioner who helped make theoretical functions work."[4] And this is demonstrated in a letter Childs wrote to a doctoral student: "The function of philosophy is the criticism of presuppositions. More specifically, this means that philosophy has the never ending task of adjusting inherited beliefs and values to advances in knowledge and in human aspirations, and to changes in our group ways of living. This philosophical undertaking finds its supreme opportunity in the enterprise of deliberate education, for it has responsibility for the continuous re-evaluation of our ways of life and thought as it seeks to nurture the young in them."[5]

It has been said that "each phase of your life is a revised and updated version of the previous one."[6] In the case of John Childs this is particularly true. The forces that molded him were in place by the time he first landed in China in 1916. From his agrarian boyhood he learned the worth of hard work, honest labor, and thrift. In school he internalized the values of democracy and the democratic temper. From his Methodist roots he became committed to good works, to which he added at Madison elements of the Wisconsin idea, primarily that of service to a wider community. From Professors Richard T. Ely and John R. Commons he came to respect and later favor unionization and to see that freedom is more than absence of restraint. His moral and religious convictions were reinforced by his long association with the YMCA. After Childs left China and had completed his doctoral studies, the "revised and updated version" of his life is the one remembered. His faith remained firm; the object of that faith changed. Childs' enthusiasm for the Christian gospel was replaced by enthusiasm for the scientific method, which never thereafter wavered. Although he retired to a Methodist home and lived there for seventeen years, thirteen of them with his wife, he took no part at all in the religious life of the community and only once attended a worship service in the home's chapel (a single Thanksgiving); he never discussed religion. During the Carbondale years, he regularly attended the Unitarian Fellowship, and the extent of his commitment to experimental inquiry is clear in the exchange he had with Henry Nelson Wieman. One can sense how much he enjoyed the debate on the topic of God's existence, but there is no retreat at all from his pragmatism. God, Jesus, and prayer, all so dear to the heart and mind of the young YMCA missionary, had been completely deposed.

Perhaps more importantly, for this is a topic that has been barely touched upon, Childs' life is a demonstration that pragmatic ethics does not seem possible outside the context of some more absolute moral code—a suggestion Childs would have been the first to deny. But the pragmatists in general do not appear to have realized that, even though one judges the moral worth of an action by its consequences, the goodness or the badness of a consequence is not usually self-evident. It is, after all, an ill wind that blows no good, so that the good for some is not necessarily the good for others. Childs might here echo the utilitarians and say that the good is the greatest good for the greatest number, but that ultimately begs the question. While it may readily be conceded that *some* consequences could clearly be described as good and others bad, most moral dilemmas do not resolve themselves clearly. More often than not the choices, especially in the classroom, are not between good and bad but between competing goods and hence the real problem for the teacher. Childs himself faced that problem when he decided to give his true-false tests. He thought to do so was, all things considered, the good, the moral choice. Even though it did in one sense accomplish its goal of getting the students to read the material, many of them in fact read for the test, concentrating more on details than on the more important but less testable content.

On the other hand, what is most conspicuous about Childs' career is that he actually lived his beliefs. In his early years he was a committed, if somewhat unorthodox, Christian. He believed in the divinity of Christ and the efficacy of prayer. He took seriously the command to go into the world and preach the gospel to every creature. His commitment to the enterprise was total. The *conversion,* and there is really no other word to describe it, to pragmatism in no way changed his zeal or his commitment, it merely changed the object of that passion. Childs' life from that point on was indeed "a revised and updated version" of the previous phase. It was as necessary for him to live the mandates of pragmatism later as it had been for him to live the biblical commandments earlier. St. James had said that faith without works is dead; Jesus had said that it was by their fruits that ye shall know them. These ideals remained central in Childs' life and work even after his conversion to pragmatism. True, his zeal did suggest a certain self-righteousness; his pragmatism was a serious business. As former student Robert Mason said in reference to Childs, "One doesn't play with ideas, toy with them; ideas and praxis are of serious moment."[7] In this respect Childs was slightly different from Counts, who, although deadly serious about the work that he had to do, found time to plant his garden, tell his jokes, drink his vodka, and enjoy his friends. Childs was altogether of sterner stuff.

There can be little doubt that Childs' advocacy of social reconstructionism was tied up with his earlier religious commitment. As C. A. Bowers reportedly argued, the work of the reconstructionists was an "expression of a long messianic tradition in American educational thought, a traditional faith in utopian reform through schooling. A large portion of them had deeply religious roots and used religious language that could have been heard at social gospel meetings."[8] The "messianic" nature of the group is clear when one remembers that Kilpatrick was a Baptist, and Counts, like Childs, a Methodist; R. Bruce Raup actually earned a bachelor of divinity degree from the Presbyterian McCormick Seminary. Harold Rugg was "one of the few members of the social reconstructionist group who did not have a strong affiliation with a religious group during his formative period."[9] It is not surprising that Childs was a Methodist, for Methodists are quite committed to a social gospel. But the entire group, led by Kilpatrick, was "interested in having educators take a more positive stand" on the social problems of the day.[10] As William E. Eaton has stated:

> It is a bit risky to summarize the basic tenets of the social reconstructionists because of the danger of over-simplification. . . . They believed, first of all, in the importance of a liberal democracy, that is, the Jeffersonian ideal of a responsive and participative government, modified by the writings of John Stuart Mill, especially his *On Liberty*. They accepted the idea that socialism complemented democratic forms and practices of equality while capitalism acted as a centrifuge forcing the "haves" and the "have nots" to opposite ends. They accepted the necessity of a cross-national view of matters, seeing international tribunals and assemblies as the best hope for the establishment and maintenance of world order. But most fundamental to any discussion of the social reconstructionists was their acceptance of the proposition that the school was the fundamental institution within modern culture.[11]

Several have called the social reconstructionists utopian, but Childs would have resented the label, for he believed that all reconstructionism must only take place in light of the "stubborn past" and the "stubborn facts" of the present. In the 1930s these were mainly economic; in the 1940s they involved nuclear weapons and the looming presence on the world scene of Soviet Russia. As late as 1952, Childs wrote to H. Gordon Hullfish that "much as we may reject 'blue prints' of the new social order, we cannot restrict education to the cultivation of personality without reference to the deep moving tendencies in a scientific and technological civilization."[12] Were he alive today, there can be little doubt that Childs would be calling for a more equitable society, a reinforcement of the commitment to democracy, a recognition of the fact that all affairs must now be conducted on a world stage, a certitude that educational reform must involve more than trying to do better what schools already do. If the new social order as dreamed by Childs and his colleagues seems now to be but the memory of a dream, there are always ideals for which to strive. The schools should not ignore these ideals, for in a dynamic society all education is necessarily a form of social reconstruction as it is of personal reconstruction.

To ask for an assessment of John Childs, particularly immediately following the centennial of his birth, is fair. How important was his work? What is his significance? It is safe to say that no one more accurately interpreted John Dewey's thinking for the educational community, as was recognized early when Paul Arthur Schilpp asked Childs to write the essay in the first volume of his distinguished series, *A Library of Living Philosophers*. It was also recognized by many people, including Dewey himself, who told Boyd Bode that he thought Childs had the best mind among the group of his followers. Dewey wrote to Childs, "Your knowledge of my position is so thorough that you don't need my assurance that you have understood it and reported it correctly."[13] In 1946, Kilpatrick received an inquiry from a graduate student who asked him to name the "Apostolic succession" at Columbia after Dewey and Kilpatrick. He replied that it passed jointly to John Childs and L. Thomas Hopkins.[14] Herbert Schneider remarked that Childs was among those closest to Dewey, both personally and professionally. Festus Chukwudi Okafor, speaking from a Third World perspective, called him, "a chief interpreter" of the leading pragmatists.[15] Childs was continually in demand to speak about Dewey's educational theory, and he participated in the celebration of Dewey's eightieth, ninetieth, and centennial birthdays. True, there was more of the reconstructionist in Childs than there was in Dewey, and for that reason Childs may be considered to have supplied the philosophical basis for the Teachers College brand of social reconstructionism, while Counts provided its sociohistorical basis. For that alone, Childs should receive more credit than he has.

In 1968 Childs was awarded an Honorary Doctorate of Humane Letters at Southern Illinois University. Ramrod straight, tall, dignified, Childs received the degree on that hot June day. The encomium not only sums up a distinguished career but catches the spirit of his work.

Scholar, teacher, author, leader of liberal causes, John Lawrence Childs has won international fame through a lifetime of dedicated service to the cause of education, both at home and abroad. A native of Wisconsin and alumnus of its State University, he received his graduate degrees from Columbia University where he spent most of his teaching career. For eleven years he served as Foreign Secretary, International Committee of the Y.M.C.A., in Peking, China. Later he was the first Chairman of Academic Freedom and the American Civil Liberties Union. An active member of the American Federation of Teachers for over twenty years, he rendered distinguished service on its National Commission on Educational Reconstruction. After receiving Emeritus status from Columbia in 1954 he was Visiting Professor at several universities, completing his active career at Southern Illinois University where he was widely known and respected for his scholarship, his uncompromising devotion to the pursuit of truth, and his incisive teaching of both undergraduate and graduate students in Education and Philosophy. Recipient of numerous awards and author of several important books, he has consistently emphasized the social nature of education and implored respect for the child and the nurturing of the young in the essential patterns of democratic life.[16]

Notes

Checklist of
    Writings by
    John L. Childs

Index

Notes

In citing sources in the notes, the following abbreviations have been used to designate libraries and collections.

ICarbS   *Special Collections, Morris Library, Southern Illinois University, Carbondale.* John L. Childs papers; George S. Counts papers; Philosophy papers.

MnU   *University of Minnesota, St. Paul.* YMCA of the USA Archives.

NNC-T   *Special Collections, Milbank Memorial Library, Teachers College, Columbia University, New York.* W. F. Russell papers; Records of the Office of Public Relations (Publicity); William H. Kilpatrick Diaries.

WU   *University of Wisconsin, Madison.* University YMCA Archives; E. A. Ross papers.

1. Introduction

1. Cliff (born in 1904) is not an abbreviation; it was the surname of his father's employer and close friend.

2. About one-fifth of the papers cataloged by Cliff Childs are still missing.

3. John L. Childs, "Unresolved Problems in the Education of American Teachers." Address delivered at University of Illinois, College of Education, November 6, 1964 [typescript], 1. ICarbS/ Childs.

4. Lawrence A. Cremin is certainly correct when he identifies Childs and Counts as the two members of Kilpatrick's Discussion Group who were active participants in political organizations; see Cremin, *Transformation of the School* (New York: Alfred A. Knopf, 1961), 229. Also Harold Rugg, *Foundations for American Education* (Yonkers-on-Hudson, New York: World Book, 1947), 579.

5. George S. Counts, "A Humble Autobiography," in *Leaders in American Education*, ed. Robert J. Havighurst. Yearbook of the National Society for the Study of Education, No. 70, Pt. 2 (Chicago: NSSE, 1971), 151–74. Gerald L. Gutek, *Educational Theory of George S. Counts* (Columbus: Ohio State University Press, 1970). Gerald L. Gutek, *George S. Counts and American Civilization* (Macon, Georgia: Mercer University Press, 1984). Lawrence J. Dennis and William Edward Eaton, eds., *George S. Counts: Educator for a New Age* (Carbondale: Southern Illinois University Press, 1980). Lawrence J. Dennis, *George S. Counts and Charles A. Beard: Collaborators for Change* (Albany: State University of New York Press, 1989).

2. Early Years

1. John L. Childs, "Genesis of an Educational Point of View." Address delivered at Boston University, May 11, 1960 [ms.], 1. ICarbS/Childs.

2. Childs, "Genesis," 3. ICarbS/Childs.

3. Lois Barland, *The Rivers Flow On* (Stevens Point, Wisconsin: Worzalla Publishing Co., 1965), 412.

4. Childs, "Genesis," 3. ICarbS/Childs.

5. Childs, "Genesis," 4. ICarbS/Childs.

6. John L. Childs, "Future of the Common School." Address

delivered at Teachers College, New York, November 9, 1956 [type-script], 3–4. ICarbS/Childs.

7. Barland, *Rivers*, 420.

8. Childs, "Genesis," 2. ICarbS/Childs.

9. Childs, "Genesis," 7. ICarbS/Childs.

10. *University of Wisconsin Catalogue 1907–8* (Madison 1908), 267.

11. Childs, "Genesis," 7. ICarbS/Childs.

12. Merle Curti and Vernon Carstensen, *University of Wisconsin: A History 1848–1925*, II (Madison: University of Wisconsin Press, 1949), 327.

13. A. L. P. Dennis was an expert in colonial history, including that history in China. Paul Samuel Reinsch left the University of Wisconsin in 1913 to become American Minister to China until 1919. He was appointed counsellor to the Chinese government and was advisor to the Chinese delegation at the Washington Arms Confer-ence. He ran for the U.S. Senate in 1920 but was defeated. He returned then to China, where he died in January 1923.

14. Childs, "Genesis," 7. ICarbS/Childs.

15. Childs' own references to both Ely and Commons can be read to suggest that they were directly his teachers, but his own transcript when matched with the university catalogs suggests oth-erwise.

16. The inscription reads, "Whatever may be the limitations which trammel inquiry elsewhere, we believe that the great state University of Wisconsin should ever encourage that continual and fearless sifting and winnowing by which alone the truth can be found." It was the censuring of Professor Edward A. Ross by the Board of Regents, and the consequent fear that academic freedom was still in danger, that prompted the class of 1910 to have the plaque cast as a class memorial.

17. Reported in "Obituary," *New York Times*, October 5, 1943, 25.

18. Childs, "Genesis," 7. ICarbS/Childs.

19. John R. Commons, *Myself* (New York: Macmillan, 1934), 129.

20. Childs, "Genesis," 9. ICarbS/Childs.

21. Curti and Carstensen, *University of Wisconsin*, II, 109.

22. John L. Childs, "The Wisconsin Idea and the Purposes of Public Education." Address delivered to the Wisconsin Chapter of Phi Delta Kappa, June 29, 1965 [typescript], 3. ICarbS/Childs.

23. Childs, "Wisconsin Idea," 7. ICarbS/Childs.

24. Childs, "Genesis," 11. ICarbS/Childs.

25. Childs, "Wisconsin Idea," 11. ICarbS/Childs.

26. *University Press*, October 1, 1871, 148 (quoted in James T. Honnold, *History of the YMCA of the University of Wisconsin: 1870–1924*. Unpublished thesis for the Master of Science in Social Work [Madison: University of Wisconsin, 1954], 26).

27. Honnold, *YMCA*, 118.

28. Arthur Jorgensen to James T. Honnold, September 7, 1953 (quoted in Honnold, *YMCA*, 126).

29. Honnold, *YMCA*, 126–27.

30. *Daily Cardinal*, October 3, 1910, 1.

31. *Daily Cardinal*, October 3, 1910, 1.

32. *Daily Cardinal*, October 25, 1910, 8.

33. *Daily Cardinal*, November 17, 1910, 1.

34. *Daily Cardinal*, December 3, 1910, 1.

35. *University of Wisconsin Catalogue 1910–11* (Madison 1911), 113.

36. John L. Childs, *A Study of the Editorials of the New York Evening Journal*. Unpublished thesis for the Bachelor of Arts in Journalism (Madison: University of Wisconsin, 1911), 52.

37. Childs, *Study of Editorials*, 63.

38. Childs, *Study of Editorials*, 6.

39. "Religion for Men," *Daily Cardinal*, November 18, 1910, 4.

40. *Daily Cardinal*, January 16, 1911, 1.

41. Shirley S. Garrett, *Social Reformers in Urban China: The Chinese YMCA 1895–1926* (Cambridge, Massachusetts: Harvard University Press, 1970), 65.

42. *Daily Cardinal*, March 11, 1910, 1.

43. John L. Childs to John R. Mott, June 15, 1922. ICarbS/Childs.

44. Alfred P. Haake to James T. Honnold, July 1, 1953. WU/YMCA.

45. Honnold, *YMCA*, 127.

46. Honnold, *YMCA*, 132.

47. Honnold, *YMCA*, 133.

48. Honnold, *YMCA*, 133–34.

49. John L. Childs to G. Sherwood Eddy, April 9, 1914. MnU/YMCA.

50. John L. Childs to G. Sherwood Eddy, April 9, 1914. MnU/YMCA.

51. Their home, 240 North Harrison Street, is now a sales lot for the truck dealer across the road.

52. John L. Childs to John R. Mott, January 29, 1916. MnU/YMCA.

53. John L. Childs to John R. Mott, January 29, 1916. MnU/YMCA.

54. John L. and Grace Childs to Fletcher S. Brockman, January 28, 1917. MnU/YMCA.

55. Garrett, *Social Reformers*, 57.

56. Garrett, *Social Reformers*, 59.

57. Garrett, *Social Reformers*, 71.

58. Garrett, *Social Reformers*, 117.

59. Garrett, *Social Reformers*, 119.

60. John L. Childs, "Quarterly Report, Period Ending December 1916" [typescript], 1. MnU/YMCA.

61. Edward A. Ross, "Wisconsin-in-China" [1916]. WU/YMCA.

62. *Wisconsin in China Committee of One Hundred*. Pamphlet, n.d., 3. WU/YMCA.

63. E. G. Hersman to E. T. Colton, June 15, 1917. WU/YMCA.

64. John L. Childs to Charles D. Hurrey, January 7, 1917. MnU/YMCA.

65. John L. Childs to Charles D. Hurrey, January 7, 1917. MnU/YMCA.

66. John L. and Grace Childs to Fletcher S. Brockman, January 28, 1917. MnU/YMCA.

67. John L. Childs, "Quarterly Report, Period Ending April 1, 1917" [typescript], 3. MnU/YMCA.

68. John L. Childs, "Quarterly Report, Period Ending December 31, 1917" [typescript]. MnU/YMCA.

69. Paul S. Reinsch, *An American Diplomat in China* (London: George Allen and Unwin, 1922), 155–56.

70. Childs wrote that a small group of Chinese under his leadership had founded the journal, which he reported as "having a wide influence among the more progressive minded people in China." John L. Childs, "Annual Administrative Report of John L. Childs, Student Secretary, Peking, China, for the year ending September 30, 1921" [typescript], 2. MnU/YMCA.

71. John L. Childs. "Annual Report Letter of J. L. Childs, Secretary, Young Men's Christian Association, Peking, China, for the year ending September 30, 1918" [typescript], 5. MnU/YMCA.

72. Childs, "Annual Report 1918," 6–7. MnU/YMCA.

73. Childs, "Annual Report 1918," 8. MnU/YMCA.

74. John L. Childs, "Result of the War Upon Missionary Work in China," *Millard's Review* (December 14, 1918): 48.

75. Childs, "Result of War," 48–49.

76. Childs, "Result of War," 50.

77. John L. Childs, "Evolution of a Missionary's Thought," *The Life* [English edition] 5 (July 1925): 10.

78. John L. Childs, "Annual Report Letter—John L. Childs, 1919–1920 Student Secretary, Young Men's Christian Association, Peking, China, for the Year Ending 30 September 1920 [typescript], 1. MnU/YMCA.

3. Transition

1. George Dykhuizen, *The Life and Mind of John Dewey* (Carbondale: Southern Illinois University Press, 1973), 194–95.

2. Dykhuizen, *Life and Mind*, 199.

3. Dykhuizen, *Life and Mind*, 196.

4. John L. Childs, *Education and the Philosophy of Experimentalism* (New York: Appleton-Century-Crofts, 1931), x.

5. Barry Keenan, *The Dewey Experiment in China* (Cambridge, Massachusetts: Council on East Asian Studies, Harvard University, 1977), 230.

6. John Dewey and Alice Chipman Dewey, *Letters from China and Japan* (New York: E.P. Dutton, 1920), 293.

7. Dewey and Dewey, *Letters*, 307–8.

8. Edward W. Lockwood, February 1921. MnU/YMCA.

9. John Dewey, "What Holds China Back," in *Middle Works of John Dewey, 1899–1924*, vol. 12, ed. Jo Ann Boydston (Carbondale: Southern Illinois University Press, 1982), 57.

10. John L. Childs, "Annual Administrative Report of John L. Childs, Student Secretary, Peking, China, for the year ending September 30, 1921" [typescript], 2. MnU/YMCA.

11. "John Lawrence Childs" September 1925 [typescript]. MnU/YMCA. This document states that the sum raised was $2,300,000 in Chinese currency.

12. "John Lawrence Childs." MnU/YMCA.

13. Shirley S. Garrett, *Social Reformers in Urban China: The Chinese YMCA 1895–1926* (Cambridge, Massachusetts: Harvard University Press, 1970), 167.

14. Childs, "Annual Administrative Report 1921," 4. MnU/YMCA.

15. John L. Childs, "The National Christian Conference," *Chinese Recorder* 52 (November 1921): 738.

16. Childs, "National Christian Conference," 737–38.

17. John L. Childs to Edward A. Ross, August 7, 1921. WU/YMCA.

18. John L. Childs to John R. Mott, June 15, 1922. ICarbS/Childs.

19. James T. Honnold, *History of the YMCA of the University of Wisconsin: 1870–1924*. Unpublished thesis for the Master of Science in Social Work (Madison: University of Wisconsin, 1954), 177. Frederick E. Wolf was General Secretary of the Madison YMCA.

20. Honnold, *YMCA*, 179. Lester C. Rogers had been student president of the Madison YMCA for the 1914–15 academic year.

21. Honnold, *YMCA*, 179.

22. Nancy D. Sachse, "Campus Pioneers for a Hundred Years: The University of Wisconsin Young Men's Christian Association," January 1964 [typescript], 29. WU/YMCA.

23. *Daily Cardinal*, October 17, 1922, 1.

24. *Daily Cardinal*, October 17, 1922, 1.

25. John L. Childs to C. V. Hibbard, January 6, 1925. ICarbS/Childs.

26. John L. Childs to C. V. Hibbard, January 6, 1925. ICarbS/Childs.

27. *Wisconsin in China*. John L. Childs file, School of Journalism, University of Wisconsin.

28. *Wisconsin in China*, 2.

29. Charles A. Herschleb to [Edward W. Lockwood], April 13, 1923. MnU/YMCA.

30. "John Lawrence Childs." MnU/YMCA.

31. *Annual Catalogue*, Union Theological Seminary, 1923–24, 82.

32. *Annual Catalogue*, Union Theological Seminary, 82.

33. *School of Education, Announcement, 1923–24* (New York: Teachers College, Columbia University), 25.

34. William Heard Kilpatrick, *Diary 1924*, 70. NNC-T.

35. Kilpatrick, *Diary 1924*, 71. NNC-T.

36. John L. Childs to E. C. Jenkins and Charles A. Herschleb, June 4, 1924. MnU/YMCA.

37. John L. Childs to C. V. Hibbard, January 6, 1925. ICarbS/Childs.

38. John L. Childs, "Letter to Bishop Norris," *Leader* (Peking) (June [25], 1925): 6.

39. John L. Childs, "Evolution of a Missionary's Thought," *The Life* [English edition] 5 (July 1925): 1.

40. Childs, "Evolution," 14.

41. Childs, "Evolution," 17. This view foreshadows the position Childs took later in life in the address, "Is Dr. Wieman's God Dispensable?"

42. Childs, "Evolution," 17.

43. Childs, "Evolution," 19–20.

44. Childs, "Evolution," 21.

45. Childs, "Evolution," 30.

46. "Quartus, a Brother," "A Modernist's 'Confession of Doubt'," *China Press*, November [27], 1925, n.p. ICarbS/Childs.

47. D. Willard Lyon to John L. Childs, November 10, 1925. ICarbS/Childs.

48. T. C. Ch'ao to Y. C. Shu, October 26, 1925. ICarbS/Childs.

49. C. G. Dittmer to John L. Childs, November 11, 1925. ICarbS/Childs.

50. George A. Coe to John L. Childs, November 11, 1925. ICarbS/Childs.

51. John L. Childs, "Some Fundamentals in Modernism." Address delivered at the Sunday morning service of the P.U.M.C., February 21, 1926. *Leader*, n.d.

52. John L. Childs to David Yui, August 9, 1926. ICarbS/Childs.

53. Garrett, *Social Reformers*, 183.

54. G. Sherwood Eddy to Richard Edwards, March 3, 1927. ICarbS/Childs.

55. Childs, *Education and the Philosophy of Experimentalism*, x.

56. John L. Childs to David Yui, May 21, 1927. ICarbS/Childs.

57. John L. Childs, "May Fourth, 1919" [1944] [typescript], 1. ICarb/Childs.

58. *Annual Catalogue*, Union Theological Seminary, 1927–28, 30.

59. *Annual Catalogue*, Union Theological Seminary, 1928–29, 41.

60. John L. Childs, Untitled. Address delivered to the "co-operators" of the *World Tomorrow* [1928] [typescript], 12. ICarbS/Childs.

61. L. Carrington Goodrich to John L. Childs, November 10, 1956. ICarbS/Childs.

62. Kilpatrick, *Diary 1928*, 82. NNC-T.

63. Kilpatrick, *Diary 1930*, 2. NNC-T.

64. Kilpatrick, *Diary 1930*, 190. NNC-T.
65. Kilpatrick, *Diary 1931*, 35. NNC-T.
66. Kilpatrick, *Diary 1931*, 37. NNC-T.
67. Kilpatrick, *Diary 1931*, 40. NNC-T.
68. Kilpatrick, *Diary 1931*, 166. NNC-T.

4. Philosopher of Reconstructionism

1. William Heard Kilpatrick to Robert Miller, March 23, 1931. ICarbS/Childs.
2. Quoted in *Time* (September 14, 1987): 81.
3. John L. Childs, *Education and the Philosophy of Experimentalism* (New York: Appleton-Century-Crofts, 1931), 108–9.
4. Childs, *Education and the Philosophy of Experimentalism*, 217.
5. Childs, *Education and the Philosophy of Experimentalism*, 80–81.
6. Childs, *Education and the Philosophy of Experimentalism*, 93.
7. Childs, *Education and the Philosophy of Experimentalism*, 89.
8. Childs, *Education and the Philosophy of Experimentalism*, 165.
9. Boyd H. Bode to John L. Childs, October 2, 1931. ICarbS/Childs.
10. Herman H. Horne, Review, *School and Society* 35 (January 30, 1932): 164.
11. Alice V. Keliher, Review, *Progressive Education* 9 (January 1932): 67.
12. Willis L. Uhl to John L. Childs, July 17, 1931. ICarbS/Childs.
13. John L. Childs, "A Way of Dealing with Experience," *Progressive Education* 8 (December 8, 1931): 695–98.
14. William Heard Kilpatrick, *Diary 1931*, 224–25. NNC-T.
15. Kilpatrick, *Diary 1931*, 230. NNC-T. Marion Y. Ostrander was Kilpatrick's longtime secretary, and in 1940, after the death of Margaret Kilpatrick in 1938, she became his third wife.
16. William Heard Kilpatrick, *Source Book in the Philosophy of Education* (New York: Macmillan, Teachers College Press, 1923).
17. Samuel Tenenbaum, *William Heard Kilpatrick: Trail Blazer in Education* (New York: Harper and Brothers, 1951).
18. Kilpatrick, *Diary 1931*, 199.

19. Kilpatrick, *Source Book in the Philosophy of Education*, revised edition (New York: Macmillan, 1934).

20. William Heard Kilpatrick, *Syllabus in the Philosophy of Education* (New York: Teachers College, 1934).

21. Kilpatrick, *Diary 1932*, 86. NNC-T.

22. Kilpatrick, *Diary 1932*, 146. NNC-T.

23. Kilpatrick, *Diary 1932*, 156. NNC-T.

24. Kilpatrick, *Diary 1932*, 201. NNC-T.

25. Kilpatrick, *Diary 1932*, 233. NNC-T.

26. Kilpatrick, *Diary 1932*, 244. NNC-T.

27. Kilpatrick, *Diary 1932*, 252–53. NNC-T.

28. Kilpatrick, *Diary 1932*, 264. NNC-T.

29. Kilpatrick, *Diary 1933*, 47. NNC-T.

30. "Memorandum to Professor Dewey on the Proposed Yearbook in the Philosophy of Education," n.d. [typescript], 2. ICarbS/Childs.

31. "Memorandum," 3. ICarbS/Childs.

32. "Comments of Professor Dewey on My Memorandum," n.d. [typescript]. ICarbS/Childs.

33. John Dewey and John L. Childs, "The Social-Economic Situation and Education," in *The Educational Frontier*, ed. William Heard Kilpatrick (New York: D. Appleton-Century, 1933), 63.

34. Dewey and Childs, "Social-Economic Situation," 61.

35. Dewey and Childs, "Social-Economic Situation," 66.

36. Dewey and Childs, "Social-Economic Situation," 71.

37. Norman Foerster, "Education Leads the Way," *American Review* 1 (September 1933): 403.

38. John Dewey and John L. Childs, "The Underlying Philosophy of Education," in *Educational Frontier*, 290.

39. Dewey and Childs, "Underlying Philosophy," 292.

40. Dewey and Childs, "Underlying Philosophy," 294.

41. Dewey and Childs, "Underlying Philosophy," 296.

42. Dewey and Childs, "Underlying Philosophy," 306.

43. Dewey and Childs, "Underlying Philosophy," 317.

44. Dewey and Childs, "Underlying Philosophy," 288.

45. Sidney Hook, "Education and Politics," *New Republic*, 75 (May 24, 1933): 49.

46. Kilpatrick, *Diary 1934*, 4. NNC-T.

47. John C. Almack, Review, *Elementary School Journal* 34 (December 1933): 310.

48. Almack, Review, 309.

49. Hook, "Education and Politics," 49.

50. A. Gordon Melvin, Review, *Progressive Education* 10 (April 1933): 238.

51. *Times (London) Literary Supplement*, June 29, 1933, 448.

52. John Dewey, "Experience, Knowledge and Value: A Rejoinder," in *Philosophy of John Dewey*, ed. Paul Arthur Schilpp (New York: Tudor Publishing, 1939), 519.

53. John L. Childs, "Educational Philosophy of John Dewey," in *Philosophy of John Dewey*, 421.

54. Childs, "Educational Philosophy," 428.

55. Childs, "Educational Philosophy," 443.

56. Childs, "Educational Philosophy," 443.

57. Childs, "Educational Philosophy," 443. Also, Dewey and Childs, "Social-Economic Situation," 64.

58. Kilpatrick, *Diary 1939*, 157. NNC-T. Schilpp himself was disposed to include the article; therefore, particularly in view of some threats of legal action by its author, V. J. McGill, Schilpp promised him space in the second volume in his *Library of Living Philosophers* series. Thus, "Russell's Political and Economic Policy" by V. J. McGill appears in the Bertrand Russell book, *Philosophy of Bertrand Russell* (New York: Tudor Publishing, 1944), 579–617. The following chapter, "Russell's Educational Philosophy," was written by Boyd H. Bode.

59. Sidney Hook, ed., *John Dewey: Philosopher of Science and Freedom* (New York: Dial Press, 1950), vi.

60. John L. Childs, "John Dewey and Education," in Hook, *John Dewey*, 157.

61. Childs, "John Dewey," 159.

62. Childs, "John Dewey," 160.

63. Childs, "John Dewey," 160, 161.

64. John Dewey to John L. Childs, October 8, 1949. ICarbS/Philosophy.

65. John L. Childs, "Enduring Elements in the Educational Thought of John Dewey," *School of Education Bulletin*, University of Michigan, 31 (November 1959): 18.

66. Childs, "Enduring Elements," 22.

67. Childs, "Enduring Elements," 24–25.

68. Childs, "Enduring Elements," 25.

69. Childs, "Enduring Elements," 26.

70. "Economic and Educational Crisis," *School and Society* 37 (February 25, 1933): 262.

71. Kilpatrick, *Diary 1933*, 10. NNC-T.

72. Kilpatrick, *Diary 1934*, 104–5. NNC-T.

73. Kilpatrick, *Diary 1938*, 232. NNC-T.

74. [George S. Counts], "Biography of George Sylvester Counts" [typescript], 3. ICarbS/Counts.

75. *New York Times*, September 17, 1934, 19.

76. Harold Rugg, "We Cannot Be Neutral," *Frontiers of Democracy* 10 (October 15, 1943): 4.

77. Harold Rugg, "Is This Leadership?" *Frontiers of Democracy* 10 (December 15, 1943): 72.

78. William Heard Kilpatrick, "Launching the *Social Frontier*," *Social Frontier* 1 (October 1934): 2.

79. The *Social Frontier* was launched with subscriptions of $500 from the Elmhurst Fund and $400 from the Christian Social Justice Fund. Its directors each contributed between $25 and $30.

80. For a full discussion of the work of the Commission on the Social Studies in the Schools, see Lawrence J. Dennis, *George S. Counts and Charles A. Beard: Collaborators for Change* (Albany: State University of New York Press, 1989).

81. John L. Childs, "Education as Statecraft," *Social Frontier* 1 (November 1934): 23.

82. Childs, "Education as Statecraft," 25.

83. Childs, "Education as Statecraft," 26.

84. Kilpatrick, *Diary 1934*, 182. NNC-T.

85. John L. Childs, "Preface to a New American Philosophy of Education," in *Social Change and Education* (Washington, D.C.: NEA, Department of Superintendence, 1935), 138.

86. Childs, "Preface to a New American Philosophy," 137.

87. Childs, "Preface to a New American Philosophy," 127.

88. Childs, "Preface to a New American Philosophy," 129.

89. Childs, "Preface to a New American Philosophy," 132.

90. Childs, "Preface to a New American Philosophy," 134.

91. Childs, "Preface to a New American Philosophy," 113.

92. *Proceedings of the National Education Association, 1935* (Washington, D.C.: NEA), 538.

93. *Proceedings of the NEA, 1935*, 552–53.

5. Political Activities

1. Lawrence A. Cremin, David A. Shannon, and Mary Evelyn Townsend, *History of Teachers College, Columbia University* (New York: Columbia University Press, 1954), 145.

2. *New York World-Telegram*. Excerpted in *Teachers College Record* 37 (October 1935): 79.

3. *New York Post*. Excerpted in *Teachers College Record* 37 (November 1935): 151.

4. See Cremin, et al., *History of Teachers College*, 141–43.

5. Notes given to Childs report that the cuts for the dining-hall workers were approximately 33⅓ percent.

6. See Cremin, et al., *History of Teachers College*, 166–71.

7. John L. Childs to William F. Russell, November 1, 1935. ICarbS/Childs.

8. William F. Russell to John L. Childs, November 7, 1935. ICarbS/Childs.

9. James E. Mendenhall and George S. Counts to John L. Childs, November 12, 1935. ICarbS/Childs.

10. *Teachers College Record* 37 (January 1936): 334.

11. Unidentified newspaper clippings. ICarbS/Childs.

12. *San Francisco Examiner*, November 27, 1935, 10.

13. This incident is described in Lawrence J. Dennis, *George S. Counts and Charles A. Beard: Collaborators for Change* (Albany: State University of New York Press, 1989), 127–36.

14. *Teachers College News*, December 10, 1935, n.p.

15. Harry Elmer Barnes, "Education Leads in Labor Policy," *New York World-Telegram*, January 22, 1936, 22.

16. George A. Coe, "Labor Unrest at Columbia University," *School and Society* 43 (January 18, 1936): 93.

17. Coe, "Labor Unrest," 94.

18. *Teachers College News*, December 10, 1935, n.p.

19. John L. Childs to William F. Russell, December 20, 1935. ICarbS/Childs.

20. *Educational Vanguard* 1 (July 23, 1936): 1, 4.

21. Cremin, et al., *History of Teachers College*, 168.

22. *Teachers College Student News*, August 5, 1936, 1.

23. *Teachers College Student News*, August 5, 1936, 3.

24. William F. Russell to John L. Childs and George S. Counts, March 26, 1943. ICarbS/Childs.

25. *American Teacher* 35 (March 1951): 12–15; (April 1951): 7–9.

26. William F. Russell to John L. Childs, September 26, 1951. ICarbS/Childs.

27. John L. Childs to William F. Russell, October 2, 1951. ICarbS/Childs.

28. John L. Childs, "Teachers Union at Teachers College." Address delivered at Teachers College, July 30, 1936 [typescript], 9. ICarbS/Childs.

29. John L. Childs to William F. Russell, October 6, 1953. ICarbS/Childs.

30. William F. Russell to John L. Childs, April 12, 1954. NNC-T/Russell.

31. John L. Childs to William F. Russell, April 20, 1954. NNC-T/Russell.

32. William Edward Eaton, *American Federation of Teachers, 1916–1961* (Carbondale: Southern Illinois University Press, 1975), 72–78, 85–121. Robert W. Iversen, *Communists and the Schools* (New York: Harcourt, Brace, 1959), 99–118.

33. *Guild Teacher* 4 (January 18, 1939), 1.

34. James Wechsler, "Twilight at Teachers College," *Nation* 147 (December 17, 1938): 662.

35. John L. Childs, Scrapbook. ICarbS/Childs.

36. George S. Counts, "Whose Twilight?" *Social Frontier* 5 (February 1939): 135–40.

37. Edmund deS. Brunner, et al., "Teachers College and Mr. Wechsler," *Nation* 147 (December 24, 1938): 703.

38. John L. Childs, Letter, *Nation* 147 (December 24, 1938): 703.

39. "Statement by Joint Board of Teachers Unions of New York City" [typescript]. ICarbS/Childs.

40. In George W. Hartmann, "Union Teachers and Intellectual Integrity," *New Republic* 98 (April 26, 1939): 340.

41. "The Post's Answers," *New York Post* [January 1939], n.p. Copy in John L. Childs, Scrapbook. ICarbS/Childs.

42. Louis M. Hacker to New York College Teachers Union, December 31, 1937 [1938]. ICarbS/Childs.

43. "Important Announcement," January 6, 1939 [typescript]. ICarbS/Childs.

44. John L. Childs to Arnold Shukotoff, January 24, 1939. ICarbS/Childs.

45. *New York Times*, March 10, 1941, 1, 10.

46. John L. Childs to George S. Counts, November 8, 1940. ICarbS/Childs.

47. George S. Counts to John L. Childs, June 18, 1941. ICarbS/Childs.

48. "New Commission Established on Education, War and Peace," *American Teacher* 27 (October 1942): 28.

49. "New Books," *American Teacher* 27 (May 1943): 20.

50. *American Teacher* 27 (April 1943): 2.

51. Norman Angell, "American Communist-Russian Equation," *Saturday Review* 26 (March 20, 1943): 18.

52. *Book-of-the-Month Club News*, May 1943.

53. "AFT's Illuminating Report on Postwar Problem No. 1," *School and Society* 57 (May 1, 1943): 493.

54. John L. Childs and George S. Counts, *America, Russia, and the Communist Party in the Postwar World* (New York: John Day, 1943), 51.

55. Childs and Counts, *America, Russia, and Communist Party*, 74.

56. Childs and Counts, *America, Russia, and Communist Party*, 76.

57. Childs and Counts, *America, Russia, and Communist Party*, 92.

58. *American Teacher*, April 1943.

59. John L. Childs to George S. Counts, December 2, 1942. ICarbS/Childs.

60. "The Commission on Educational Reconstruction," *American Teacher* 29 (October 1944): 21.

61. *American Teacher* 30 (October 1945): 10.

62. John L. Childs, "Education and Authority," *Religious Education* 33 (July–September 1938): 150.

63. Childs, "Education and Authority," 151.

64. Childs, "Education and Authority," 152.

65. Childs, "Education and Authority," 153.

66. John L. Childs, "Spiritual Values of the Secular Public School," in *Public Schools and Spiritual Values*, ed. John S. Brubacher. Yearbook of the John Dewey Society, No. 7 (New York: Harper and Brothers 1944), 64.

67. John L. Childs, "Spiritual Values in Public Education," *Teachers College Record* 48 (March 1947): 367.

68. Childs, "Spiritual Values of the Secular Public School," 66.

69. Childs, "Spiritual Values of the Secular Public School," 67.

70. Childs, "Spiritual Values of the Secular Public School," 68–69.

71. Childs, "Spiritual Values of the Secular Public School," 70.

72. Childs, "Spiritual Values of the Secular Public School," 78.

73. Childs, "Spiritual Values in Public Education," 367.

74. Childs, "Spiritual Values in Public Education," 373.

75. John L. Childs, "American Democracy and the Common School System," *Jewish Education* 21 (Winter 1949): 37.

76. John L. Childs to William F. Russell, October 6, 1953. NNC-T/Childs.

77. *Tablet*, August 23, 1947, 9.

78. John L. Childs, George S. Counts, and Floyd W. Reeves, *To Provide for the Common Defense* (Chicago: American Federation of Teachers, 1948), 8.

79. Childs, et al., *To Provide for the Common Defense*, 9.

80. Childs et al., *To Provide for the Common Defense*, 10.

81. *Organizing the Teaching Profession* (Glencoe, Illinois: Free Press, 1955).

82. John L. Childs to Matthew Woll, November 30, 1942. ICarbS/Childs.

83. John L. Childs to William Green, December 16, 1942. ICarbS/Childs.

84. John L. Childs, "AFL Post War Committee Holds Two-Day Meeting," *American Teacher* 27 (May 1943): 4.

85. John L. Childs, "David Dubinsky and the Work of the A.F.L. Postwar Planning Committee" [typescript], 1–4, 6, 8–12. ICarbS/Childs.

86. David Dubinsky and A. H. Raskin, *David Dubinsky: A Life with Labor* (New York: Simon and Schuster, 1977), 271–72.

87. Max D. Danish, *The World of David Dubinsky* (Cleveland and New York: World Publishing Co., 1957), 142.

88. Dubinsky and Raskin, *David Dubinsky*, 286–87.

89. Lawrence J. Dennis and William Edward Eaton, eds., *George S. Counts: Educator for a New Age* (Carbondale: Southern Illinois University Press, 1980), 13–14.

90. *New York Herald Tribune*, April 24, 1944, 26.

91. *Declaration and Platform*, Liberal Party of New York State, 1944, 43–45.

92. *Justice*, June 15, 1944, 6.

93. [William F. Russell to John L. Childs, n.d.]. NNC-T/Russell.

94. *New York Times*, August 3, 1944, 11.

95. *New York Times*, November 6, 1944, 20.

96. *New York Times*, December 20, 1944, 22.

97. *New York Times*, December 22, 1944, 16.

98. Unidentified newspaper clipping, May 29, 1945, 25. ICarbS/Childs.

99. *New York Times*, July 27, 1945, 3.

100. *New York Times*, July 31, 1946, 3.

101. *New York Times*, October 8, 1946, 15.

102. *New York Times*, October 20, 1946, 15.

103. *New York Times*, September 2, 1946, 18.

104. *New York Times*, November 6, 1946, 8.

105. John L. Childs to David Dubinsky, December 12, 1946. ICarbS/Childs.

106. *New York Times*, April 16, 1948, 16.

107. John L. Childs, Untitled [typescript]. ICarbS/Childs.

108. John L. Childs to David Dubinsky, December 12, 1946. ICarbS/Childs.

109. John L. Childs to Irving Lesnich, April 28, 1953. ICarbS/Childs.

110. Louis B. Sohn, "Introduction," in *Building Peace: Reports of the Commission To Study the Organization of Peace, 1939–1972* (Metuchen, New Jersey: Scarecrow Press, 1973), xi.

111. Sohn, "Introduction," xii.

112. John L. Childs, *American Pragmatism and Education* (New York: Henry Holt, 1956), iv.

6. The Great Debate

1. Norman Woelfel, *Molders of the American Mind* (New York: Columbia University Press, 1933), 219.

2. Boyd H. Bode, "Which Way Democracy?" *Social Studies* 25 (November 1934): 346.

3. Bode, "Which Way Democracy?" 345.

4. John L. Childs, "Professor Bode on 'Faith in Intelligence'," *Social Frontier* 1 (March 1935): 20.

5. Boyd H. Bode to John L. Childs, March 14, 1935. ICarbS/Childs.

6. John L. Childs, "Bode at the Crossroads," *Social Frontier* 4 (May 1938): 268.

7. Boyd H. Bode to John L. Childs, May 16, 1938. ICarbS/Childs.

8. Boyd H. Bode, "Dr. Childs and Education for Democracy," *Social Frontier* 5 (November 1938): 39.

9. Bode, "Dr. Childs and Education," 40.

10. Bode, "Dr. Childs and Education," 39.

11. John L. Childs, "Dr. Bode on 'Authentic' Democracy," *Social Frontier* 5 (November 1938): 41.

12. Childs, "Dr. Bode on 'Authentic' Democracy," 42.

13. Boyd H. Bode to John L. Childs, December 6, 1938. ICarbS/Childs.

14. John Dewey, "Education, Democracy, and Socialized Economy," *Social Frontier* 5 (December 1938): 71.

15. Dewey, "Education, Democracy, and Socialized Economy," 72.

16. Boyd H. Bode, "Democratic Education and Conflicting Cultural Values," *Social Frontier* 5 (January 1939): 104.

17. Bode, "Democratic Education," 105.

18. *Teachers College Record* 42 (November 1940): 99–115.

19. Boyd H. Bode to John L. Childs, September 28, 1940. ICarbS/Childs.

20. Boyd H. Bode, *How We Learn* (Boston: D.C. Heath, 1940).

21. Boyd H. Bode to John L. Childs, October 31, 1940. ICarbS/Childs.

22. John L. Childs, Review of *How We Learn* by Boyd H. Bode, *Curriculum Journal* 11 (October 1940): 280.

23. Childs, Review of *How We Learn*, 279.

24. Clifford Woody, ed., *Adjustments in Education To Meet War and Postwar Needs*. Yearbook of the National Society of College Teachers of Education, No. 29 (Ann Arbor, Michigan: Ann Arbor Press, 1944).

25. George S. Counts, "A Memorable Occasion," *Teachers College Record* 49 (January 1948): 265.

26. Boyd H. Bode, "Education for Freedom," *Teachers College Record* 49 (January 1948): 282.

27. John L. Childs, "Bode in American Philosophy of Education," *Teachers College Record* 49 (January 1948): 287–88.

28. R. Bruce Raup, "Introductory Statement," *Teachers College Record* 49 (January 1948): 264.

29. Childs, "Bode in American Philosophy," 286.

30. John L. Childs to Archibald Anderson, October 20, 1953. ICarbS/Childs.

31. Boyd H. Bode to John L. Childs, November 2, 1952. ICarbS/Childs.

32. John L. Childs, "John Dewey and Education," in *John Dewey: Philosopher of Science and Freedom*, ed. Sidney Hook (New York: Dial Press, 1950), 161.

33. Childs, "John Dewey," in Hook, *John Dewey*, 161.

34. Childs, "John Dewey," 162.

35. Boyd H. Bode to John L. Childs, April 25, 1950. ICarbS/Childs.

36. Boyd H. Bode to John L. Childs, May 6, 1950. ICarbS/ Childs.

37. John L. Childs to Harvey Wedell, August 4, 1969. ICarbS/ Childs.

38. John L. Childs, *Education and Morals: An Experimentalist Philosophy of Education* (New York: Appleton-Century-Crofts, 1950), 107.

39. Childs, *Education and Morals*, 9.

40. Childs, *Education and Morals*, 20.

41. Childs, *Education and Morals*, 17.

42. Childs, *Education and Morals*, 102–5.

43. Childs, *Education and Morals*, 108.

44. Childs, *Education and Morals*, 176–77.

45. Childs, *Education and Morals*, 178.

46. Childs, *Education and Morals*, 236.

47. Childs, *Education and Morals*, 238.

48. Childs, *Education and Morals*, 262.

49. Childs, *Education and Morals*, 293.

50. Childs, *Education and Morals*, 263–64.

51. Dana H. Ferrin to John L. Childs, June 5, 1951. ICarbS/ Childs.

52. [Paul R. Hanna] [January 23, 1950] [typescript], 1. ICarbS/ Childs.

53. *Educational Administration and Supervision* 37 (October 1951): 382.

54. Irvin R. Kuenzli to John L. Childs, June 8, 1951. ICarbS/ Childs.

55. William W. Brickman, "Philosophy of Education," *School and Society* 72 (October 28, 1950): 278.

56. "The Middle Way in American Education," *American Teacher*, 35 (December 1950): 11–13.

57. Ordway Tead, "Searchlight on the Schools," *Survey* 87 (January 1951): 40.

58. John L. Childs, "From an Author," *Survey* 87 (March 1951): 98.

59. Charles F. Donovan, "Secularism: Two Views," *America* 84 (January 27, 1951): 497.

60. "Childs' Morals and Education: A Review," *Harvard Educational Review* 21 (Fall 1951): 203–20.

61. Arthur I. Gates to John L. Childs, May 2, 1950. ICarbS/ Childs.

62. Robert King Hall to John L. Childs, April 26, 1950. ICarbS/ Childs.

63. *Educational Leadership* 9 (October 1951): 49.

64. H. Gordon Hullfish to John L. Childs, April 17, 1950. ICarbS/Childs.

65. John L. Childs to Boyd H. Bode, July 10, 1950. ICarbS/ Childs.

66. Boyd H. Bode to John L. Childs, July 20, 1950. ICarbS/ Childs.

67. Grayson Kirk to John L. Childs, May 30, 1950. NNC-T/ Russell.

68. Boyd H. Bode to John L. Childs, June 8, 1951. ICarbS/ Childs.

69. Boyd H. Bode to John L. Childs, July 9, 1951. ICarbS/Childs.

70. John L. Childs to Boyd H. Bode, July 24, 1951. ICarbS/ Childs.

71. Boyd H. Bode to John L. Childs, August 12, 1951. ICarbS/ Childs.

72. John L. Childs to Boyd H. Bode, August 18, 1951. ICarbS/ Childs.

73. Boyd H. Bode to John L. Childs, September 1, 1951. ICarbS/ Childs.

74. Sidney Hook, *Metaphysics of Pragmatism* (Chicago: Open Court, 1927), 6.

75. John L. Childs to Boyd H. Bode, September 17, 1951. ICarbS/ Childs.

76. Boyd H. Bode to John L. Childs, September 25, 1951. ICarbS/ Childs.

77. John L. Childs, "Democratic Resolution of Conflicts," in *Educational Freedom in an Age of Anxiety*, ed. H. Gordon Hullfish. Yearbook of the John Dewey Society, No. 12 (New York: Harper and Brothers, 1953), 202.

78. Childs, "Democratic Resolution," 203–4.

79. Childs, "Democratic Resolution," 205.

80. Childs, "Democratic Resolution," 185.

81. Robert V. Bullough, Jr., *Democracy in Education: Boyd H. Bode* (New York: General Hall, 1981), 208.

82. Eleanor Bode Browne to John L. Childs, June 5, 1952. ICarbS/Childs.

83. Boyd H. Bode, "John Dewey: Philosopher of Science and Democracy," *Progressive Education* 30 (October 1952): 2–5.

84. Boyd H. Bode to John L. Childs, August 10, 1952. ICarbS/Childs.

85. Boyd H. Bode to John L. Childs, August 29, 1952. ICarbS/Childs.

86. Frederick Burkhardt, ed., *Cleavage in Our Culture* (Boston: Beacon Press, 1952).

87. John L. Childs to Boyd H. Bode, October 24, 1952. ICarbS/Childs.

88. John L. Childs to Boyd H. Bode, November 14, 1952. ICarbS/Childs.

89. John L. Childs, *American Pragmatism and Education* (New York: Henry Holt, 1956), vi.

90. H. Gordon Hullfish to John L. Childs, February 5, 1953. ICarbS/Childs.

91. John L. Childs to H. Gordon Hullfish, February 10, 1953. ICarbS/Childs.

92. John L. Childs, "Boyd H. Bode and the Experimentalists," *Teachers College Record* 55 (October 1953): 9.

7. Retirement

1. John L. Childs, *American Pragmatism and Education* (New York: Henry Holt, 1956), 3–4.

2. Childs, *American Pragmatism and Education*, 111.

3. Childs, *American Pragmatism and Education*, 113.

4. Childs, *American Pragmatism and Education*, 114.

5. Childs, *American Pragmatism and Education*, 298.

6. Childs, *American Pragmatism and Education*, 309.

7. Childs, *American Pragmatism and Education*, 336.

8. Childs, *American Pragmatism and Education*, 355.

9. Raymond E. Callahan to John L. Childs, February 11, 1971. ICarbS/Childs.

10. John L. Childs to Raymond E. Callahan, February 22, 1971. ICarbS/Childs.

11. John L. Childs, "Our Future Philosophy of Education." Address delivered to Faculties Association, State University of New York Colleges of Education, Albany, New York, October 14, 1960 [typescript], 2. ICarbS/Childs.

12. H. Gordon Hullfish, "American Pragmatism and Education in Review," *Teachers College Record* 58 (January 1957): 231.

13. Irving Robbins to John L. Childs, May 31, 1956. ICarbS/Childs.

14. Raymond E. Callahan to John L. Childs, October 3, 1956. ICarbS/Childs.

15. B. Othaniel Smith, July 24, 1956. ICarbS/Childs. George E. Axtelle to John L. Childs, May 3, 1956. ICarbS/Childs.

16. Max Otto to John L. Childs, May 7, 1957. ICarbS/Childs.

17. William Heard Kilpatrick to John L. Childs, July 12, 1958. ICarbS/Childs.

18. John L. Childs to William Heard Kilpatrick, June 25, 1956. ICarbS/Childs.

19. John L. Childs, "Future of Our Common School." Address delivered at Teachers College, New York, November 9, 1956 [typescript], 2–3. ICarbS/Childs.

20. William Heard Kilpatrick to John L. Childs, March 29, 1957. ICarbS/Childs.

21. John L. Childs, "William Heard Kilpatrick: Teacher and Democratic Statesman," *Teachers College Record* 53 (February 1952): 242.

22. See Lawrence A. Cremin, "William H. Kilpatrick Birthday Records," *Teachers College Record* 53 (February 1952): 281.

23. John L. Childs, "To the Members and the Friends of the League for Industrial Democracy," March 19, 1959 [typescript]. ICarbS/Childs.

24. Frederick C. Neff to John L. Childs, April 15, 1971. ICarbS/Childs.

25. Lawrence A. Cremin, *The Transformation of the School* (New York: Alfred A. Knopf, 1961), 10.

26. [Six-page typescript]. ICarbS/Childs.

27. John L. Childs to Claude Eggertsen, September 22, 1960. ICarbS/Childs.

28. John L. Childs, "The Civilizational Functions of Philosophy and Education," in *John Dewey and the World Views*, eds. Douglas E. Lawson and Arthur E. Lean (Carbondale: Southern Illinois University Press, 1966), 4.

29. Childs, "Civilization Functions," 8–9.

30. Childs, "Civilization Functions," 14.

31. William Heard Kilpatrick to John L. Childs, July 12, 1958. ICarbS/Childs.

32. John L. Childs, "Is Dr. Wieman's God Dispensable?" Address delivered at the Unitarian Fellowship, Carbondale, November 22, 1964 [typescript], 7. ICarbS/Childs.

33. John L. Childs, Class Discussion Notes, July 6, 1965. ICarbS/Childs.

34. John L. Childs, Class Discussion Notes—Topic II, July 2, 1965. ICarbS/Childs.

35. John L. Childs, Class Discussion Notes—Topic II, July 6, 1965. ICarbS/Childs.

36. John L. Childs, Outline of Class Discussion, July 8, 1965. ICarbS/Childs.

37. John L. Childs, Attached to Class Outline, July 15, 1965. ICarbS/Childs.

38. John L. Childs to Alice and Willard Miel, May 19, 1974. ICarbS/Childs.

39. John L. Childs to George S. Counts, April 24, 1971. Two slightly different versions are extant. ICarbS/Childs.

40. Carl J. Megel to John L. Childs, April 30, 1971. ICarbS/Childs.

41. Lawrence A. Cremin to John L. Childs, October 5, 1972. ICarbS/Childs.

42. William Burton to John L. Childs, November 8, 1972. ICarbS/Childs.

43. John L. Childs to Arthur Jorgensen, September 5, 1970. ICarbS/Childs.

44. John L. Childs to Delyte W. Morris, August 1, 1970. ICarbS/Childs.

45. John L. Childs to Patricia Strandt, February [10], 1968. ICarbS/Childs.

46. John L. Childs to Eugene and Berta Barnett, June 14, 1970. ICarbS/Childs.

47. John L. Childs to Lois and Martha Counts, November 11, 1974. ICarbS/Childs.

48. John L. Childs, "Teachers Union at Teachers College." Address delivered at Teachers College, July 30, 1936 [typescript], 1. ICarbS/Childs.

8. Conclusion

1. R. Freeman Butts, "Reflections on Forty Years in the Foundations Department at Teachers College." Address delivered Alumni Day, April 11, 1975 [typescript], 17.

2. Alice Miel to John L. Childs, May 24, 1974. ICarbS/Childs.

3. Donald Arnstine to Lawrence J. Dennis, August 24, 1988.

4. Carl J. Megel to John L. Childs, January 2, 1975. ICarbS/ Childs.

5. John L. Childs to John Knox Coit, October 22, 1953. ICarbS/ Childs.

6. *Who Is Sylvia? The Diary of a Biography*, ed. Lynley Hood (Dunedin, New Zealand: John McIndoe, 1990), 39. Quoted by Phyllis Povell, "The Biographer as Autobiographer: A Working Paper." Address delivered at University of Toronto, April 26, 1991 [typescript], 9.

7. Telephone interview with Robert E. Mason, March 26, 1988.

8. David Tyack, Robert Lowe, and Elisabeth Hansot, *Public Schools in Hard Times* (Cambridge, Massachusetts: Harvard University Press, 1984), 25.

9. C. A. Bowers, *Progressive Education and the Depression* (New York: Random House, 1969), 81.

10. William Heard Kilpatrick, *Diary 1935*, 235. NNC-T.

11. William E. Eaton, "Historical Background of Social Reconstruction." Address delivered at AERA, San Francisco, California, April 28, 1989 [typescript], 4–5.

12. John L. Childs to H. Gordon Hullfish, December 9, 1952. ICarbS/Childs.

13. John Dewey to John L. Childs, October 8, 1949. ICarbS/ Philosophy.

14. Hugh Weir Smeaton to William Heard Kilpatrick, n.d. [January 1946]. L. Thomas Hopkins (1889–1982) received his doctorate from Teachers College and taught curriculum and learning theory there for half his career. He then went to Texas and retired from the University of Maine in 1971.

15. Festus Chukwudi Okafor, *Philosophy of Education and Third World Perspective* (Lawrenceville, Virginia: Brunswick Publishing Co., 1981), 54.

16. "Commencement Program," Southern Illinois University, Carbondale, June 7, 1968, 1.

Checklist of Writings by John L. Childs

1910

Childs, John L. "Substitute for Hazing." *Western Intercollegiate Magazine* 2 (November 1910): 44–47.

1917

———. "Students Are Leading China—Whither?" *Foreign Mail* 24 (July–August 1917): 23–25.

1918

———. "Result of the War Upon Missionary Work in China." *Millard's Review* (December 14, 1918): 46–51.

1921

———. "National Christian Conference." *Chinese Recorder* (Shanghai) 52 (November 1921): 737–43.

1925

——. "Evolution of a Missionary's Thought." *The Life* (English edition) 5 (July 1925): 1–37. Extracted in *Bible for China* (February 1926): 6–9.

——. Letter. *Leader* (Peking) (June 21, 1925): n.p.

——. "Letter to Bishop Norris." *Leader* (Peking) (June [25], 1925): 6.

1926

——. "Some Fundamentals in Modernism." *Leader* (Peking) (n.d. [1926]): n.p.

1931

——. *Education and the Philosophy of Experimentalism.* New York: Century, 1931.

——. "Way of Dealing with Experience." *Progressive Education* 8 (December 1931): 695–98.

1933

Childs, John L., and John Dewey. "Social-Economic Situation and Education," and "Underlying Philosophy of Education." In *Educational Frontier*, ed. William Heard Kilpatrick. New York: D. Appleton-Century, 1933, 32–72, 287–319.

Kilpatrick, William Heard, John L. Childs, et al. "Economic and Educational Crisis." *School and Society* 37 (February 25, 1933): 259–62.

1934

Childs, John L. "Education as Statecraft." Review of *Conclusions and Recommendations* by the American Historical Association's Commission on the Social Studies in the Schools. *Social Frontier* 1 (November 1934): 23–26.

——. "Education Faces the Future." *Childhood Education* 10 (April 1934): 334–47.

——. "School and the Social Order." *School and Home* 15 (March 1934): 300–305.

Kilpatrick, William Heard. *Source Book in the Philosophy of Education.* Revised edition. New York: Macmillan, 1934. (Childs contributed to the first four chapters, pp. 1–95.)

1935

Childs, John L. "Academic Freedom in a Period of Transition." *National Education Association Proceedings* (1935): 233–37.

———. "New Education in Contemporary Society." *Parent Education* 1 (February 15, 1935): 11–16, 20.

———. "Preface to a New American Philosophy of Education." In *Social Change and Education*, Yearbook of the National Education Association, Department of Superintendence, No. 13 (1935): 113–39.

———. "Professor Bode on 'Faith in Intelligence'." *Social Frontier* 1 (March 1935): 20–24.

———. "Should the School Seek Actively To Reconstruct Society?" *Annals of the American Academy of Political and Social Science* 182 (November 1935): 1–9. *Educational Digest* 1 (February 1936): 1–4. Reprinted in *Teacher, Student, and Society*, eds. Sterling Fishman, Andreas M. Kazamial, and Herbert M. Kliebard. Boston: Little, Brown and Co., 1974, 216–24.

———. *Ten Theses on Education and American Culture.* Greenwich, Connecticut: Edgewood School Press, 1935.

Childs, John L., et al. "Full Text of Report of Dining Hall Committee." *Teachers College News*, December 10, 1935.

1936

Childs, John L. "Can Teachers Stay Out of the Class Struggle?" *Social Frontier* 2 (April 1936): 219–22.

———. "Democracy, Education, and the Class Struggle." *Social Frontier* 2 (June 1936): 274–78.

———. "Mr. Laski's Half-Truths." *Social Frontier* 3 (October 1936): 16–18.

———. "Social Assumptions and Education." Review of *Social Ideas of American Educators* by Merle Curti. *Social Frontier* 2 (January 1936): 121–22.

———. "Whither Progressive Education?" *Progressive Education* 13 (December 1936): 583–89. Excerpts: *Education Digest* 2 (March 1937): 42–44.

1937

———. "American Interests and the Far East." *Far Eastern Magazine* 1 (November 1937): 9–13. And *Social Frontier* 4 (December 1937): 32–34.

———. "Religion of Naturalism." Review of *Faith in an Age of Fact* by Edward H. Reisner. *Social Frontier* 4 (October 1937): 31–32.

1938

————. "Bode at the Crossroads." Review of *Progressive Education at the Crossroads* by Boyd H. Bode. *Social Frontier* 4 (May 1938): 267–68.

————. "Can We Take Sides in Social Conflicts?" *Womans Press* 32 (January 1938): 12–13.

————. "Dr. Bode on 'Authentic' Democracy." *Social Frontier* 5 (November 1938): 40–43.

————. "Education and Authority." *Religious Education* 33 (July–September 1938): 149–53.

Childs, John L., and John Dewey. "Implications of Idea of Education as a Social Operation." *Progressive Education* 15 (March 1938): 244–45. Excerpt from *Educational Frontier*, chapter 2.

Childs, John L., et al. "Teachers College and Mr. Wechsler." *Nation* 147 (December 24, 1938): 703.

1939

Childs, John L. "Changing Scene." *Frontiers of Democracy* 6 (October 1939): 4.

————. "Changing Scene." *Frontiers of Democracy* 6 (November 15, 1939): 35.

————. "Changing Scene." *Frontiers of Democracy* 6 (December 15, 1939): 67–68.

————. "Democracy and Educational Method." *Progressive Education* 16 (February 1939): 119–22.

————. "Educational Philosophy of John Dewey" and "Preface" with William Heard Kilpatrick. In *John Dewey as Educator*. New York: Progressive Education Association, 1939, 419–43. Also in *Philosophy of John Dewey*, ed. Paul Arthur Schilpp. New York: Tudor Publishing, 1939.

————. "John Dewey and the Educational Frontier." In *Educational Frontier* (Progressive Education Association, Booklet No. 13, 1939): 5–12.

————. "Philosophy and Educational Research." *Advanced School Digest* (May–June 1939): 6–8.

————. "Progressive Education and the Secondary School." *Progressive Education* 16 (October 1939): 411–17.

————. "Teachers' Union vs. Professor Childs." *Nation* 149 (January 14, 1939): 76.

Childs, John L., and George S. Counts. "Statement." *Independent* 1. *New York Times*, January 21, 1939, 2. *New York Sun*, January 20, 1939, 10.

Childs, John L., et al. "Manifesto." *New Leader*, May 20, 1939, 1, 6. *New York Times*, May 15, 1939, 13. (This manifesto was put out by the Committee for Cultural Freedom. See Sidney Hook, *Out of Step*, 248–74.)

1940

Childs, John L. "Bertrand Russell and American Higher Education." *Frontiers of Democracy* 6 (April 15, 1940): 197.

———. "Catholic Church and the Social Order." *Frontiers of Democracy* 6 (March 15, 1940): 164.

———. "Changing Scene." *Frontiers of Democracy* 6 (February 15, 1940): 132.

———. "Changing Scene." *Frontiers of Democracy* 6 (March 15, 1940): 164.

———. "Church and War." *Frontiers of Democracy* 6 (April 15, 1940): 198.

———. "Defeat for Liberal Education." *Frontiers of Democracy* 7 (November 15, 1940): 36–37.

———. "Liberalism and National Defense." *Frontiers of Democracy* 7 (October 15, 1940): 5–6.

———. "Meaning of the Term: Experimentalism." *Frontiers of Democracy* 6 (January 15, 1940): 105–9.

———. "New Deal in the Far East." *Frontiers of Democracy* 6 (January 15, 1940): 100–101.

———. "Politics and Education." *Frontiers of Democracy* 6 (May 15, 1940): 229–30.

———. "Progressive Education and the War." *Frontiers of Democracy* 7 (December 15, 1940): 69–70.

———. Review of *How We Learn* by Boyd H. Bode. *Curriculum Journal* 11 (October 1940): 279–80.

Childs, John L., et al. "Manifesto on Democracy and Education in the Current Crisis." *Teachers College Record* 42 (November 1940): 100–115. (The manifesto was actually prepared by a faculty committee consisting of Thomas H. Briggs, John K. Norton, and John L. Childs.)

1941

Childs, John L., "Brandeis: Liberal Judge and Educator." *Frontiers of Democracy* 8 (November 15, 1941): 38–39.

———. "Future of the NYA and CCC in Public Education." *Frontiers of Democracy* 8 (November 15, 1941): 36–37.

————. "No 'Munich' in the Far East." *Frontiers of Democracy* 8 (October 15, 1941): 5–6.

————. "Philosophy and Social Reconstruction." Review of *Reason, Social Myths, and Democracy* by Sidney Hook. *Frontiers of Democracy* 7 (January 15, 1941): 123–25.

————. "Philosophy and the Education of Teachers." *Frontiers of Democracy* 7 (March 15, 1941): 166–67.

————. "Reply . . ." *Frontiers of Democracy* 8 (October 15, 1941): 14–15.

————. "Russia and Japan." *Frontiers of Democracy* 7 (May 15, 1941): 228–29.

————. "Russia and the United States." *Frontiers of Democracy* 8 (December 15, 1941): 69.

Childs, John L., et al. Statement. *New York Times*, February 28, 1941, 21.

Childs, John L., et al. "This War and America." *Frontiers of Democracy* 8 (October 15, 1941): 10–11.

1942

Childs, John L. "Comments by John L. Childs on Dr. Dewey's Letter." *Frontiers of Democracy* 8 (March 1942): 181–82.

————. "East and the West in the War and the Peace." *Teachers College Record* 44 (November 1942): 84–91.

————. "Progressive Education and the War and the Peace." *Progressive Education* 19 (March 1942): 142–45.

————. "Public Schools and the Needs of Youth." *Frontiers of Democracy* 8 (January 15, 1942): 107–9.

————. "Teachers and Boards of Education in a War Period." *Frontiers of Democracy* 8 (March 15, 1942): 166.

————. "This War and American Education." *Frontiers of Democracy* 8 (January 15, 1942): 102.

————. "Twilight of the White Man's Domination." *Frontiers of Democracy* 8 (April 15, 1942): 196–97.

————. "War and the Processes of Democracy." *Frontiers of Democracy* 8 (February 15, 1942): 132–33.

1943

————. "AFL Post War Committee Holds Two-Day Meeting." *American Teacher* 27 (May 1943): 4–5.

————. "American Teachers and a People's Peace." *American Teacher* 27 (April 1943): 5–8.

————. "Common Stake of Labor and Education in the Making of the Peace." *Teachers College Record* 45 (October 1943): 43–50.

————. "Education and the Post-War World." *American Teacher* 27 (February 1943): 8–9.

————. "End of the Comintern." *New Leader* (June 5, 1943), 2.

————. "Experimentalism and American Education." *Teachers College Record* 44 (May 1943): 539–43. Also in *Educational Digest* 9 (October 1943): 36–38. Reprinted in *Nature, Aims, and Policy*, ed. Adrian Dupuis. Urbana: University of Illinois Press, 1970, 109–13.

————. "Experimental Morality and the Post-War World." *Frontiers of Democracy* 9 (April 15, 1943): 197–200.

————. "Moscow Charter and the Peace." *American Teacher* 28 (December 1943): 11–13.

————. "Total War and Youth." *Teachers College Record* 44 (January 1943): 260–66.

Childs, John L., and George S. Counts. *America, Russia, and the Communist Party in the Postwar World.* New York: John Day Co., 1943.

1944

Childs, John L. "AFL Plans for Postwar World." *American Teacher* 28 (May 1944): 6–8. Also "Labor and a Democratic Peace: A. F. of L. Plans for Postwar World." *New Leader* 27 (April 22, 1944): 4.

————. "Aims of Liberals Discussed." *New York Times*, December 22, 1944, 16.

————. "American Labor Conference on International Affairs Issues Quarterly Review." Review of *International Postwar Problems*, vol. 1. *American Teacher* 28 (February 1944): 23–24.

————. "Can We Build a Permanent Peace?" *Chicago Union Teacher* 9 (April 1944): 4–6.

————. "Childs Sees Liberal Party as Instrument of Progress." *Justice* 26 (June 15, 1944): 6. (Verbatim report of most of an address delivered by John L. Childs to International Ladies Garment Workers Union, May 31, 1944.)

————. "Foreword." *Declaration and Platform*. New York Liberal Party Pamphlet, May 19–20, 1944, 4–5.

————. "Foreword." *For Victory and Lasting Peace*. New York: Liberal Party of New York State, December 27, 1944, 3–4.

———. "Labor in the Postwar World." I: "Labor and the Patterns of the Peace" (January 15, 1944); II: "Labor and the Economy of Postwar America" (February 15, 1944); III: "Tolerance and Intolerance in American Democracy" (March 15, 1944); IV: "A Strategy for Organized Labor in Postwar America" (April 15, 1944); V: "Labor and the Winning of the Peace" (May 15, 1944); VI: "Labor's Postwar Domestic Task" (June 15, 1944). Workers Education Bureau of America, 1944.

———. "New York's Liberal Party." *Justice* 26 (September 1, 1944): 3.

———. "Spiritual Values of the Secular Public School." In *Public Schools and Spiritual Values*. Yearbook of the John Dewey Society, No. 7. New York: Harper, 1944, 58–79.

Childs, John L., and Dean Alfange. *Call for a New Party*. Pamphlet by Liberal and Labor Committee, 1944.

Childs, John L., John Brubacher, and Boyde [*sic*] H. Bode. "Adjustments in Philosophy of Education in Meeting War and Postwar Needs." In *Adjustments in Education To Meet War and Postwar Needs*, ed. Clifford Woody. Yearbook of the National Society of College Teachers of Education, No. 29. Ann Arbor, Michigan: Ann Arbor Press, [1944], 1–13.

Childs, John L., Layne Lane, and Dorothy Leil. "Foreword." *American Teacher* 28 (April 1944): 2.

Childs, John L., et al. "Who Will Vote for Roosevelt, Truman, Wagner." Advertisement in the *New York Times*. October 31, 1944, 14. (The advertisement also appeared in other papers.)

1945

Childs, John L., and Dean Alfange. "Foreword." *For Our City*. New York: Liberal Party of New York State Pamphlet, 1945, 4–7.

1946

Childs, John L. *America's First Need: A Political Realignment*. Pamphlet by Liberal Party of New York State, September 1946.

1947

———. "American Liberalism Today." *Modern Review* 1 (March 1947): 26–33.

———. "Spiritual Values in Public Education." *Teachers College Record* 48 (March 1947): 367–73. Excerpted in "Government Funds for Private Religious Schools?" *Clearing House* 22 (December 1947): 235.

Childs, John L., George S. Counts, et al. Joint Statement: "European Aid Program Merits Liberal Backing." *Liberal* 1 (November 25, 1947), 1–2.

Childs, John L., et al. *Federal Aid and the Crisis in American Education.* Report by the Commission on Educational Reconstruction of the American Federation of Teachers (1947). Also in *American Teacher* 32 (October 1947): 18–21. (Pamphlet includes "Statement by John L. Childs on Welfare Services and Aid to Children.")

Childs, John L., et al. "Sectarian Education." *New York Times,* October 1, 1947, 28. (Childs signed but William Heard Kilpatrick was the author of this letter.)

1948

Childs, John L. "Bode in American Philosophy of Education." *Teachers College Record* 49 (January 1948): 285–88.

————. "8 Tribal Myths of American Liberalism." *Liberal,* March 2, 1948, 3.

————. "Free American Education!" *Christian Century* 65 (April 1948): 378–80. Reprinted as "New Threats to the Principle of Separation." *Progressive Education* 26 (February 1949): 112–15.

Childs, John L., George S. Counts, and Floyd W. Reeves. *To Provide for the Common Defense.* Chicago: American Federation of Teachers, 1948.

1949

Childs, John L. "American Democracy and the Common School System." *Jewish Education* 21 (Winter 1949): 32–27. Reprinted in *Religion and the Public School.* New York: American Association for Jewish Education, n.d., 1–6.

————. "Communists and the Right to Teach." *Nation* 168 (February 26, 1949): 230–33.

————. "Cultural Factors in Dewey's Philosophy of Education." *Teachers College Record* 51 (December 1949): 130–32.

————. "Laboratory for 'Personhood'." *Saturday Review of Literature* 32 (October 1949): 11–12, 36–38. Also in German, "Erziehung zum denkenden Menschen." *Erziehung* 4 (February 1951): 1–3.

————. "Morality of Science and the Values of Democracy." *Science Education* 33 (October 1949): 261–66.

————. "Student of Public Affairs Views the Problem of Curriculum

Development." *Teachers College Record* 50 (January 1949): 232–40.

1950

———. "Defending Rights." *New York Times Magazine*, July 30, 1950, sec. 6, p. 2.

———. *Education and Morals: An Experimentalist Philosophy of Education.* New York: Appleton-Century-Crofts, 1950.

———. "John Dewey and Education." In *John Dewey: Philosopher of Science and Freedom*, ed. Sidney Hook. New York: Dial Press, 1950, 153–63.

———. "Teachers and the Democratic Struggle." *Progressive Education* 27 (February 1950): 116–20.

1951

———. "From an Author." *Survey* 87 (March 1951): 98.

———. "William H. Kilpatrick—Pioneer in Education *in* and *for* Democracy." *American Teacher* 36 (November 1951): 9–13.

1952

———. "Experimentalism and Educational Values." *Harvard Educational Review* 22 (1952): 219–28.

———. "William Heard Kilpatrick: Teacher and Democratic Statesman." *Teachers College Record* 53 (February 1952): 241–44.

1953

———. "Boyd H. Bode and the Experimentalists." *Teachers College Record* 55 (October 1953): 1–9.

———. "Clarifies Professors Stand." *Columbia Spectator*, April 28, 1953, 2.

———. "Democratic Resolution of Conflicts." In *Educational Freedom in an Age of Anxiety*, ed. by H. Gordon Hullfish. Yearbook of the John Dewey Society, No. 12. New York: Harper, 1953, 185–205.

1954

———. "Education and the Crisis in American Democracy." Review of *Education and Social Integration* by William O. Stanley. *Progressive Education* 31 (January 1954): 91–94.

———. "Has Pragmatism Undermined Basic Values in Education?" *Teachers College Record* 56 (October 1954): 25–30.

———. " 'Objective' Teaching of Religion." In *Role of the Public School in Dealing with Religion*. Pamphlet published by the Joint Advisory Committee of the Synagogue Council of America, 1954, 14–15.

———. "Some Ambiguities in Value Theory in Education." In *American Elementary School*, ed. by Harold G. Shane. Yearbook of the John Dewey Society, No. 13.New York: Harper, 1954, 9–27.

1955

———. "Not a Dogmatist, Nor Sentimentalist." *Social Democrat* (July 1955): 9.

Childs, John L., et al. "Freedom to Teach." *Washington Post*, April 1, 1955, 34. Also as "Classroom Freedom." *Christian Science Monitor*, April 7, 1955, 14.

Commission on Educational Reconstruction of the American Federation of Teachers. *Organizing the Teaching Profession*. Glencoe, Illinois: Free Press, 1955. (Childs was a member of the commission, but he seems to have edited some of the chapters rather than having written any.)

1956

Childs, John L. *American Pragmatism and Education: An Interpretation and Criticism*. New York: Henry Holt and Co., 1956. Also in Spanish, *Pragmatismo Y Educación*. Buenos Aires: Editorial Nova, n.d.

1957

———. "America in the Educational Thought of Dr. Kilpatrick." *Progressive Education* 34 (March 1957): 33–34.

———. "Assessment of the Experimentalist Educational Theory." *Bode Memorial Lectures, 1957*. Columbus: College of Education, Ohio State University, 1957.

———. "Education and Politics in the Soviet Union." *Teachers College Record* 58 (April 1957): 351–54.

———. "Future of the Common School." *Educational Forum* 21 (January 1957): 133–41.

1958

———. "Can We Take Sides in Social Conflicts?" *Womans Press* 32 (January 1958): 12–13.

———. "Evaluation of Dewey's Theory of Education." *School of Education Bulletin*, University of Michigan 29 (May 1958):

113–21. *Journal of the Michigan Schoolmaster's Club* 61 (March 2, 1960): 7–14.

———. "Preface." *Education and Morals.* Japanese edition. Translated by Keizo Miksuzumi and Eijiro Hattori. Tokyo: Riso Sha, 1958, 1–3.

1959

———. "Education and the American Scene." 88 *Daedalus* (Winter 1959): 91–106. Also John L. Childs, Arthur Bestor, and Panel. "Education and the American Scene." In *Education in the Age of Science.* New York: Basic Books, 1959, 53–114 (75–90).

———. "Enduring Elements in the Educational Thought of John Dewey." *School of Education Bulletin.* University of Michigan 31 (November 1959).

———. "John Dewey and American Education." *Teachers College Record* 61 (December 1959): 128–33.

———. "John Dewey and American Thought." *Progressive* 23 (November 1959): 28–30.

———. Untitled biographical sketch, prepared by John L. Childs. *Educational Forum* 23 (May 1959): 503j–4j.

1961

———. "American Democracy and Higher Education." Review of *Policies and Practices in Higher Education* by Algo D. Henderson. *Educational Forum* 25 (March 1961): 389–92.

———. "Value Conflicts and the Education of Our Young." In *Aspects of Value,* ed. Frederick C. Gruber. Philadelphia: University of Pennsylvania Press, 1959, 73–88.

1963

———. "Noted U.S. Educator Salutes Role of ILG." *Justice* 45 (February 1963): 3.

———. Review of *Eclectic Philosophy of Education* by John S. Brubacher. *Educational Forum* 27 (March 1963): 375–76.

1964

———. "William Heard Kilpatrick: A Recollection." New York: Teachers College, Columbia University Press, 1964.

1966

———. "Civilizational Functions of Philosophy and Education." In *John Dewey and the World View,* ed. Douglas E. Lawson and

Arthur E. Lean. Carbondale: Southern Illinois University Press, 1966, 3–14. Also in *John Dewey: Visión e Influencia de un Pedagogo.* Buenos Aires: Editorial Nova, n.d., 13–28.

―――. "Discussion: Graduate Study of Education." *Harvard Educational Review* 36 (Spring 1966): 162–68. *Universities Quarterly* 20 (September 1966): 443–50.

―――. "John Dewey, Lectures in the Philosophy of Education: 1899. Ed. by Reginald Archambault." *Studies in Philosophy and Education* 5 (Winter 1966–67): 60–76.

―――. "Tribute to Dubinsky." *New York Times*, March 24, 1966, 38.

1967

―――. Review of *Genius of American Education* by Lawrence A. Cremin. *History of Education Quarterly* 7 (Spring 1967): 102–7.

―――. "A Second Look at Dr. Conant's Report." *Educational Forum* 31 (March 1967): 265–74.

1968

―――. "Comments on Studies." *Studies in Philosophy and Education, A Prospectus* [January 1968].

1969

―――. "Review Article—Berkson Re-evaluates Experimentalism." *Educational Theory* 19 (Winter 1969): 88–98.

Index

Bleyer, William G., 12, 15, 19
Bode, Boyd H., 15, 61, 63, 65, 66,
    74, 91, 128–36, 143–54, 157,
    162, 167, 176, 195
Borchardt, Selma, 100
Borge, Victor, 119
Borrowman, Merle, 182
Bossing, Nelson, 173
Bowers, C. A., 193
Brickman, William W., 141, 173
Brockman, Stephen, 53
Browne, Eleanor (née Bode), 152
Brubacher, John S., 133
Bruce, William F., 141
Brunner, Edmund deS., 77
Bullough, Robert V., Jr., 151
Burgess, John Stewart, 25
Burgum, Edwin Berry, 94
Burkhardt, Frederick, 152
Burton, William, 185
Butts, R. Freeman, 77, 190

Cairns, William B., 12
Callahan, Raymond E., 158–59,
    161, 190
Carbondale, Illinois, 1, 2, 3, 173–
    75, 180–81, 192
Caswell, Hollis L., 161, 163
Catell, James McKeen, 77
Center for Dewey Studies (SIUC),
    2, 7
Champlin, Nathaniel, 161
Childs, Cliff, 2, 181, 187, 200
Childs, Grace Mary (née Fowler),
    23, 24, 40, 45, 46, 52–56, 59,
    64, 92, 102, 155, 172, 174, 179,
    181, 184, 187, 189, 192
Childs, Helen Janette (née Smith),
    9, 125
Childs, John Lawrence (see related
    topics): American Pragmatism
    and Education, 92, 135, 152–53,
    155–62, 166, 176; Educational
    Frontier, ed. William Heard Kil-
    patrick, 54, 65–72, 73–74, 75,
    80, 128, 131; Education and
    Morals, 104, 125, 136–44, 160,

176; Education and the Philoso-
    phy of Experimentation, 37, 54,
    59–63, 65, 128; and George S.
    Counts, America, Russia, and the
    Communist Party in the Postwar
    World, 90, 100–102
Childs, John Nelson, 8–9
Childs, Marshall, 26–27
China, 5–6, 21, 23–40, 42–44,
    46–54, 56, 58, 84, 127, 186,
    191, 196, 201n.13
Churchill, Winston S., 121
Clement, Mrs. S. M., 25
Coe, George A., 43, 45, 48, 50, 53,
    88–89
Columbia University, 2, 4, 36, 44,
    55, 75, 84, 95–96, 114–16,
    124–25, 171, 186, 195, 196
Commission on Educational Recon-
    struction (AFT), 103, 107–8,
    196
Commission on Education and the
    Postwar World (AFT), 99–102,
    109
Commission on Education and the
    Problems of the War and the
    Peace (AFT), 78, 102
Commission on Education for New
    Social and Economic Relation-
    ships (NEA), 81
Commission on the Social Studies
    in the Schools (AHA), 66, 80–
    81, 128–29, 183, 210n.80
Commission To Study the Organi-
    zation of Peace (Shotwell Com-
    mission), 125
Commons, John R., 12–14, 191,
    201n.15
Communism, 6–7, 87, 89, 93, 95,
    98–99, 100–101, 114, 116, 123,
    139, 183
Comte, Auguste, 148
Counts, George S., 2, 3, 5, 6–7,
    55, 56, 57, 63, 66, 69, 71, 72,
    77, 78, 80, 85, 86, 87, 90, 93,
    95, 96–102, 107, 108–9, 114–
    15, 119, 121, 123–24, 127–29,

Lawrence J. Dennis was born in England and trained as a pianist. He lived in Montreal for a decade, where he did much performing for the CBC. He received his Ph.D. in educational foundations at Southern Illinois University, Carbondale, where he now teaches. He has written extensively on the progressives, and in recent years he has concentrated particularly on the work of George S. Counts as well as John L. Childs.